WHY JOHNNY CAN'T
COME HOME!

UPDATED 2024

Noreen N. Gosch

Copyright November 2024
Noreen N. Gosch & OfficalJohnnyGosch.com

All rights reserved. No part of this book may be reproduced or transmitted in any form or by any means, electronic or mechanical including photo copying, recording or by any information storage and retrieval system, without permission in writing from the publisher.

Contact the above for permission to excerpt larger sections of this book for magazine and other forms of reproduction.

As a citizen of the United States, I have the constitutional right under the First Amendment to disseminate the autobiographical account of my 42-year journey to find my son and solve the case.

My detailed account is accurate and totally documented. Law enforcement ignored court documented evidence and did not assume responsibility in this case.

ONE OF THE MOST FAMOUS KIDNAPPING CASES IN THE NATIONS HISTORY

DEDICATION

This book is dedicated:

To my son, Johnny, who has suffered the pain
of being kidnaped abused and tortured.

May he know that I tried with all my strength to find him,
to solve the case and finally bring his story out
before the public.

May he know his family loves him and he is not forgotten.

To the countless other kidnapped children
may they not give up hope.

To the parents of kidnapped and murdered children....
May this book give you hope to go on, when the
pain is so great and the world looks bleak.

IN APPRECIATION

FOR THE

SUPPORT, KINDNESS AND LOVE

TO

Natalie Regan – My Mother

Rita Turner – My Aunt

Bob Duitch – Family

Jim Mascaro – Family

Johnny Gosch – Members

The Faithful Public Who Cared

WITHOUT THEIR HELP ...

THIS BOOK

WOULD NOT HAVE BEEN POSSIBLE

Natalie Regan – My Mother

George Hartney – My Husband

Gordon Gratias – Private Investigator

Ted Gunderson – FBI Special Agent

Jeff Blunk – Computer Specialist

TABLE OF CONTENTS

INTRODUCTION 1
PREFACE 12

SECTION ONE 17
THEY HAVE NO CRIME.... I HAVE NO SON!!!! 18
SURVIVAL.... A WAY OF LIFE FOR NOREEN 71
CENTRAL INTELLIGENCE AGENCY ON THE SCENE–1983 88
JOHN GOSCH... JOHNNY'S FATHER 103
JOHNNY DOESN'T LIVE HERE ANYMORE 125
.... BILL 134
ON THE AUCTION BLOCK 140

SECTION TWO 149
THE FRANKLIN COVER–UP 150
PAUL BONACCI 163
BONACCI DOCUMENTS 183
A MAN CALLED RUSTY 195
JOHN DECAMP... RELUCTANT HERO 214
TED GUNDERSON – MAN WITH A MISSION 229
FBI FRIEND OR FOE? 240
NAMBLA 251
SATANISM IN AMERICA 262
MIND CONTROL, MONARCH & MK ULTRA 281

SECTION THREE 311
INTRODUCTION TO 2024 312
MY THANKS AND GRATITUDE TO 349
LOCKED UP AT ABC 352
GRIEF BY LOSS OF A CHILD BY NOREEN N. GOSCH 366
RECOMMENDED READING 378

INTRODUCTION

For those who say Johnny was kidnapped over 18 years ago... what does this have to do with today? The reader should know that this story is as hot as the Internet. On June 28, 2000, a package of information about Russell Nelson, was sent across the Internet to everyone ... from the President to the Pope. Nelson is one of the key witnesses in the Johnny Gosch case. Nelson testified in 1999, in Federal Court, he had seen and photographed Johnny Gosch in 1998.

Ted Gunderson, Senior Special Agent In Charge FBI (Retired), John DeCamp, former Nebraska State Senator, Captain in the military under William Colby.... who later became the director of the CIA, all got involved in the Johnny Gosch case, through the Franklin Credit Union investigation by the Nebraska Legislature.

Johnny became a victim of a multi-level governmental project under the umbrella of MKUltra (beyond TOP SECRET), which singled out children to be used in mind war experiments. Its roots began as a top-secret project at the end of World War II masterminded by the Pentagon. Former Secret Service Agent Mark Philips reports of Mindwar experiments on human beings "would make Dr Frankenstein blush...I say blanche. The chapter "MKUltra, Monarch and Mindwar explains this in detail.

INTRODUCTION

The Pentagon believed that the knowledge of top Nazi scientists out weighed the horrible crimes they had committed. Although Harry Truman insisted that no scientist who had committed crimes be allowed into this country, the Pentagon issued false passports, laundered any reports that would have revealed the charges against them.

Vile human experiments conducted in the death camps in Nazi Germany were considered so valuable that the scientists, who had conducted them, were brought to this country, given unlimited resources to experiment on any human subject under the command of the Pentagon. When the draft was eliminated the federal government no longer had a ready source of soldiers to be used as human guinea pigs.

This book will prove that the CIA set up as a proprietary company called "The Finders" who recruited mothers to bred children. These children were then sold around the world. The Chapter on "The Finders" will shock you, as you learn about a Washington D.C. based organization that "buys and sells children. " The Finders still operates in Washington D.C. under CIA protection yet today.

Everything you will read in this careful chronological account should make the hair stand up on the back of your neck. As any good Hollywood mystery film should. Only this is not Hollywood fiction, this is the cold and gritty truth proven with police records, congressional documents, and congressionally suppressed videotape. Evidence was obtained despite the total lack of co-operation from law enforcement. With absolute certainty the highest levels of law enforcement in this country are compromised. These law enforcement officials do not protect the public! It appears their job is to protect the pedophiles in this country, whose names ring "the social register."

Only those who listen to short wave radio, would know that across the world in England, Belgium and Holland there is an uprising against these highly connected pedophiles. BBC Radio recently reported parents and children marching on the houses of known pedophiles, as the London newspapers print their addresses. After an eight-year-old girl was found raped and murdered in the London area.

Who Is Noreen Gosch?

She is above all else mother of Johnny Gosch. The Noreen Gosch, I have known over the last ten years has let nothing stand in the way of finding out what happened to her son and why.

She has the answers. Answers, which will shock and confound every parent who reads this book. The answers have come at great costs to her personally. She has thrust her story forward with all the power and determination of SuperMom. Knowing her for more than ten years… it would not surprise me to hear that she could leap tall buildings. She certainly has fought her way over, under, around or thru every obstacle placed in her path.

It is not all grimness and evil…you will get to know SuperMom Noreen Gosch, who went from working Mom to CIA asset. She had to learn on her feet how to survive death threats, physical beatings and being thrown from a moving car. But nothing, not the ridicule of the Des Moines Register, not an attempt to portray her as a grasping publicity hungry mother, could stop her quest for the truth of Johnny's fate.

She was instead a spy, a super sleuth who used ever skill she possessed…you will laugh when you read about "Iowa's Deep Throat". As a mother and a workingwoman, she held down a full time position as an office manager for twenty-two years and Yoga Instructor in Des Moines for thirty years to earn the money that financed continued private investigation. She also gave seven hundred programs/speeches during this time period to educate parents about the "profile of a pedophile."

How many children knew what to do when a molester approached them? FEW, MANY or NONE until Noreen Gosch spoke out before thousands of children throughout the country. Noreen ripped the cover of

INTRODUCTION

naiveté off Des Moines, Iowa and America. Suddenly parents were faced with the reality that in every community, there were predators waiting to target their children.

Would it surprise you to know that she and her family were threatened with death because she exposed "the international child kidnap/ child drug trafficking, child slavery network " that operates from the U.S. I think ever reader of this book will be horrified by what has hap-

pened to the Gosch family and think there but for the grace of God go I. Noreen more than any other parent of a kidnapped child made the America people aware of kidnapped and missing children. For those of you who believe the kidnapping of children stopped with Johnny Gosch, Eugene Martin and Jacob Wetterling... better think again.

Call up the index of any major newspaper and check the number of kidnappings involving women and children. I found 279 references listed for the U.S. in the Des Moines Register, over less than a ten-year period. Multiple these by major papers around the country who deal with only their own area. Or go on the Internet to www.amf.com and check for each states registered sex offender list. There are 3,641 for the state of Iowa, 474 in Polk County, reported by the Iowa Division of Criminal Investigation.

It took nearly 14 years to confirm what Noreen suspected from the beginning. She learned there was an alliance between the kidnappers, certain elements of the government and law enforcement. I predict that this book will leave many with their mouth hanging open! Parents will realize the children are not safe in school or even in church.

You will read how the Satanists and the North American Man Boy Love Association (NAMBLA) under the protection of the Federal Government infiltrated every organization where children might be found.

NAMBLA, in fact published in their June 1983 newsletter, a warning for all members "Not to submit to questioning on the Johnny Gosch case by the FBI". They are also known as the Church of the Beloved Disciple and have a 501-C3 (Tax deductible/ non-profit exempt) rating with the IRS.

Understand that there has been a tremendous increase in violence against and by children. Could this be because pedophiles have infiltrated many professions dealing with the treatment of children? Could it also be at the behest and with the sponsorship of the ruling elite…now in the top positions in our government? You will learn about the all-encompassing National Security Act of 1947, it gave unlimited power to the CIA and other military covert operations. This power led one kidnapper to brag, "The FBI lets me do what ever I want with kids"!

In 1997, Johnny Gosch came home to tell his mother that he had been kidnapped for Project Monarch, a government program that had involved him as a prostitute, in pornography, drugs and special covert operations.

Johnny came home with faith in his mother, knowing that she had not forgotten him. He came as a man, believing that his mother could do something to bring these evil men to justice. Noreen knew when she promised to help her son, that she could not do it alone… She needed to mount a campaign to tell Johnny's story and the horrendous scandal to the United States.

Noreen Gosch is doing her best to demonstrate the length and depth of the cover-up. She has been working for years, with former State Senator John DeCamp. DeCamp represented a young man, Paul Bonacci and notified the Gosch's after Paul confessed to his participation in the kidnapping of Johnny Gosch. Noreen Gosch found him to be credible. He had knowledge only about Johnny that only the family knew. Paul Boncci filled in the missing pieces of the Johnny Gosch story. His story is pivotal to the Johnny Gosch case.

Take the time to read the transcript of the "Conspiracy of Silence" documentary, which I have transcribed. What you are reading is the documentary video that shook the White House and Congress enough that they spared no effort to see it destroyed. I did not know until Noreen Gosch and I were viewing this videotape that one of those prostituted children, who toured the White House twice, was none other than Paul Bonacci.

INTRODUCTION

Noreen Gosch has obtained it for the Johnny Gosch Foundation. It affects all the children in this country whose lives and honor may be in jeopardy. You the American people have the duty to see that your own children remain safe.

In 1982, Reader"s Digest claimed in an article that 100,000 children a year are kidnapped. Multiply this by the child who runs away because of abuse, or abusive parents, who literally throw children away. Their children are often forced to prostitute themselves on the streets of America.

Sister Mary Rose McGeady, director of Covenant House in New York City, which provides shelter for homeless children, states in her book "Are You Out There God? ... there are over one million homeless children! Others have stated the figure far higher. As many as one child in 66 doesn't have a home.

It is estimated that one girl in three will be molested before she is sixteen and one boy in five. A radio program featuring Colonel James "Bo" Gritz, one of the most decorated Green Berets to come out of Viet Nam, talked about dangers to children. As a boy scout, he said, "two scoutmasters tried to molest him." He was narrating this in conjunction with the story on the news about the scoutmaster, who hung three boys upside down naked in the woods and carved a "T" on their chests. The man was a saddest. Gritz makes the point ....get involved with your children as a scoutmaster or coach of the Little League. If you don't the pedophiles surely will. See the chapter on NAMBLA.

In July 1993, Reader's Digest in an article called "Savior of the Streets" a Bridgeport businessman, set out to help the teen prostitutes of New York City. The story contains a reference to a pimp, who goes to Florida visits another pimp and admires one of his "kittens," the girl is 14 and buys her for $3,000. The girl is a runaway, throwaway who was forced into prostitution and is now obviously a slave. See the chapter on Slavery.

You have all watched major network shows such as 20/20, 60 Minutes etc. You will see what is happening to poor Russian children, Bosnian children, etc., or kids living in sewers in Rio de Janeiro but you will not see the children living in New York Sewers, or Chicago sewers, but they are there.

There continues to be an insidious plan to silence Noreen Gosch, because she has become the spokesperson for "the lost " children. How many are there? If you believe the Reader's Digest Article of 1982 and multiply 100,000 a year times 30 years. Then you have 3,000,000 that is more than all the soldiers, who have died in all the wars from the wars that we have fought from the Revolutionary War to the present.

What is your picture of America? Are children safe in its streets? In its schools? What you are about to read will change your view of America, the government and the very history of this country.

Who today believes that the lone gunmen, Lee Harvey Oswald, shot John F. Kennedy? No one it seems but the major news anchors of NBC, CBS, ABC, and CNN. Most of us know that it was a conspiracy….a coverup. If you follow all the books and articles that have been done on Kennedy, you will discover that many were involved in the assassination and many who were in Dealey Square died because they saw too much.

Since that time the "new media" and "university types" are fond of calling reason and reasonable accounts as conspiracy theories. If one and one make two, it is a fact not a theory.

One day an envelope with no return address came to me from Nebraska. It was a copy of a report. It told the story of the Franklin Investigation going on at the Nebraska Legislature. It involved important political figures and the use of Nebraska children for sexually purposes. It was the story mainly of Paul Bonacci, who had been forced as a boy to participate in the making of "snuff films. " As a long time reporter for Associated Press and Milwaukee Journal, etc. I did not take these stories for granted. I called repeatedly Senator Loren Schmit, in charge of the Franklin Credit Union Investigation for the Nebraska Legislature. Finally, he returned my call and for forty-five minutes, he told me of important political figures and

INTRODUCTION

businessmen, who were using and abusing children. Schmit said, " I believe they are going to get away with it."

It was then; I called Noreen Gosch and explained that I felt the Nebraska investigation might provide some leads to what happened to Johnny. I had been given access to a casebook by Ted Gunderson, Retired Senior Agent In Charge FBI, California. Gunderson's investigations since his retirement in 1979, had lead him to the McMartin Day Care Center and proof that 800 children had been molested in Satanic rituals. He had hundreds of newspaper clippings dealing with missing and kidnapped children connected to the satanic and North American Man Boy Love Association. See chapter on Gunderson.

Noreen Gosch, West Des Moines

In the fall of 1991, I decided to make a video about the Johnny Gosch case for cable access television in Iowa City, Iowa. John Herbst, a young student video and film maker, whose father was the director of Channel 2 in Cedar Rapids, accompanied me to West Des Moines Sitting in the her living room, Noreen Gosch unfolded the story of her son's kidnapping and what it had done to the family over the past nine years.

Noreen spoke forcefully and well, as an interviewing journalist, I did not have to do much, only an occasional question. She had by now given every detail of the story many times but she came across as someone who had a mission and no obstacle would stop her for long.

This video, which is still available, became not just Johnny's story but the story of what was happening to children across this country and internationally. I read and showed the Newspaper article from June 29, 1989, Washington Times saying: Call Boys Given Midnight Tour of Bush/Reagan White House, to a church group. My presentation was filmed for a video, which I finally titled "America's MIA Children", which stands for Missing/Murdered In America.

Noreen is a woman of tremendous compassion. She is a busy woman holding down as many as three jobs at one time, but if someone needs her she is there. When she knew, she had her emotions firmly under control; she went to see the young man Paul Bonacci in the Nebraska prison. She was not prepared to like the man, who had helped to kidnapped her son, but her heart opened to the tortured young man, who had been forced into that situation and had done his best to help Johnny survive. Paul was only one of a number of prisoners Noreen visited to gain information. Pedophiles, murderers and serial killers were among the informants. See Bonacci chapters.

When the West Des Moines Police, FBI and news media portrayed Paul Bonacci, as a pathetic liar and a nut. She stood by him and testified for him in a federal court hearing in February 1999, where Judge Urbom stated he was telling the truth and granted him a million dollars in real and punitive damages from Larry "Lawrence" King, from Omaha, Nebraska. King now sits in a country club style prison in Colorado. Struck from the list of those who had a part in Paul Bonacci torture and degradation was the Archdiocese of Omaha, a millionaire department store heir and others to whom a million dollar judgment would have been a minor inconvenience. See DeCamp chapter.

At Paul's trial, Noreen met another young man, Russell Nelson. He was a young photographer, who got involved with Larry King. He went from taking pictures of guests at parties to taking compromising photos of important politicians with children. . He was forced by threats and intimidation to go deeper and deeper into the photographing of children with important political figures surreptitiously …. without their knowledge. Today more than twelve years after he disappeared from the Omaha area, he is back in prison in Oregon after having been granted his freedom through the efforts of Attorney John DeCamp.

Today even as Noreen is looking for a job to replace the one she was downsized out of after more than 20 years, she has taken the time to help Russell Nelson, who as been re-imprisoned with a trumped up charge of parole violation. Assisting Retired FBI Agent Ted Gunderson, she has E-

INTRODUCTION

mailed a 50-page packet of information to everyone from the President to the Pope. See A Man Called Rusty

For nearly 19 years, Noreen has fought to uncover who kidnapped Johnny and why. Today, she can give you the name of all four kidnappers, she can take you to the house in Sioux City, Iowa, where Johnny was held prior to being picked up by a government agent...called the Colonel. Paul Bonacci identifies him as Colonel Michael Aquino. See chapter on Michael Aquino and Satanism.

Noreen has endured threats against her own person until she is numb...someone beating on the door of her house in West Des Moines...rocks thrown against the side of the house. Explicit phone calls telling her she was marked for death if she did not shut up.

When she testified in Washington DC, at a Senate hearing armed guards were stationed outside her door. A Mafia figure, she is going to call Bill called her to let her know a hit had been put out on her life and he was sending men to protect her. Of all the people, Noreen has met over the years, Bill has been the most compassionate and helpful, the FBI has been the most spiteful.

For a woman, who grew up watching Efrem Zimbalist Jr. in "The FBI Story", where the agents always helped the people, not till Noreen met retired agent Ted Gunderson did she met a man to match the TV Image. Ted Gunderson a highly respected retired agent and became a whistleblower as a civilian private investigator; he exposed the FBI covering up murder evidence. Ted has been ostracized from the organization of retired agents for his failure to follow the party line. See Gunderson chapter. See FBI chapter.

Noreen has become the secretary, the office manager, friend, confidant, mother confessor, angel and even servant to a whole host of people...from the injured children, now injured adults and mindwar survivors.... In addition to the men and women, who have lost wives, husbands and children in the pursuit of truth.

Noreen Gosch is still standing tall, still determined to get Johnny's story on paper and in print. Since I first met her, I have been amazed at her ability to change direction on a dime. In the midst of doing this book, she took time to ship Ted Gunderson's text in an attempt to save Rusty Nelson's life.

In September 1982 Noreen Gosch lost a son. In the struggle to find him she has adopted a very large family…all with the same aim….to bring to justice those who abuse and murder children, thinking they are above the law.

The Rest of the Story

Anyone who has listened to Paul Harvey 's Radio broadcast is well familiar with this phase. Most of Harvey's true tails have a twist. The book that you are about to read has more twists and turns in it than a Victorian maze.

PREFACE

I have chosen to write this book to bring forth the truth for the first time. Sharing with all, who will take the time to read. The Who, How and Why... my son Johnny was kidnapped.

Some who read this book might find it difficult to believe and wonder how could anything such as this happen in America. I will share with you, the words of a brilliant detective. He told me very early in the case, "Just because you don't believe something.... Does not mean that it isn't true. Keep your mind open and be willing to investigate every lead or clue that comes to you. If you do these things, you will solve your son's case, you will have the answers." As the most horrific facts, began to surface in the case, I had to remind myself, sometimes several times a day, the words of this man. I kept saying to myself... "It is only a matter of time and I will have all the pieces to this tragic puzzle."

Our family was shattered by the loss of Johnny, no one should have to go through this pain. But unfortunately, it happens across our country daily, at the hands of the most evil predator alive... the pedophile. I had never heard the word pedophile before Johnny was kidnapped. I knew it happened by watching the news but that was somewhere else in the country... I didn't realize or feel the impact. I was shocked to find out how prevalent pedophilia is in America. The National Average of Pedophiles is... **one active**

pedophile to every 500 people in our population. I feel this is a very conservative estimate... the numbers are much larger.

It has taken me many years to find the answers; I had every obstacle thrown before me, from ridicule to death threats. I have lived through and survived every parent's nightmare.... **SOMEONE TAKING YOUR CHILD!** If you have ever lost your child in a supermarket or a crowd for even a few minutes, you know the panic in your heart until you find them. Multiply that by 18 years of searching and you will know what it has been like to walk in my shoes.

It is easy to become despondent, angry, vicious and bitter when this happens. I realized from the beginning.... I must always remember "Johnny is the true victim in this case" I have been left with a terrible heartache and huge problem to solve but he is the victim. No matter what or how I feel.... He is going through "worse". Keeping this thought focused in my mind at all times, enabled me to be effective in not only the investigation but helping other families.

My calmness before the public has often been "misjudged" as a lack of caring or being somehow aloof. It is neither... it was the only way I was able to survive. I had to learn how to remove the painful, emotional parts of this situation in order to continue on the path. My skin had to become "thick... almost bullet proof" to ward off some of the things which were said and done to me. I knew when I had a spot on national television ... that I would only have a few minutes to get my message across and show Johnny's picture. I could not waste those precious moments falling apart on television.

Losing my son is the most difficult, painful thing I have ever endured. It is a nightmare; you lose control of your entire life. It is in the hands of the kidnapper, the police and the media. You want so much to have the answers; but you hit brick walls everywhere you turn. The tragedy becomes (and rightly so) your entire focus. Being a devout person, I would pray but answers did not come for years... I would say out loud **"God, did you hear** me? God... are you there? My son's life is at stake! Help me! I need to know the truth... all of it!" I would then try reminding myself, it will come if you wait long enough and work hard enough. But at three a.m., when you can't sleep and are pacing the floor, it is hard to remember these affirmations. It took making a decision and remaining determined. If I quit, fell apart and lost it.... Then who would look for Johnny?

Later, when the pieces fit together, despite the fact it was the most vile upsetting things one could ever be told, I was grateful, for my prayers had been answered. I finally knew what happened to Johnny. Even though, he is not here with me, I know he is alive... I know he is safe and has the skills to survive. It saddened me to learn of the torture he endured.

I have developed many survival tips throughout the years... I call it my "survival kit", in fact, I teach a course called "Your Survival Kit". The practical things you need to know to survive a tragedy emotionally and physically. Many of the people, who contact me have not had their child kidnapped but still need ways to survive tragedies in their lives..

There are sad things in life, which we must all face. It is my intention to give "hope and help" to many who will read this book. Even though I do not like what happened to my son and it brought terrible heartaches for me...I am at peace.

We can all be handed a **"basket of lemons in life"** but it is our individual decision whether we **"suck on the lemons and become bitter or we make lemonade"**. I feel no anger or bitterness.

No matter what happens to us in life....
The situation remains the same...
It is how we happen to "IT"
that makes us or breaks us
physically and emotionally!

This didn't happen overnight... I had to work at it **DAILY**. I made it a policy to find something to be "thankful for" each and every day. Some days it was tough, almost impossible... I focused on little things because the big things were so out of control in my life.

Recently, as I was having a lunch break in a restaurant, a lady sat down and said, "You don't know me but how are you"? I answered, "Just fine, how are you." She went on to say "I knew you would say fine... I knew you would ... how do you do that? You are always fine no matter what is happening in your life. You know the secret to surviving, will you teach me?" I knew by the last question this woman needed some assistance and that she no doubt had trouble or sadness in her life. I did share with her some things, which work for me. I then told her about the classes in Survival that I teach. She was so grateful for time we spent together talking. By just taking a little time, I knew I had helped her... if only on a temporary basis.

If this unspeakable crime has happened in your life, if you have suffered a loss of a loved one through another type of violent crime, or if you have lost hope due to a tragedy of any kind in your life...then please read this book with an open mind, you will be both amazed and glad you did.

..**Noreen N. Gosch**

SECTION ONE

THEY HAVE NO CRIME....
I HAVE NO SON!!!!

THE FIRST TWO YEARS

My story really begins on Sept. 3, 1982; we had attended a Valley High school football game to watch our older son play. Johnny asked if he could buy some popcorn, as he walked down the bleachers toward the concession stand, a policeman approached him. They visited briefly, my husband then went down and asked Johnny to stand near the playing field, so we could see him from where we were sitting. Johnny obeyed and stood by the railing, the policeman had followed him and continued their conversation.

A few moments later, I looked down and Johnny was no longer by the railing. Again, my husband went down to locate him, he discovered him under the bleachers in the darkness talking to the policeman once again. John brought Johnny up to sit with us. A short time later the game was over and, on the way, out of the stadium, Johnny pointed to the policeman and said… "He was really nice, maybe I should think about being a policeman when I grow up." We went home. I thought at the time this was very unusual behavior on the part of the policeman and as we left the stadium, I turned around and memorized his face. This incident became very important in the days to come.

The following day, Saturday, September 4, 1982, Johnny went to a movie in the afternoon with his friend Mark. That evening, my daughter and her boyfriend came from college, our older son was also home, I fixed a nice dinner. It was so nice to have all of them home at the same time. We had what I call "the last supper." I remember how much fun the kids had that night, joking with each other, laughing, and enjoying being together. About nine thirty p.m., Johnny jumped up saying "I am going to bed, I have to do the paper route in the morning before we go to the lake". Before saying good night to everyone, he asked "Can I do my paper route alone tomorrow morning"? His Dad said, "I guess it would be okay.". I immediately said "No, your dad will go with you like always, it is so dark at six a.m., and I don't want you out on the street alone." Johnny said, "good night", gave everyone a hug and went upstairs to bed. A few moments later, Johnny was back in the kitchen standing next to me as I was cleaning up after dinner. He gave me another hug and said "Mom, I will always love you... you are the best"! He then went to the stairs, turned looked at me, smiled, and then disappeared up the stairs. This was to be the last time I would see my son for over fourteen years. (5,293) days.

Early on September 5, 1982, our phone rang, I looked at the clock and it was one thirty a.m. My husband took the call saying, "Yes, alright, yes, alright, okay" and then hung up. I asked him who it was, and he replied, "It was a wrong number." I remember thinking it was very odd; we had been receiving calls like this every Sunday morning at the same time... for the past four weeks. Never had my husband spoken to anyone until this call but he always said they were just "hang up calls."

A few hours later, our phone started ringing again, the neighbors were saying they did not receive their Sunday paper and wanted to know if Johnny was running late. I got up to check if Johnny had overslept, he was not in his room, I went downstairs and noticed Johnny's wagon was also gone. My husband said "he is probably running late. I will go help him. Why don't you start breakfast, then we can leave for the lake when we are finished." It was a beautiful Labor Day weekend, and we had plans to go boating at the lake. I began to fix breakfast and suddenly, I felt something was very wrong. I walked to the refrigerator and put all of the things back, which I had taken out for breakfast and sat at the kitchen table.

John, Johnny's father burst through the door yelling "**JOHNNY IS GONE... HIS WAGON IS SITTING TWO BLOCKS AWAY FULL OF NEWSPAPER, CALL THE POLICE SOMETHING HAS HAPPENED TO HIM**". By then the phone was ringing off the hook, everyone wanted their newspapers, I told the neighbors something had happened to Johnny, the papers would be delivered as soon as possible but we had an emergency. One man said, "We just want our paper". I immediately called the West Des Moines Police Dept. While a neighbor helped my husband deliver the papers. We waited 45 minutes for the police to arrive (we live 10 blocks from the police station)! I telephoned our daughter at college and our other son at his job, asking each of them to come home immediately. I knew it was serious and I wanted my family all together.

I then telephoned Johnny's, District Manager at the Des Moines Register to ask for the names of the other boys, picking up newspapers at the corner paper drop. She came right to the house after hearing what had happened. I made phone calls to the other news carriers, they each told me a man was seen talking to Johnny, he was driving a blue car and stopped him for directions, as he walked away towards the corner to pick up his bundles of papers. Johnny continued to walk with our little dog, Gretchen, towards the corner and did not at any time go over to the car. The driver then made a U-turn in the street and followed Johnny back to the corner, where the other children were also folding newspapers. Soon an attorney, John Rossi arrived to pick up newspapers for his children, he also talked to the driver of the blue car.

Mike Seskis, a paper carrier, 16 yrs. old at the time told me, "Johnny said quietly this guy is weird, something is wrong with him, I am scared and am going home." Johnny started to walk away; suddenly the driver of the blue car started the engine, backed up and drove away from the scene. The attorney had left while Mike remained on the corner. Mike reported" just before the driver pulled away ... he flicked the dome light on and off in his car 3 times." Just then, Mike saw a man come out from between two houses and follow Johnny down the street, around the corner and out of sight. He watched until he saw Johnny turn the corner out of sight. The second man followed Johnny around the corner, he also said, "I heard your dog growl, but nothing else seemed wrong at the time" and continued folding his papers.

At that moment, the two Bosen brothers were approaching the area, also pulling their wagon on the way to pick up their newspapers. They reported seeing Johnny sitting on his wagon slumped over, but the boys were in a hurry and went on. Seconds later, all of the witnesses heard the slamming of a car door, screeching of tires and the car leaving the area at a high rate of speed, running the stop sign and traveling North on 42nd street towards the Interstate. Another neighbor, P.J. Smith also heard the car door slam, looked out his bedroom window as the car pulled away. All that was left on the sidewalk was Johnny's wagon still full of newspapers... Johnny was gone.

The police finally arrived to make out a missing person's report. I had collected all this information from witnesses before they arrived. I answered all the entire questions; the police officer then looked at me and said, "Has your son ever run away before?" I couldn't believe what I was hearing, after sharing all the information with the witnesses. How could he even ask such a question. I replied "my son has never run away.... not in the past and not now"! The officer acted unconcerned as if this was normal, just another runaway in his mind. He left the house, and we heard nothing from the police department for the next eight hours.

While waiting for the police to contact us again, I telephoned friends and relatives all over the Des Moines area to let them know what happened, giving them the description of the car, asking for help in a search. We started searching the immediate neighborhood and then expanded the search.

THEY HAVE NO CRIME.... I HAVE NO SON!!!!

Large groups of people were beginning to form, helping us search parks, near the rivers, any secluded area which might be a crime scene. I stayed near the phone handling all the calls which were coming in and telephoning police departments in other areas. I soon discovered no one outside our area knew Johnny was missing. The West Des Moines Police had not sent out any report to other areas. Approximately three thirty p.m., two detectives returned to the house and requested a picture of Johnny, asked a few questions and left.

I called the parents of the witnesses again, they told me two police men came to their home, listened to the report but had not brought a clip board or a piece of paper to write anything down. These parents were very upset with the police, they knew nothing was being done to help us locate Johnny and reported it to me.

Soon the word began to spread that a child in West Des Moines was missing, and reporters appeared on the front porch wanting pictures and a story. We handed out photos of Johnny, telling them we would appreciate it if they would publicize his picture and ask for any information possible. The police meanwhile were not doing anything... They were using their legal right at that time to not take any action on the case for 72 hours. It would be two years before a law was passed in Iowa to force the police to act immediately when a child is missing for whatever reason. Johnny was clearly kidnapped, and we could not get any type of police investigative action for 72 hours. We had to get friends, relatives and neighbors to form search parties to look for Johnny.

The police chief Orval Cooney instructed us not to talk to the media but to sit in our house and not to even participate in searches. We of course did not listen to him, continued to search throughout the entire night all wooded areas, along country roads, ditches, any place a crime might have taken place. We feared the worst and kept our eyes trained to look for a body. The evening news carried Johnny's pictures and our phone was ringing constantly. It was complete bedlam at the house. We were in shock that the police were treating this so lightly and we could not get any kind of help for Johnny.

As darkness fell, it started to rain, our relatives soon began arriving during the long night to help in any way they possibly could and to show support. Most of them lived several hours from Des Moines. We simply could not believe something like this could happen two blocks from our home. Johnny had never gone on the paper route alone, his father always went with him, until that one morning. Why! Johnny's older brother had gotten up early to go to work and knocked on Johnny's door to be sure he was up. Johnny had always come in to wake his dad to do the route together. We do not know to this day why he went by himself. It all happened so quickly, our son was gone, we knew he had been kidnapped from the reports of the five witnesses and here we are alone, the police would not help. What were we going to do?

The phone rang again, it was a representative of the Des Moines Register, Johnny's employer… they wanted us to find a replacement for him to deliver the papers. There was very little consideration from the Des Moines Register. At this point, I lost my temper and called the editor James Gannon, reported to him what had happened to our son and how the circulation department of the paper had treated us. I then told him exactly what he could do with their typewriters, press and paper. The lack of response by the police and Des Moines Register was about more than I could take. Mr. Gannon apparently made some calls and called back shortly to tell me that the newspaper was going to offer a reward of

$5,000 for information.

No one slept the first night, as all the relatives gathered to show support, I said "we are going to leave the **porch light** on… one of my children isn't home yet." The porch light was to remain on for eleven years. The next day, more than 1,000 people arrived at the police department volunteering to search for Johnny on foot. A call was placed to Governor Robert Ray to ask for use of the National Guard helicopters for an aerial search. His response was "you must prove it is life and death, then there would be a fee of $750 per hour to use the helicopters.... And a fee to be paid to the pilots". It was simple... we did not have the money. As the people searched throughout the day, the police were not helpful in any way in organizing the search or directing it. It was a "do it yourself project". One search team after another would return to the house to give us a report. The report was the same at each search site... the police chief would arrive use a loudspeaker and say to the crowd "Go home folks, the kid is probably just a damn runaway." I was stunned and couldn't believe what I was hearing. Why was this man behaving this way, was he drunk or just stupid? My little boy was gone; he had done nothing to anyone. Johnny was only twelve years old.

Our Police Chief, Orval Cooney had a reputation as the town drunk, only a few months before the kidnapping; he had beaten a man in a local bar while intoxicated. It was quite a news item for a while, but Mayor George Mills allowed the man to keep his job. There had been a full-scale investigation of the West Des Moines Police Department after twenty of his own officers filed reports of negligence, among other charges. It was evident that we were working with a police department incapable or unwilling to handle a crime of this magnitude.

After hearing these reports from the search teams, I made another trip to the police station. Orval Cooney and Gene Meyer. Dept. of Criminal Investigation were sitting in the chief's office when I arrived at the station. I confronted the Chief about his remarks to the search teams, Gene Meyer interrupted by saying "We do not consider Johnny to be in danger, until you (his parents) prove his life is in danger." I asked them if they had begun any type of investigation on the vehicle, as one witness had given a partial license plate number, the name of the county and state on the plate. Both the Chief and Meyer reported they were not going to decide to do a motor vehicle license search for at least another day. The Chief then said, "We have never had a case like this, we aren't sure what to do." I replied, "I don't fault you for this, but please call other police departments for assistance." The chief told me "He would not do that because they wanted to handle it themselves!

Again, I couldn't believe what I was hearing…. My son's life was at stake and the Police Chief had an ego problem. I returned home, frustrated, angry and made the decision to call the media. I scheduled the first of what was to be hundreds of television interviews. It was Sept. 7th and the police continued to wait another day to begin an investigation. I later learned from three Sheriff's departments in neighboring counties… they had sent men to assist in the search for Johnny, and were told by the Chief "go home, we do not want your help." He was refusing any type of help for our son…. What is wrong with his man? Is he a lunatic or just stupid or was he protecting someone?

During the first TV interview, I made a "plea for my son's life, to beg his kidnappers to contact us and we would meet their demands, we wanted our son and loved him very much". I also included a special message to Johnny to remember he is loved and try to stay strong until we find you. Following the news showing the interview, every nut in the city began calling our home and driving by our house. Although there were some people who were very sympathetic, others were cruel and said, "your son is dead and begin laughing, then hang up the phone". Some called to criticize me for not crying on television.

The most unbelievable expressions of humanity began to surface. Due to the interviews, we began to receive leads and would call the police to report them. Each time, the police would say "it is probably nothing."

It was evident by their lack of professionalism that they were not investigating this case. I had no choice but to become my own investigator, checking out all these calls one by one. Many of them were a dead end but everything had to be checked, just in case it might yield a clue. The ground searches continued for one more day… people then had to go back to their jobs, the long holiday weekend was over. Our relatives had to also return to their own lives. The reality began to sink in "Johnny was gone and no one but his family was going to do anything about it."

A few other businesses contributed to a reward fund which had been started to find Johnny, which had been started by the Des Moines Register.

THEY HAVE NO CRIME.... I HAVE NO SON!!!!

We added $40,000, the equity in our home, to the $20,000 already being offered. We stipulated our portion of the reward was "for the safe return of Johnny".

I knew it was necessary to create a missing persons poster to send them out. But I didn't know how to begin this project. I assumed the police departments assisted parents with this... they informed me that wasn't their job. There were no Missing Children's organizations to turn to at this time. Many were created following Johnny's kidnapping. The FBI was nowhere in sight... why were they not involved? Kidnapping is a Federal Crime.... if you are wealthy enough, apparently, we weren't!

My heart was heavy, I felt, I was going to completely fall apart but knew if I did, there would be no one to help Johnny, certainly not the local law enforcement. Our family had never experienced a violent crime, nor had any problems with the police in our lives. This was all new to us, it seemed there was nowhere to turn.

The media did continue each day to call us, doing interviews with updates, new pleas to the kidnappers and reports on the growing reward fund. The media became more instrumental in our case than the police department. At least they were helping us to circulate Johnny's picture locally and to other areas of the state.

I made another trip to the police department to plead with the police chief. While I was at the station, I overheard an officer say "Why does that stupid family leave the porch light on for a kid that will never come home". The officer saw me standing there.... Why such cruel remarks? But this was just the beginning as I was about to discover.

By Sept. 8th, the police now wanted to ask questions. They asked if we had threatening phone calls, anything unusual happen in the week prior to Johnny's kidnapping. I reported to them the phone calls in the middle of the night prior to the kidnapping and about the policeman at the football game on 9/3/82...I was told neither was important. This concerned me, as the man at the football game resembled the description from witnesses of the driver of the blue car, kidnapping Johnny. However, the police chief would not pursue the matter and told me to forget it.

During this most tragic time of our lives, suddenly we were forced to be investigators, fund raisers, do interviews on television, and continue to keep our jobs and our sanity. How are we going to do it? I had no training in these things.

The Police Chief kept telling me that the FBI would not be entering the case. I decided to call the local FBI office and request an agent to come to my home. They sent Special Agents Ed Mall and David Oxler. When they arrived, they sat down at the table and told me they would not be entering the case because, in their words "WE HAVE NO CRIME." I responded, "I have no son, he was kidnapped, you have all the information from the witness's, kidnapping is a Federal Crime." The agents informed me the Police Chief, Orval Cooney had briefed them telling them there was no need for them to enter the case… That he could handle the situation. I could not believe what was happening. It seemed the world had gone completely nuts. A young boy was kidnapped off the street and the FBI would not enter the case. I grew up watching the FBI Story with Effram Ziembalist Jr. and really believed that they entered kidnap cases and set up a command post in the homes of the families. NOT TRUE…. It is nothing like TV … not one thing in this case would I consider to be a real investigation.

It seemed all hope was gone, then someone called and suggested Child Find in New York, I called them and arranged to have all the material sent for registration for Johnny. I sent the check for the initial fee and in the following months, continued to receive requests for more money, we had finally over the months sent several hundred dollars. Each time, Child Find would tell us that it was for printing and distribution costs on our son's case. And that just as soon as Johnny's picture was placed in their national book it would be distributed all over the country. Unfortunately, they overestimated their ability to help or their budget, because it was over eighteen months before my son's picture finally was printed in their book and distributed....it to dentist's offices and doctors' offices etc. There was no way Johnny would be in a dentist's office to have his teeth cleaned and be recognized. It was a complete waste of our money and our time. At that time their organization was set up to help victims of "parental kidnapping."

I was scheduled to be at a school board meeting to discuss the kidnapping. At that time, we took turns covering the telephone at home. The police instructed us to tape record phone calls and let them know where we were at all times. I reported to them I was attending the meeting. The police then telephoned John at home, saying they wanted to see him at the police station right away to go over material on car license plates. They sent the Police Chief and Gene Meyer to the house to cover the phone while John was gone. I happened to come home early and discovered both men searching our home without a search warrant...I asked them to leave my home. I never received an apology for their conduct or deception.

The following day... I made a trip to the police department.... The Police Chief said, "you people are so straight, we couldn't find anything wrong or illegal about you when we looked through your house." He sounded positively disappointed. I then told him that the case needed more concentrated investigation, he replied "They were going to put the case on the back burner because it was becoming very quiet, and nothing was happening.... the phones just aren't ringing."

It was only three weeks after the kidnapping at that point. I took care of that immediately, upon returning home, I called a few friends and asked each of them if they would call four friends, asking each to call the Police Chief and demand to know what was being done in the Gosch kidnapping case. Soon the police were flooded with calls, and they could not put the case on any back burner.... It had suddenly come "alive" once again.

The week of September 24th, a small article appeared in the Des Moines Register, about the attempted abduction of two young children in a small town just outside of Des Moines. The man arrested was from Omaha, Neb. and was connected to a pornography ring. I took the newspaper clipping to the Police Chief, Orval Cooney, asking him to investigate and call the Police Chief in Omaha, Robert Wadman. Our Police Chief refused saying, "I don't have a feel for this, so I am not going to do anything." I then went to the FBI office and was told once again "they did not intend to enter the case, because the Police Chief told them he didn't need their help." In desperation, I called a press conference and raised "holy hell" releasing the information that neither the police nor the FBI would investigate my son's kidnapping.

Within an hour of my press conference, I received my first of many death threats. A male voice on the phone said, "Stop making waves or you will die…. you bitch! " What I did not realize at the time was that I was knocking on the back door of what became the Franklin Credit Union Sex Scandal conducted by the Nebraska Legislature. John DeCamp, a longtime Nebraska State senator detailed it in a book, The Franklin Cover-Up on "child abuse, Satanism and murder, which went far beyond the confines of Nebraska. It is no wonder our police chief would not investigate this matter. I was so close to discovering what happened to my son within three weeks after he was taken, they had to find some way to stop me…. The death threat and the refusal of authorities to investigate severely limited me in trying to find my child.

The West Des Moines Police Chief was considered an authority in Johnny's case and was invited to speak at a number of civic organization meetings. It was reported to me that Orval Cooney began spreading a story that Johnny was not our child but adopted and ran away to find his parents. I had to produce his birth certificate and publish it in the newspaper to prove Johnny was my son. This ludicrous behavior by professional law enforcement official was hurting our chances of having public support to locate our son. I could not understand why he would behave in this manner when a child's life was at stake. Looking back on it today, it is perfectly clear why the Police Chief did not pursue an active investigation to find Johnny. You will read why in later chapters of this book.

It became clear that we would receive more help from a private detective than the police. I began collecting names of investigators to be interviewed.

THEY HAVE NO CRIME.... I HAVE NO SON!!!!

I had also contacted several national TV shows 60 Minutes, 20/20, Mike Douglas, Phil Donahue, Nightline programs to tell them what was happening here. They were very nice but told me to submit the story in writing with clippings. This was their policy, but it takes longer.

I decided to tell the police I planned to hire a private detective. When I told Police Chief Cooney, he became outraged. He began yelling and threatening me. He shouted: "You have no right to bring in an outsider!" I replied, "You cannot tell me what I can or cannot do to find my son. I will hire a private detective…If you have a problem with that … stick it up your ass!" I walked out of the police station and returned home. I made arrangements to travel to Omaha Nebraska the following day to interview a private detective.

At four p.m., the same day our doorbell rang. There stood the Police Captain, Bob Rushing, with his hat in his hand, saying the Police Chief now wanted us to take a polygraph test. He told me: "They would try make an effort to keep it out of the press, so as not to embarrass us." I couldn't believe what I was hearing! My son is gone. They handled the case negligently from the beginning and now just after I announced hiring a private investigator…. They were demanding a polygraph test. That conversation ended with my asking the Captain to stay, while I called the media and arranged a press conference to announce; We were being harassed by the police, simply because we had planned to hire a private detective. He could not stand the heat and left before the press arrived. I did the interview and received many calls of support from people in the community.

The following day, I traveled to Omaha, Nebraska to interview and hire Dennis Whalen, a private investigator. He was recommended to me because he had solved a case of a missing child in Carter Lake, Iowa. He located Todd Bequette who had been kidnapped, held for two years by a man who repeatedly sexually abused him. To pay the retainer fee, I used all the cash value in my life insurance policies and money in savings for the children's education. We made all the arrangements with Dennis to come to Des Moines and begin work within a few days.

I returned home that evening, and the phone rang. It was Good Morning America asking us to be on their show on October 11, 1982. I accepted and made plans to travel to New York. This was to be the first of over 50 network appearances over the years. It was wonderful to have this opportunity to show our son's picture on Good Morning America to millions of people. I lived in the hope that there would be one solid lead, which would give us the answer. It would help us solve the case and find Johnny. On October 9th, the night before I was to leave for New York, I received a phone call from a man asking for $10,000 ransom. I notified the West Des Moines, who again said "it is probably nothing". This call was not investigated by any law enforcement.

The following morning, I left for New York and the Good Morning America program. We arrived in the city, as I rode in the taxi, I kept looking out the window thinking Johnny could have been taken to a large city such as New York. The hotel accommodations were very nice, but I kept wondering why they allowed all the horses along Central Park to "poop" all over the place. This was my first trip to New York, and I was somewhat surprised by the "aroma". It is called the "city that never sleeps", I felt fortunate to have this opportunity. That evening, I did find a little time to unwind, as it had been non-stop stress from the moment Johnny was kidnapped, I was operating on very little sleep. I went downstairs in the hotel and had dinner just observing all the people who were no doubt living a "normal life" …. something, which was taken from me. I no longer had anything that resembled a normal life.

The following morning, I got up, got ready to go to the studio, there was no way I could even think about eating food. As I was waiting in the lobby for the limo to arrive, a woman sailed in from the dining room, introducing herself as Kristin Cole Brown from Child Find in New York. She was to appear on the program with me. I kept my distance from her as I could remember all of the checks, I had written to Child Find and my son's picture had still not appeared in their book. I knew that Child Find primarily

THEY HAVE NO CRIME.... I HAVE NO SON!!!!

worked on "parental kidnappings" not "stranger" so perhaps that is why they were not effective in Johnny's case. However, they continued to ask for money until I shut off the spigot.

Kristin was just too bubbly for the occasion, she chirped in the limo about how her make up would look on TV that day. I remember thinking at the time, my son is gone, I am turning inside out here, and this woman is concerned about her eyeliner. However, when we got to the studio and we were called into the makeup room, they had to do an "overhaul on Kristin and the make-up artist said to me "your make up is beautiful Mrs. Gosch, what products do you use? We don't have to add a thing ... you are ready to go on the air. "I hadn't done anything special... just got ready for the day as though I were going to work.

Finally, I was escorted to the studio and introduced to David Hartman. He is a very tall man, extended his hand to shake mine and made me feel welcome immediately. We were seated on stage; the soundmen were installing microphones on us. David continued in a very kind sensitive manner to ask for more details about Johnny, the case and asked to see the photo I brought with me. He took it in his hands shaking his head, looked back up at me and said, "I am so sorry this happened to your son." The show began, I was able to give the entire description of the kidnapping, show Johnny's picture and answering questions that David Hartman asked concerning the case.

Kristin Cole Brown was then brought on stage with us, and she gave information to the public about Child Find and all they do for parents of missing children. I did not get another opportunity to set the record straight about the difference between parental and stranger kidnappings....and that this organization primarily worked on parental. They may have changed their format by now.

As I walked out of the studio, I decided not to take the limo back to the hotel. Instead, I walked and about twenty people came up to me, who had seen the program. They were so kind, telling me they were praying for my son. It was surprising to me in a city that large that people would take the time to share their kind comments with me.

When I returned home from New York, the local media reported on the Good Morning America appearance…they gave it good exposure. A number of people called saying they were happy we had the opportunity to show Johnny's picture on national TV and hoped it would bring results. The downside of this (and there seems to always be a downside to everything) some in the city called to say, "You looked too good on the show, your make up, your outfit … how can you be suffering?" Two friends who owned beauty shops also called to tell me the topic of discussion in the shops for a few days was "How Noreen Gosch looked on TV… she looked too good… she can't be suffering… she is in this for just the publicity".

Those that gossiped and criticized me did not understand that I would always present my "best foot forward", in case my son would see the show. I wanted him to see a positive reinforcement, to hear that his mother was working very hard to find him and would not give up. On a network show you are only given a few precious minutes to tell your story. I wasn't going to waste it by sitting there crying and being unable to speak, nor would I go in looking like I had just crawled out of bed.

On October 13, 1982, I spent the day with the private detective. My husband left for a business trip, my mother, older son and private detective were all talking over details of the case. Shortly before, midnight the same man, who had called two days earlier with a ransom demand, called again and "told me to drive to a phone booth at the corner of Hickman Road and Merle Hay Road, that I would find the ransom demand there. He told me, I only had a short time to comply with the demand or I would not see my son again." My private detective told me to grab a pair of gloves to handle the note and off we went. I didn't know if there would be a note or if it was a hoax, but I had to check. When I arrived at the phone booth, I got out of the car, slid my gloved hand across the top of the booth and sure enough there was a note. I ran back to the car, got in and we could see the note was addressed to Mrs. Gosch. I drove home and called the FBI after reading the instructions.

I first called the West Des Moines Police; they of course said it was nothing. I then called the FBI demanding an agent come to my home, reporting we had received a ransom demand. Agent David Oxler, at first refused to come to the house, saying "it is probably nothing!" I explained what the note contained, and he finally agreed to come to the house. When he arrived, he took one look at the note and said, "this does not pertain to Johnny, and we are not going to do anything". How could he say that… the note was addressed to me, and they talked about Johnny in the note? I couldn't believe or accept what he was saying, **THE FBI REFUSING TO ACT ON A RANSOM DEMAND.**

I couldn't think of anything else to do so I grabbed a piece of paper and "asked Agent Oxler to sign it, date it and state that he was refusing to act on this ransom demand, and we would all sign as witness's, my mother, Dennis Whalen (private detective), my older son and myself". Then if my son were killed due to his refusal to act, I would file charges against the FBI for negligence.

Agent Oxler then said, "if you put it that way, we will check it out, but you will have to drive your own car to the area, we will not put one of our agents in to drive it." It was a very bad section of town, there had been a gang murder there just ten days prior. And now the FBI would not send anyone with me for protection nor allow our private detective to go along. The private detective told Agent Oxler "He was going with me regardless!"

Just then the phone rang … I turned on the tape recorder and answered the call. It was the police chief, Orval Cooney, asking for Agent Oxler. I handed him the phone, after they finished talking, he walked back to the table and sat down. I noticed the tape recorder was still running, I had forgotten to shut it off. So, I reached over and turned it off. Agent Oxler got up and threatened to arrest me for tape-recording their conversation. I told him, "It was not intentional, and I had been instructed by the police record every incoming call." He wouldn't listen, grabbed me, shoving me into a wall, taking the tape recording out of the machine and put it in his pocket. To this day, we have never recovered it, I am sure it contained off color remarks about me that they did not want me to hear.

At 1:45 a.m. the FBI called and told me to proceed over to the address in the ransom note and make the money drop. The result of the ransom demand was a disaster the police & FBI waited so long to get into formation. Just before I left the house, the man called back to tell me time was up…**we had waited too long!** Nevertheless, I followed instructions drove to the location, dropped the bag on the corner but the man never surfaced to pick it up. Dennis Whalen and I returned home to wait the rest of the night. The despair that followed this episode was unbelievable. I had always believed that the FBI would handle these cases and that they would respond to a ransom demand. I was so disappointed with every aspect of this case and how it was being handled. The true victim here was Johnny, and no one was doing their job.

The only conclusion, I can arrive at for survival in this time and place, is the fact that from the beginning; I was plagued with people placing obstacles before me. I literally had to fight to go over, around or through them for Johnny's life. I had never been through anything like this in my life… having to fight for everything. There was no time for "pity parties" or falling apart even though I felt so badly. Johnny was the victim, and I kept that focus. My heart hurt: there was actual pain in my chest, which never went away, day or night. The pain remained with me for four years, three months and twenty-six days.

Years later, I began working with the Polk County Victims Association, giving talks for their support group meetings. I learned that all of the other victims, who had lost a loved one to violent crime, also shared the same physical pain in their heart area that I had experienced. The counselors at the Association explained to me that it is very common for victim survivors to have the pain in the heart region, lasting from the onset of the crime up to ten years. They were very interested in the actual time my pain was present before waking up one morning to discover it had vanished. I looked it up in my daily journal and I had recorded the day, I woke up without my pain. Which was four years, three months and twenty-six days after Johnny was kidnapped.

The following day, the story was all over the media in Des Moines, television, radio, and newspaper that there was a ransom demand. During the interviews I shared with the public that the FBI refused to help on that night. The usual public uproar took place, which amounted to dozens of phone calls to our home once again. The phone rang every fifteen minutes day and night. Some people were praying for me and others wanted to criticize me. The law enforcement then began to harass our private detectives, refusing to work with them.

The police forced our investigators to come into the department, telling them they would not accept their P.I. licenses because they were from the state of Nebraska. This caused us a delay. Our investigators had to find a P.I. in the state of Iowa who would issue them a license under his agency. This was also another outlay of money, which we could not afford. The detectives were able to finally begin working. The first morning they were doing a "stake out" of the kidnap scene to determine times, lighting, and distance of the cars from the witnesses. The West Des Moines police drove up and once again forced our detectives to come into the station to explain what they were doing on the street corner at 5:56 a.m. This was a continued type of harassment by the West Des Moines police. They were not willing to investigate the kidnapping, but it seemed they were not about to let us do it either.

THE BIG "DO IT YOURSELF" PROJECT

I continued with our massive flyer program and to finance all of this and private detectives, it was suggested that we sell **"WORLDS FINEST CANDY BARS",** with Johnny's name on the candy wrapper. Many children's groups have used this kind of fundraiser at some time to raise money. In the history of this company, it was reported to me that The Johnny Gosch Foundation sold more candy bars than any other group in the United States. Over a three-year period, we sold 400,000 candy bars, which we received fifty cents profit per bar. That did raise $200,000 to help pay for private investigators and the additional expenses, which accompany a kidnapping and search for a missing child.

I chose November 12, 1982, Johnny's 13th birthday, to have our first meeting of the Johnny Gosch Foundation. Twenty volunteers came, some were old friends, but many new acquaintances that were dedicated to helping us find Johnny and change the system for the positive. We elected a board of directors, Bill Hornbostel, an attorney to file for incorporation/non-profit tax-exempt status and Bob Duitch volunteered his services as an accountant to handle all money incoming and outgoing. We kept all of this as a separate entity. John and I had absolutely nothing to do with the finances other than to work with all the volunteers at the fundraisers. The board of directors managed the Foundation.

Word began to spread throughout the country via the media … JOHNNY GOSCH'S PARENTS ARE SELLING CHOCOLATE TO RAISE MONEY TO FIND THEIR CHILD. For a time, it became quite a humaninterest story, but for a very touching reason. A reporter for the Washington Post wrote a very compelling story about a set of parents "selling chocolate to save their son." We had candy bars in 80 stores; weekly volunteers from the organization would pick up the money and replenish the candy supply. Candy bars were being sold in other parts of Iowa, Illinois and Minnesota. Many people realized that we were average working people, who could not withstand the expense of an ongoing private investigation alone. I borrowed all the money I could from my life insurance cash value, our families helped as much as they could. Our resources could only go so far but it was imperative, we had to keep the private investigation going otherwise we would never know what happened to Johnny.

I decided to go public with our case for several reasons:

1. To find Johnny
2. Educate parents throughout the country.
3. Bring positive change in legislation forcing police to treat "stranger" kidnap cases with priority.
4. To give other parents hope – to convey the idea of "not giving up on your missing child".
5. To help other parents cope with the tragic loss of their child.

When it was first suggested that we sell candy bars and then Johnny Gosch bumper stickers…. I was upset to think that in this country of wealth and waste a parent would have to do this to recover their kidnapped child. **KIDNAPPING IS AGAINST THE LAW. BUT WHERE WAS THE LAW? IT IS A FEDERAL CRIME!**

It is difficult to convey sometimes to others how desperate a parent feels when they do not receive assistance from law enforcement. In our community, it was as though people found this to be unpleasant and preferred not to talk about it. A West Des Moines City Councilman told me "I was embarrassing the city on national TV!" I was treated as "modern day leper" for some time. No one thought it could happen to them that the Johnny Gosch case was an isolated incident. Readers Digest reported in a article that there are as many as 100,000 children kidnapped in the United States each year. What makes people in this area think it couldn't happen to them?

Due to all the publicity, I received the biggest break of the entire case; Ken Wooden called our home after reading articles about Johnny and wanted to visit with me. He had been at Iowa State University doing a week of being a "guest professor". He suggested Perkins Restaurant near the airport. When I arrived Mr. Wooden and Professor Colson of Iowa State University were waiting at a table. We sat down to talk, when suddenly Mr. Wooden asked me "Do you really want your son back or is this all an act?" I was so stunned, I just stood up and said, "I am not sure where that came from, but I do not have time to talk with you" and prepared to leave. He quickly said Professor Colson "I like her.... She has spunk."

He asked me to sit back down and explained that he had worked for ABC and CBS as an investigative reporter. He done a great deal of research on pedophiles, how they molest and kill children. He also wrote the "Children of Jonestown" the story of Guyana and the massacre that took place. He had been following the progress of the case through the media as well as many others in the country. He told me "IT WAS TIME TO ENTER THE NATIONAL ARENA!" He said, "Johnny is probably no longer in the state of Iowa." He also said he wanted to see how strong and determined I was....

He asked me to go forward with an awareness program, telling the truth of what is happening to our children and to fight for better legislation on both a state and federal level. He said he would help me every step of the way, share information with our private detective and me to make an impact in this country. He reported to us the grim statistics of other families destroyed by this tragedy and crime. Divorces and the suicides which so common among parents. He had asked me to speak for so many of the children whose parents could not do it.

The day I met Ken Wooden was one of the best days I had experienced since the kidnapping. A man from outside of Iowa, who cared enough about our son to really give me some "hands on advice."

He said, "it might get rough, the public and press will doubt you, laugh at you and try to discredit you, because the truth you will bring out will be difficult to accept." Then he looked at me and said, "are you willing to fight for you son?" I agreed to do whatever was necessary to find my son. I had no idea of the roller coaster ride that was ahead of me. All Ken warned me about and then some was about to begin. I have never had to fight so hard for anything in my life up to this point.

It was through Ken, I learned about the organized aspect of these kidnappings and how children were used. Organizations such as

THEY HAVE NO CRIME.... I HAVE NO SON!!!!

NAMBLA.... North American Man Boy Love Association, The Rene Guyeon Society and others. The first targets sex with little boys, the second sex with little girls. Both their mottos seem be "sex before eight or it is too late." It was very difficult for a time to cope with this new information. It made me feel ill knowing someone has taken my son to be used in the same way. But when I would weaken, I would look at Johnny's picture and remind myself **"HE IS THE VICTIM, THIS IS NOT THE TIME TO CRUMBLE."**

Ken took time to teach me how to write a press release, which would be noticed when it was sent to a radio or television station or program. He did not forget about Johnny after he left Des Moines, he continued to work very closely with me. In an effort to find Johnny but to also achieve progress in this country. He was a turning point in this case and in my life.

Ken sent me the names of every producer to contact on the entire big network TV shows. I began the long process of letter writing and sending packages of materials to these producers, in hopes of being selected for the shows. Within six months, I began receiving invitations to appear on talk shows, magazine shows and special productions.

One day, as I neared the elevator in the building where I worked, a man approached, shook hands with me and said "Hello, I am Terry Branstad, and I am running for Governor". I replied, "Hi, I am Noreen Gosch, my son was kidnapped, and I need to talk to you." With that I hopped on the elevator with him and his press secretary/campaign manger. I told him I needed help and had ideas for legislation. He said to his press secretary..." make a note for me to get in touch with Noreen after the election." Terry Branstad was elected Governor of Iowa, and he didn't forget what he said in the elevator that day. Soon after the election was over and he got settled in office, I was able to schedule an appointment with him to discuss legislation changes concerning not only Johnny's case but also abused children needed for the state of Iowa.

The next big event that shaped our investigation on a national level was being chosen for an **HBO Documentary Movie** called **"Missing."** Dave Bell

Associates was the film company hired to do the project. The filming was to take place during Thanksgiving week in November of 1982. The producer Terry Meurer Dunn, the film crew, and soundmen ... the entire entourage came to West Des Moines. This was a documentary film, and we were to play ourselves. They did use local people to reenact the kidnapping of Johnny. Our interview lasted five straight hours; it was exhausting... They showed how hard we worked to raise money to find him and also the never-ending faith we displayed that someday we would see Johnny again.

They filmed all types of day-to-day activities. The producers and crew planned to stay with us through the "first Thanksgiving without Johnny," showing how we as a family coped.

The producer wanted to film me shopping for the Thanksgiving turkey at the local Hy-Vee grocery store. They chose the busiest time of the day, with many customers in the store. So much controversy, speculation and publicity had taken place, that I felt as though I were on public display. I grabbed for a 24-pound turkey, hoisted it up to the cart, it slipped out of my hands and bounced along the floor, drawing even more attention to the scene. At that point, there was nothing to do but have a good "laugh" .... something I probably needed.... comic relief. The film crew, producers and I stood in the aisle at the busy grocery store laughing till tears ran down our cheeks. I am sure the other customers thought we had lost our minds.

They recreated the crime scene, interviewed many people in the Des Moines area, including the Police Chief Orval Cooney. Cooney stated in his interview **"the Goschs are damn stupid people"**. The producer Terry Dunn was so stunned the police chief would utter such a crude comment, that she gave us the "sound bite" on a tape to prove his remark. I couldn't understand why a public official, one who was supposed to be looking for my son would say such a hurtful remark about us.

Terry Dunn, the Producer asked the police chief if they had any fingerprints of Johnny Gosch? His response was..." Mrs. Gosch wanted us to fingerprint her son's room, but it makes such a hell of a mess, we decided not to do it".

The HBO film "Missing" aired for the first time in June 1983. Many people having missing children began to contact The Johnny Gosch Foundation for help after seeing the film. They wanted to know how to begin a search on their own cases. By going public with our case, it was the beginning of an increased awareness for families. Many will search indefinitely for their children and probably will never have an answer. It began a movement in this country, which was heard from coast to coast. An awareness of the danger to children falling prey to pedophiles, either in a sexual abuse situation within their community or being kidnapped from their hometowns across the country.

Today you cannot pick up a paper anywhere in the country without seeing an article of someone sexually abusing a child. Seldom do you see an article about kidnapped children. Yet it continues to go on between stranger and parental kidnappings numbers over a half a million per year. An added situation today is the throw away children which add another half a million to the number.

Our organization had become very active in fund raising and awareness programs. I was asked to be a speaker at many schools. I developed a comprehensive program with films to be shown to parents and children, called **"IN DEFENSE OF CHILDREN"**. Ken Wooden assisted with information and statistics, I could share in my talks. During my programs, I gave parents the profile of a pedophile enabling them to see more clearly those who might be abusing children in their communities. In many communities, following one of my programs there would be arrests of pedophiles, which had been operating in secrecy for many years. This program was very necessary and also enabled us to qualify for the nonprofit classification as we were providing a very needed service within our state for all children.

Our detectives advised us to find a good composite artist to do a sketch of the kidnapper. I called the Des Moines Art Center; they were very kind and recommended a fine young artist. He worked with each of the witnesses separately, then all together to create and refine the composite picture of the suspect. This is another area, which Police failed to complete. As soon as the composite drawing was finished, I again called another press conference to release the picture. As soon as our sketch was released, the police then did a composite drawing also and it resembled a **"MR. POTATOHEAD!"** Even the witnesses said it did not look like the driver of the car, the suspect. We added this picture to our missing persons posters, which have numbered into the millions sent out across the country.

I decided to make an appeal to the Des Moines Register editor... James Gannon, only to make someone aware of things the police were not doing in the investigation. I had made repeated efforts to gain cooperation between the police and our detectives from the beginning of the case. They simply would not.

The result of my letter pleading for help was another disaster. Mr. Gannon published it on the front page of the paper and allowed the police to dissect it in print and make crude remarks. The letter was never intended to be used for publicity ... only as a plea for help for my little boy. It was another blow to our family, the impact left me shell shocked, unable to sleep, severe loss of weight because I simply could not eat under all the stress.

I was afraid to open the newspaper each morning, because I didn't know who would attack us next. Nor could I understand "why!" I kept asking this question daily how they could do this and why?

What were their motives? Why would Gannon, the editor of the Des Moines Register encourages and assisted in the attacks against parents to find their child. Today, we know many important people in business and in government are themselves pedophiles or for one reason or another are sympathetic to those who are. Pedophiles can be in any walk of life, male or female teachers, coaches, scout leaders, politicians and police at all levels.

I felt a deep commitment to establish new legislation regarding the "period of time" in which the police wait in a missing person case. Most often they wait 72 hours as they did in Johnny's case. This is valuable precious time in the missing person's life. I gathered all of my materials on

THEY HAVE NO CRIME.... I HAVE NO SON!!!!

legislation for my appointment with Governor Terry Branstad. I worked with an attorney, telling him of the ideas I had for a bill, he helped me write it in the proper language. When I presented all of my ideas and suggestions, I was so pleased to discover Governor Branstad, a kind man who listened. He had an open mind and said," He would read it over and do what he could to help." We did meet again later with a revised edition of the bill after the Governor and his legislative staff had an opportunity to look it over. It was decided that a bill would be drafted.... it was to be called THE JOHNNY GOSCH BILL.

At first, no one wanted to sponsor the bill... they all felt it would be too upsetting to law enforcement, but I continued to talk to both Senators and Representatives, eventually Vic Stueland, from my hometown, who knew me from the time I was a baby, sponsored the bill in the House. A short time later the Senate sponsored the bill.

I was then informed by well-meaning people that if I really wanted the bill to be passed, I would have to wine and dine the legislators. Just as the lobbyists do. I refused to do it that way; I had a full-time job, a part time job and the search for my son... I didn't have time or money to wine and dine legislator I did another press release to this effect. This launched the most hectic schedule for the next full year, as Johnny Gosch Bill did not make it out of committee the first year and we would have to begin all over again on the following session of 1983/1984.

Speaking engagement invitations were coming to every part of the state of Iowa and other states. I was booked every night of the week and weekends. My program, "In Defense of Children" gives a very in-depth presentation, on prevention but also the Profile of a Pedophile and how they operate in a community. Not only for the kidnapped child but the many who are molested, and the cases never resolved. I worked closely with our private detective and Ken Wooden in gathering material for this project.

Each morning, I would go to work, as soon as I got off work, I would be on the road to present another program. I was blessed to have volunteers in the Johnny Gosch Foundation, who took turns traveling with me and handling the literature table. I had several brochures and information for the parents to take home to educate their children on safety. We had huge operating costs in the first few years, due to the amount of printing for all our literature and legislative material. So we always carried a supply of World's Finest Candy Bars to sell at the programs to help defray the cost of printing.

Then came a devastating blow in April 1983. Another boy from West Des Moines was reported kidnapped. Immediately the FBI were called in.... very different than Johnny's case, when they stated, "THEY HAD NO CRIME". It was the son of a very wealthy man in West Des Moines, a very prominent family. Listening to the news reports was like reliving Johnny's kidnapping all over again. The FBI solved the case in 36 hours. They did pay a call to our home at eight a.m. the following day. As they entered our home, Special Agent Herb Hawkins, in charge of a five-state region, stated **"WE REALLY HAD TO MOVE FAST ON THAT CASE,**

THERE WAS A HUMAN LIFE AT STAKE." I couldn't take it anymore and said to Hawkins..." WHAT DO YOU CONSIDER OUR SON..... DOGFOOD?"

Herb Hawkins was sitting in Johnny's chair at the table drinking coffee and replied, "Mrs. Gosch, there is something you don't understand... the other boy kidnapped.... their family is more prominent, their son was worth more money, we had to act fast". Again, I couldn't believe what had just been said to me. In essence "the rich and influential... the FBI will work to find, but sorry you are out of luck."

I completely lost my temper, after many months of this type of treatment, they finally told me the truth...." *JOHNNY DIDN'T MATTER BECAUSE WE WERE NOT RICH AND PROMINENT IN THIS COMMUNITY".*

I honestly do not remember throwing my cup of coffee across the table and just missing the head of Special Agent Hawkins by half an inch. The FBI quickly left our home very quickly after the flying coffee cup. I realized; I needed a new plan; I had to do something different ... because nothing was

THEY HAVE NO CRIME.... I HAVE NO SON!!!!

working. At that moment, I didn't think I would ever be all right again. I decided after that blow... to pack a bag and leave town for several days. I did not tell anyone where I was going and traveled several hundred miles away, checked into a hotel to rest, I needed it so badly.

The police called the house to talk to me and couldn't reach me. They then called my husband saying, "They would put out an alert because there were concerned something had happened to me and I might be missing." My husband told them, "You can't put out an alert, she isn't missing, she is over 21 and it hasn't been 72 hours yet." Essentially their 72-hour rule was being reversed on them.

During the time away from Des Moines, I did rest but more importantly all alone in that hotel... **I HIT BOTTOM AND GUESS WHAT.... I SURVIVED.** I had never felt such despair...I wasn't sure what to do next. That FBI Agent did me a favor, even though it was cruel on his part to say such a thing. He had given me the "tools" to create national interest in Johnny's case.

The night I returned home from my short "rest", the phone rang; it was Ken Wooden. He had heard about the coffee cup incident in Washington D.C., while at a dinner meeting with William Webster, Director of the FBI. Mr. Webster said, "Some crazy lady in Des Moines Iowa, threw a cup of hot coffee at one of my agents." Ken Wooden asked Mr. Webster "what was the woman's name?" Webster replied, "that newspaper boy's mother, that Gosch woman". Ken replied to Webster "If Noreen Gosch threw a cup of coffee at your Agent, he must have done something herrendous... because she has displayed tremendous courage and control throughout this entire nightmare." In his call to me, shortly after his dinner with Webster, Ken said to me "The next time you throw a cup of coffee at an FBI agent... I don't want to hear that you missed".

Ken suggested I send all of this information once again to all of the talk show contacts and he would do what he could on the situation. I began receiving invitations to CBS Morning Show, Hour Magazine, Phil Donahue,

ABC Morning and Nightly News, and many more. The story about the coffee cup became public with my appearance on Donahue. I related the entire story on national TV. In a newspaper article, Agent Hawkins first denied it, and then said, "Mrs. Gosch is mistaken", then finally "admitted he had said every word". He no longer is in this part of the United States. He was moved to another area and has nothing more to do with our case. Some years later he died but had also been discharged from the FBI for sexual misconduct.

Within six months of the kidnapping, a young man identifying himself as Paul Bishop contacted me by phone. He told me an international kidnapping/pornography ring had taken my son. I asked, "How do you know that to be true, can you prove it!" He replied, I work for a government agency which is investigating pedophile organizations. And there are indicators in your case that suggest your son was taken by such an organization. We feel he is being used for pornography and prostitution." All clues were pointing to the kidnapping being organized and not that of a "lone criminal". I found it difficult to believe and accept that my son could have been targeted by such an organization. It was only in later years; I was to learn the possible reason Johnny was selected

Again it was brought to my attention that Orval Cooney; police chief was continuing his tirades against our family. He was constantly making derogatory remarks about Johnny, our family and me. In desperation, I telephoned several members of the West Des Moines City Council, on a Friday afternoon. I told each of them I was filing a 20 million dollar lawsuit against the city on Monday morning, naming the Police Chief as being negligent in my son's case.

Stunned, the city council called an emergency unpublished meeting on Sunday evening, in the basement of the police department. The following morning, it was announced the police chief would retire, as he was too ill to continue in the job, he went out on medical leave, it was the only way he could keep his pension. His real fate was being fired. Finally, he was no longer making negligent decisions on Johnny's case. I never intended to file the lawsuit, but I wanted them to think so. Approximately three months after he left the office, Orval Cooney was arrested for shoplifting at a Target Store; he took videotape and some mollies plug screws for hanging plants from the ceiling.

We had the State director of DCI (State Police) Gerald Shanahan followed for two months by detectives and then a little list was presented to his superiors as to his activities during this time. A short time later, he resigned. During the first 18 months on our case, several people were removed from their positions, which gave fresh people to the case. This eased the frustration level of having to deal with the people who treated my son's case with such little regard. We hoped the new people in these positions would have more of an open mind.

We received an invitation to speak at the "10th National Conference of Juvenile Justice Judges & District Attorney's Assoc.", in Hilton Head, North Carolina, sharing the podium with Ken Wooden. Due to the collective talent and contacts in our audience this resulted in much more publicity all over the country. It gave me the opportunity to work on Federal legislation, which was the Missing Children's Act of 1983. The audience of judges and district attorneys numbered to three hundred. It was an excellent opportunity to become more visible concerning Johnny's case and convey what we were trying to accomplish in Iowa and on the national level. It was also the first time I was introduced to John Walsh, father of Adam Walsh kidnapped and murdered in Florida in 1981. John was working on federal legislation, and he mentioned that our "paths would cross again to work together."

In December 1983, Ken Wooden invited me to testify before the Justice Department at Sam Houston University in Houston Texas. Parents of missing children gathered and were asked to tell their story on video camera, naming names and sharing what went wrong in their cases. I met John Walsh for the second time, he came to share his story about his son

Adam, who was murdered a year before my son was kidnapped. While I was there, I met many people from all over the country, all carrying the same burden pain. It seemed apparent that in every case, the police reacted very slowly or not at all. The families were left with the frustration of not knowing what happened to their child.

All of the videotaped testimonies were taken to Washington D.C. and a few months later the Justice Department appropriated the first ten million dollars to start the Center for Missing and Exploited Children. I was invited to the White House for the dedication of the new Center for Missing Children. It was a huge success to have this Center created; it meant that parents had for the first time a place for help, support and guidance when their child was taken. The Center was designed to act as a liaison between law enforcement and the families, to help create and distribute missing persons posters, and an 800 number for calls on sightings of missing children …1-800-843-5678. They had people to handle the caseloads and keep in communication with the families. This was important so parents did not feel so isolated and alone in their tragedy, as we had before the creation of the Center.

The Johnny Gosch Foundation was constantly growing, and the speaking engagements were continuing. Over a period of six years, I presented seven hundred programs, all over the country.

A very special young couple came to meet with us; he was the editor of the Ankeny Press Citizen in a neighboring town. They joined our organization, and he began to write a series of articles on Johnny's case, telling the true story. Ron and Luann Sampson played a very large role in shaping this entire investigation.

The Des Moines Register was ignoring any kind of helpful publicity (no one could understand why…. (Johnny worked for them), so we worked with other forms of the press, in and outside our state. I received a phone call in the spring of 1983, a woman saying, she worked at the Des Moines Register in the newsroom…. She reported, "Shortly after the kidnapping, the editor at that time, came into the newsroom and announced …all articles written about the Gosch boy WILL be slanted against the family and for the police." She would not give me her name… she was afraid of losing her job. I now knew what was happening but didn't understand "why"!

Ron's articles really began to shake people up and finally for the first time, they were made aware of how our family had been treated. We had an avenue of communication in our case, which was fair. We spent many hours together formulating this project; later Ron became the President of the Johnny Gosch Foundation. I felt such gratitude for all of the people who helped us, prior to and following this series of articles. It made me more determined than ever to continue to work towards a safer environment for all children.

As I traveled, giving speeches throughout Iowa, I collected legislative contacts in every community. I circulated a clipboard to my audiences asking everyone of voting age to sign their name, if they were interested in being a "legislative contact". I explained a "legislative contact", would be called if we had a bill being held hostage, if we needed them to call their legislator to put pressure on them to vote for a certain bill for children. We would also ask them to call as many people as possible for them to do the same. Many times, bills are held "hostage" in a committee. Logic would seem to dictate that any bill concerning the welfare of children should be a top priority instead of being used as a "pawn" in a political catfight. In all, I collected nearly a thousand names, with the help of Teresa Burriola, a volunteer in the Johnny Gosch Foundation, who worked as a lobbyist. The names were sorted and placed in folders according to their counties/districts with the names of their Representative and Senator.

Word reached Governor Branstad office about my legislative contact project. On a number of occasions, the Governor called and asked me to activate our massive telephone tree, we could generate over 500 calls to legislators within an hour and did so many times. Putting pressure on the Senator or Representative, deliberately holding a bill hostage.

My work with Governor Branstad proved to be very rewarding; he is a fair and honest person. We created many positive legislative changes in the state of Iowa, which have been copied in other states. Finally in the second year 1984, the Johnny Gosch Bill passed into law. It felt like such a victory. It had made all of the late nights, driving, speaking and work worthwhile. At the signing ceremony on July 1, 1984, the Governor said to me quietly "I had an extra pen done for Johnny, if he is found, I want him to have it. None of this would have happened if it hadn't been for the tragedy of his kidnapping and all your work".

Those words meant a great deal to me, the Governor had gone out of his way many times on a personal level to assist me with kindness. It is refreshing after all the other difficulties and obstacles. The police now must begin an investigation immediately when a child is missing. IT IS THE LAW. Needless to say, a few policemen in the state did not care for the idea but a surprising number appreciate having it in black and white on paper.

Despite the victory of the Johnny Gosch Law being passed, there were several disgruntled lobbyists and legislators who said to me… "You got your bill passed but now who will provide the money to enforce it… we are on the finance committee, and we are not going to allocate dollars for this…" I reported these comments from the lobbyists and legislators to the Governor's office and said it was necessary for this law to be enforced the next time a child was taken. Little did I know that only a month from that day, another paperboy would be kidnapped from Des Moines?

THE SECOND KIDNAPPING

I received a phone call from Sam Soda, a local private investigator. He claimed to have valuable information for me and wanted to meet as soon as possible. We arranged to meet at his office the evening of June 13, 1984. This was another of the tons of calls from people trying to help, I had no idea if his information was something I could use or not. Many of the leads turned out to be nothing. But I accepted the meeting with him.

THEY HAVE NO CRIME.... I HAVE NO SON!!!!

I brought a tape recorder along and placed it on the table. Sam raised no objection to being taped. During this meeting, he disclosed information about a "second kidnapping in Des Moines". He claimed this came from his informant. The kidnapping was to occur on the second weekend in August, on the South Side of Des Moines and that it would be another paperboy. I thought it strange that he would be telling me this and not the police. When I questioned him on this point, he claimed that I should be the one to take the information to the Des Moines Police, as it would be their jurisdiction. I thanked him for the information and left. I thought that if this information were on the level... it would be a chance to prevent another kidnapping. I believed him but still questioned why he told me and not the police.

I went the very next day to the Des Moines Police Dept., asking if I could play the tape of the meeting with Mr. Soda for them. The uniformed officer at the front desk would not allow me to talk to a Detective, he insisted, "If they felt my information was of importance, they would call me". Repeatedly, I told him that I had a tape recording and in a couple of months, there would be another paperboy kidnapped. They treated me as though I had lost my mind and didn't want to be bothered with me. I was shocked, my son was kidnapped, and they were rejecting information to prevent another crime.

When I left the Police Dept., I contacted WHO, WOI & KCCI TV station program managers. I did speak to each of them and relayed the information, telling them I also had a tape recording of this conversation. I was shocked to find out that even though they listened to me, no one wanted to listen to the tape.

I was very uneasy about the whole situation and felt that Mr. Soda had given me important information. Someone needed to take it seriously. I contacted Frank Santiago, Des Moines Register reporter, who had been assigned to Johnny's story since the beginning. He was the only one who really listened to the information. He asked if I had been to the police. I told him "Yes and to the TV stations". He showed concern and then thanked me for the information. But the Des Moines Register did not do any type of article on this new information. A couple months, later after Eugene Martin was kidnapped, I went back to the Des Moines Police Department and asked if they were "ready to talk to me about the contents of the Sam Soda tape." I was told "no, they had too much to do with the new kidnapping to investigate and for me not to talk to the press or the Martin family about the contents of the tape". One officer also said "We can get a gag order placed on you if necessary!"

DEEP THROAT

Just as in the movie "All the President's Men", Des Moines also had its "Deep Throat". It has become increasingly important to have certain information released in the press at precise times. I knew that if I approached them…. the information would not be taken seriously or have the impact as if it came from an anonymous informant who was accurate. I hired a man to make the phone calls, supplying the reporter with accurate information. I knew the clock was ticking closer to the date in August, which was predicted for the next kidnapping of a Des Moines Register paperboy.

When I had information to be released, I would call Deep Throat; he would go to a pay phone, placing a call to the "newspaper reporter", giving him the information, with the facts for him to verify everything. Within a couple hours, I would receive a phone call from "the reporter" saying "that his anonymous informant had just given him new information and that every word of it was true because he was able to confirm it." There would then be a story, which followed in the newspaper.

At these times, it was imperative that information be released strategically to obtain a desired effect from the "guilty parties" involved locally in the case. It was then and then only; I would know if I was on the right path of investigation. To some people it might seem or sound a bit "calculating" but I was up against many powerful people. When your child

THEY HAVE NO CRIME.... I HAVE NO SON!!!!

is taken and you are forced to do your own investigation, you do what you must do.

After a succession of appearances on Good Morning America, The Today Show, CBS Morning & Evening News, Charles Kuralt Sunday Morning, Phil Donahue, Inside Edition, ABC Morning & Evening News, NBC Morning & Evening News, and 48 Hours, where I was able to share my story about my son and alert the public to the ever-present and growing danger of child kidnapping. I received a call from Karen Burnes, a producer with ABC's 20/20 in July of 1984, asking to present Johnny's story.

This was the beginning of a long relationship with not only Karen Burnes but also ABC's 20/20. The show depicted the effort I had to make to cope with the loss of my son, which required me to become a public speaker, fundraiser, detective and "thorn in the side of police, FBI and political bureaucrats." It seemed the only way to get anything done on Johnny's case was to shout long and loud on any forum I could find.... from the stage of a church or school, newspaper, magazines to a radio or TV studio. Plans were made with Karen Burnes to film Johnny's Story with 20/20, on the second weekend in August.

Paul Bishop, made another short trip to Des Moines, July 31, 1984. It was at this time, he reported the name of the man who was the "spotter".... in Johnny's kidnapping. Paul explained that a spotter is the person who secures a photo of a victim prior to a kidnapping. Years later in 1991, I learned from Private Investigator Roy Stephens, that Paul Bonacci, (who participated in Johnny's kidnapping) positively identified a photo of Sam Soda as the man, who brought photos of Johnny to the kidnappers, who stayed in a motel room in West Des Moines, on September 4, 1982, the night before the kidnapping.

When Paul spoke his name, I said, "Paul, you need to listen to this tape." I played a recording of my meeting with Sam Soda. He listened...I then told him of my attempts to share the information with the police department and media. Paul was not shocked at what he heard on the tape and paid a visit to

Sam Soda, questioning him concerning the source of the information on a second kidnapping. Sam was not too cooperative, became annoyed with Bishop, asking him to leave his office. There is indication today that these two individuals knew each other prior to this time. Before Paul left Des Moines, he created a very intricate map of Johnny's crime scene, indicating time sequence of each aspect of the kidnapping. Paul dated and initialed the map using GPB (George Paul Bishop) After Paul flew back to Washington, I began to hear from Sam.

Soda on a regular basis. He wanted to be the investigator for Johnny's case. He asked for a bank account to be set up for him to draw upon for a salary. I explained to him we already had a private investigator and could not afford another. He continued to attempt to be involved in any way he could in the case.

I think this suggests how intricate are the manipulations of those involved in the kidnapping and exploitation of children like Johnny. Eventually, I had reports from not only Paul Bishop but also Paul Bonacci (See Bonacci chapter) implicating Sam. What better way for them to keep track of my progress in this case than to plant someone in our very midst? To this very day no police agency has ever conducted a thorough investigation of Sam Soda's alleged participation in Johnny's case.

During this time, I had also been working with Senator Grassley from Iowa, he had been particularly helpful in facilitating with the FBI. A short time later, I received my invitation to testify in Washington D.C. before Senator Arlan Specter's Hearing on **Organized Crime and its Re-Relationship to Kidnapping.** Senator Grassley's office made all of my arrangements.

I was instructed by Senator Grassley's office to Federal Express a copy of my testimony and to carry a copy on the plane when I flew to Washington D.C. In testifying before Congress or State Legislature, you are required to prepare a written presentation of your testimony. Paul Bishop met the plane and escorted me to the hotel. I checked in and then he took me on a tour of

THEY HAVE NO CRIME.... I HAVE NO SON!!!!

Washington, followed by showing me some of the blighted places in D.C. Where children as young as ten years old hang out on the streets late at night. Today those blighted areas include places like the White House Mall at night. Even Congressmen are not safe on the steps of the Capitol.

Later that evening, Paul and I spent time going over every word of my testimony. I wanted to be sure that when I presented my information the following morning that it was clear to the committee, "an Organized Pedophile Group" took my son. Again and again, I have met with denial on the part of individuals and organizations that any such groups could exist in this country. For my protection, two men, dressed in suits were posted outside of my hotel room door all night. A major disturbance occurred downstairs in the lobby during the night, the police were called and arrested the man causing the problem. I have no idea if it was related to me.

The following morning, Paul Bishop, accompanied by two men arrived at the hotel to drive me to the Capitol for the Hearing. The bodyguards accompanied us always a few steps behind us. They were dressed well but business casual rather than suits. Paul looked very polished wearing a dark brown suit. As I entered the room, I noted there were reporters everywhere from ABC, NBC, CBS television, radio, newspaper and magazine. I recognized Special Agent Kenneth Lanning, a member of the Behavioral Science Unit of the FBI Training Division at Quantico, VA, I walked towards him, saying, "Hello, I am Noreen Gosch", extending my hand to shake his.... he pulled back and said, "We know who you are". With that statement there was a definite chill in the air. It was as though the FBI resented me being asked to testify.

Paul sat beside me at the table, the two bodyguards blended into the background, as I testified to my knowledge of the slave auctions in the

U.S. During my testimony, Senator Specter asked several questions about my son's kidnapping and the investigation. I explained the FBI refused to enter the case, because they wanted me to prove my son's life was in danger. The lack of response from the local authorities created the need for private investigators.

At this hearing were books made available by the FBI showing children in a mail order type catalog and offering them for sale. How much more needed to be proven about the existence of organizations national and international that were buying and selling children. This book was spiral bound about seventy-five to a hundred black and white pages, with six or seven children's pictures on a page. Below each child's picture was offered details about the child, hair and eye color, weight etc. The question that must be asked is that with this information in the hands of the FBI and the Senate, clearly indicating that an organization capable of not only photographing children around the U.S. but offering them for sale and kidnapping to order, why is this still unknown to most Americans. I have made repeated attempts to obtain copies of this catalog, which would prove beyond a shadow of a doubt the existence of an organization or organizations that do buy and sell children.

Councilwoman of the City Council of Philadelphia, Joan Specter stated "I found it rather shocking to hear there was a book "How to Have Sex with Kids", and I decided to verify the fact that it was indeed obtained at the bookstore. I called the bookstore and asked if they had a pamphlet of how to have sex with kids. They said, "let me check", they returned to the phone and said, "we did have the pamphlet and are out of it but we can reorder it." I said thank you and hung up. And then the pamphlet was delivered to my office. I looked at the pamphlet and saw that it was a How to Do It Pamphlet. It described how to find children, how to go to playgrounds, how to get babysitting jobs, and then it described how a man who is over 200 pounds can have sex with a child.

It seemed to me that if you have a pamphlet available in a bookstore, which was not a pornographic bookstore, and someone goes in and buys that pamphlet, there is a sense that there is nothing wrong with having sex with kids. Because, after all, here is the book in a regular bookstore available to anyone who comes in. This is taken from the minutes August 8, 1984, (the same hearing where I testified) of the Organized Crime Hearings and its Relationship to Missing Children

Senator Specter asked Paul Bishop of his relationship to the case, to me and did he know this to be true. Paul indicated he was an investigator and that every word of my testimony was accurate. Paul remained by my side during the hearing; answering questions asked by Senator Specter, these were the only words he spoke. This struck me as very unusual but then I had never been in this arena before to observe how a CIA man would conduct himself. At no time did Paul ever identify himself as CIA Asset during the hearing or afterward during the interviews with the Washington Press. He withdrew from the view of the cameras. All attempts on my part to obtain photos from the hearing were unsuccessful.

Following the hearing, I requested from one of the staff members a copy of Mr. Lannings testimony and the pedophile material that was displayed on the table, including the catalog. She asked, "Mrs. Gosch would like a copy of the material presented by Mr. Lanning" and an FBI Agent told her "This is the property of the FBI, and it was acquired from a pedophiles lair, it cannot be given to anyone".

It was appalling to me to me that with all this material in the hands of the FBI, presented by Ken Lanning to Senator Specters committee and examined by the National media, that there is ever any question today in the year 2000, about the existence of national and international kidnap organizations. Today children are a commodity used in TV commercials and magazine ads in a sexually provocative manner. Is it any wonder that children are no longer safe in our schools because the pedophiles have managed to become their teachers, coaches, and become mentors to young children.

My own private investigator attended a slave auction with naked children paraded on a stage. Paul Bonnaci, who assisted in kidnapping my son claims to have attended many auctions. Everyone from psychiatrist to policemen report talking to people who have attended or been a participant in such auctions. If there is any doubt that Slavery is alive and well in America in the year 2000, there should not be. I examined the same FBI evidence in August 8, 1984, that Senators and the entire news media present examined.

Is there a plot to conceal this from the America public? FBI and countless witnesses such as I have repeatedly presented ample proof before the U. S. Congress. Yet the average America thinks you are crazy if you declare Slavery exists and is a well-guarded U.S. Government secret. I have a book in my possession, which identifies various members of the

U.S. Congress as compromised by having had sex with children, or owning slaves themselves. Paul Bonnaci who participated in the kidnapping of Johnny also stated, he was repeatedly sent to Washington D.C. to have sex with Massachusetts Representative Barney Frank. The Washington Times published a front-page story stating a child prostitution ring was being run out of his D.C. apartment.

It has now been sixteen years since Senator Arlen Specter has been given these materials. To my knowledge, no major report was given to Congress about the growing and influential pedophiles operating throughout the United States. What happened to the new media who immediately surrounded me following the hearing anxious for more details about Johnny? They had the same access to that catalog that I did. Why hasn't it become a major national story? I testified that slave auctions were being held in the U.S. The catalog clearly confirmed my testimony.

My schedule was so tight, I flew immediately back to Des Moines as the crew from ABC 20/20 were arriving. The following day, Karen Burnes and the film crew from 20/20 arrived in town. It was a beautiful Saturday and the second weekend in August. They filmed locations around Des Moines and West Des Moines, including the site where Johnny was kidnapped. Later when we arrived back at our home. I decided to share the information regarding a second kidnapping, supposed to occur the following day. I

THEY HAVE NO CRIME…. I HAVE NO SON!!!!

played the Sam Soda tape recording for Karen and shared how I had been to the Des Moines Police Dept., telling her of the reaction I received.

I had hoped they would at least patrol the paper drop areas on the South Side of Des Moines. I also told Karen; I had given the information to the News Directors at the local TV stations. She showed great interest in the information.

After we finished filming for the day, the crew went to the airport and flew back to New York. Karen remained in Des Moines and stayed at the Marriott hotel. The next morning began with the shock of the phone ringing very early. It was a reporter at the local ABC TV station, telling me "The second kidnapping had just taken place". He kept saying, "It happened just as you said it would Mrs. Gosch".

I asked the reporter how he knew what I had reported, as I only talked with his manager. He replied, "they spread it around the newsroom …everyone thought you were nuts!" He informed me the police were calling it a kidnapping immediately and the FBI were bringing in twenty-two agents from Quantico, VA to assist in the investigation and search. The young boy kidnapped was Eugene Martin, a newspaper carrier, preparing to deliver his papers on the South Side of Des Moines.

In Johnny's case, the FBI refused to enter the case, the reason they verbally gave me in my home was that "they had no crime, and it was my responsibility to prove my son's life was in danger". Why now with Eugene Martin's kidnapping under identical circumstances was the FBI coming forward with a bevy of FBI agents. Could it be that somewhere during the months of Johnny's kidnapping ……the law enforcement here learned something?

Based on this phone call alone, I called Karen at the hotel and told her the "second kidnapping had just happened", exactly as Sam Soda had told me on June 13, 1984. She immediately swung into action contacting her network and arranging for a film crew to come back to Des Moines, when the crew arrived, they went directly to the Des Moines police department.

The police department was in a state of confusion; Karen placed, put, shoved a microphone in the police chief's face and demanded the answers to the following questions. Are you bringing in FBI Agents for this case? They didn't for Johnny Gosch! Are you going to use canine search teams? They didn't for Johnny Gosch! Will you do an aerial search? They wouldn't for Johnny Gosch! The Police Chief had no comment about the Johnny Gosch case and stated the department would do everything in their power to solve the Martin kidnapping. The police went all out using FBI, SWAT Teams, Canine Searches, and Aerial searches but like Johnny, Eugene Martin was probably quickly taken out of the immediate search area. This case appeared to be a duplicate of Johnny's kidnapping.

Karen stayed in Des Moines for several days, interviewing and gathering information on this latest tragedy. The story about Eugene Martin and Johnny appeared immediately on ABC news. Karen and I continued to keep in touch as the years rolled by.

After the Martin kidnapping, I expected the Des Moines Police Dept, to contact me and want to discuss the information I received from Sam Soda. Even though my information proved to be valid, the police never asked to listen to the tape. Sam Soda knew another boy was going to be kidnapped. Shouldn't the police have asked how did Sam Soda know? Who did Sam Soda know? Did Sam Soda also have the information that would have solved or prevented this crime?

Instead... I was warned not to talk about it to the press and certainly not the Martin family. I could not believe what I was hearing. But it certainly can be explained; they had the opportunity to prevent the second kidnapping, due to the advanced information. Instead of listening to the information, I tried to give them; I was treated like a "nut" and dismissed. If the newspaper drops points had been patrolled, Eugene Martin might not have been taken. If the local media had created pressure about the tape, police might have been forced to take action. But neither the police nor the media wanted to listen to the tape recording. Where the kidnapping of children is concerned it is difficult to arouse the social conscious.

Suddenly an apathetic law enforcement body…. And The Des Moines Register, who now had **TWO KIDNAPPED PAPERBOYS**, began to act. We continued to pay for our own investigation. Money was donated to reward funds. The newspaper printed thousands of missing person's flyers to distribute all over the United States. We printed and paid for distribution of our son's posters. The change of attitude was amazing.

Jim Gannon, the same newspaper editor, who smugly ignored our case except to do damaging articles and instruct the staff to slant articles against us… wrote an article **"MAD AS HELL THAT TWO CARRIERS WERE KIDNAPPED"**.

President Ronald Reagan telephoned Jim Gannon to tell him what a good job the Des Moines Register was doing publicizing these kidnappings. I questioned why did it take two children kidnapped to shake the social conscience of this newspaper editor? How tragic and sad for the children.

We were still selling candy bars to pay for all of our flyers, watching this same newspaper rollover and do it for another family was very painful. I am glad that all of our work had brought this kind of awareness and progress but at the same time, my heart ached for my son. Going through the first few days of the second kidnapping was like reliving Johnny's. Every bit of the pain was still there and had not lessened.

I thought my life was busy before but after the second kidnapping the speaking engagements and public appearances mushroomed. People felt threatened… would their child be next?

A few days later, NBC Today Show contacted me, asking if I could get in touch with the Martins, as they had been unsuccessful. It seems the FBI (was this the Efrem Zimbalist Jr. from the FBI TV Show, I had been waiting for) had more or less set up a command post in the Martin home and calls were being screened. The Today show wanted to interview both the Martins and us the following day. I called the Martin home, an FBI Agent answered the phone, I posed as a relative and asked to speak with either of the Martins. He handed the phone to Don, Eugene's father. At that time, I identified myself, told Mr. Martin "They want us on the Today Show … tomorrow!"

We then made the plans to do the Today show from the local WHO-TV studio in Des Moines, the NBC affiliate. When I met them at the TV studio, the Martins told me "The FBI told us not to talk to you!"

In a total reversal Sam Soda, began to contact the Des Moines Police telling them that Paul Bishop (my CIA contact) had been in Des Moines a short time before the Martin kidnapping and was somehow involved. Sam must have bent the ear of some influential people because shortly afterward a Federal Grand Jury Hearing was scheduled; Paul Bishop was subpoenaed to testify.

He returned one more time to Des Moines. Following the hearing, Paul took a taxi to my home. He had been questioned about Eugene Martin, what he was doing in Des Moines, who he talked to in Des Moines for over six hours. While he was sharing the details of the hearing, the phone rang a number of times. It was Sam Soda each time wanting to know if Paul Bishop was there. He became very agitated when I told him Paul was not there. He claimed he needed to talk with Paul and could not find him. We felt it best for Paul to change his travel plans, I made arrangements with friends for Paul to stay the night at their home. He flew back to Washington D.C. a couple of days later, under another name.

I received two more phone calls from Paul in the following week, that was to be the last time I saw or spoke with Paul. The phone number to call Paul at Langley Air Force Base was no longer working.

Shortly after that visit, Paul Bishop or Robert LaVeck vanished without a trace. What happened to Paul Bishop, we have never been able to discover. Paul used to call me "Mom." He was a young person in his twenties, and I sometimes wonder, had he been used in some manner by the very element that took my son? Was he sent here to share with me the threads of truth, which would unfold later? It was years before the CIA was revealed as a part of this problem of missing children in our country and the world.

A reporter asked me to describe in a few words one time something positive about this experience, if there was such a thing. I said, "I have had the opportunity and privilege to meet so many fine people… together we have made a difference in this country. People I would not have met otherwise, and it is sad that it had to be at the expense of a child's life. I feel that all of what I have accomplished has been done in Johnny's name, so that his kidnapping did not happen without any progress in our country. I just hope in some way he is able to know we did everything possible to save him. If I had not fought hard to save him, I would not be able to now look at myself in the mirror or at his picture." ***The first sound of the words still echoes in my mind from the*** Police and FBI...." Mrs. Gosch, we have no crime...." My reply has always been "But I have no son... Kidnapping is a Federal Crime!"

worked against the odds to overcome and go on. If anything, this was the biggest "do it yourself project had ever encountered." Most parents do not realize that much of the search for their child will be up to them. If they drop the ball so to speak... there goes their child's case.

Some in the country have called me a "nut or troublemaker" and have said, "I should just shut up and quit." Would they quit if it were their child missing? It is easy to judge when it hasn't happened to you. I have learned to live with all the elements that go with this tragedy...from the pain of losing a child in a violent crime to living in a fishbowl.

My entire world was shattered on the morning of September 5, 1982 and yet somehow, I received the energy, support and guidance to go on with my life, rising above the tragedy to accomplish many things, which will last for others.

WHY JOHNNY CAN'T COME HOME!

KIDNAPPED
JOHN DAVID GOSCH

Taken 81/82 School Year

Composite Of Suspect
5'9", 175 lbs., dark eyes, black eyebrows, older, early to mid 40's, black hair, combed back, full in back, black mustache, heavy beard or unshaven appearance, Latin appearance.
This man may be driving a two tone blue car, real dark top and light blue bottom -mid size - 79 to 81 model -clean inside and outside - no vinyl top -plush interior -Iowa plate.

DESCRIPTION: Age: 13 years old, D.O.B.: Nov. 12, 1969, Ht.: 5'7" Wt.: 145 lbs. Hair: light brown, Eyes: blue, Complexion: medium Teeth: gaps between front teeth, Shoe Size: 9½-10, Marks/Scars: freckles, large birthmark upper left chest, horseshoe shaped scar on tongue, large lower lip. Stature: At 13 years old, John has the physical appearance of a boy 15 or older.

John David Gosch was last seen on Sunday, September 5, 1982 at approximately 6:06 A.M. He was believed to have been kidnapped when starting his paper route at 42nd and Marcourt Lane in West Des Moines, Iowa.

John was believed to have been wearing a white sweat shirt with the words KIM'S ACADEMY on the back of it along with black warm up pants and blue rubber thongs. Missing also with John is his yellow paperbag and wire cutters.

REWARD

A $90,000.00 REWARD has been offered for the safe return of John David Gosch in addition to a $10,000.00 REWARD for information leading to his whereabouts.

Anyone having information to John's whereabouts, please call: LOCAL F.B.I OFFICE or INVESTIGATIVE RESEARCH AGENCY, INC. (312) 745-1111 or John's parents JOHN and NOREEN GOSCH at (515) 225-7456.

THEY HAVE NO CRIME.... I HAVE NO SON!!!!

Type of car in Gosch case

Below: One of the many "candy bar" fund raisers ...

Fund-raising

Search for Johnny Gosch continues

WHY JOHNNY CAN'T COME HOME!

KIDNAPPED
JOHN DAVID GOSCH

ken 81/82 School Year

Composite Of Suspect
5'9", 175 lbs., dark eyes, black eyebrows, older, early to mid 40's, black hair, combed back, full in back, black mustache, heavy beard or unshaven appearance, Latin appearance.
This man may be driving a two tone blue car, real dark top and light blue bottom -mid size - 79 to 81 model -clean inside and outside - no vinyl top -plush interior -Iowa plate.

Sam Soda
"I think I was entitled to them"

Composite Of Suspect
5'9", 175 lbs., dark eyes, black eyebrows, older, early to mid 40's, black hair, combed back, full in back, black mustache, heavy beard or unshaven appearance, Latin appearance.
This man may be driving a two tone blue car, real dark top and light blue bottom -mid size - 79 to 81 model -clean inside and outside - no vinyl top -plush interior -Iowa plate.

This poster was sent anonymously to me and a number of others in Des Moines ... Shortly after Eugene Martin was kidnapped...1984

THEY HAVE NO CRIME.... I HAVE NO SON!!!!

HAVE YOU SEEN EITHER OF THESE YOUNG MEN?

Both of these young men disappeared while delivering the Des Moines Sunday Register. John Gosch has been missing since Sept. 5, 1982. Eugene Martin disappeared on Aug. 12, 1984. If you have information concerning either boy call the Des Moines, Iowa, Police Department Hotline
COLLECT 515-246-9988.

John Gosch was 12 years old when he disappeared on Sept. 5, 1982, while delivering newspapers in West Des Moines, Iowa. He was described as 5 feet, 7 inches tall, weighing 140 pounds, with blue eyes and light brown hair.

Eugene Martin of Des Moines, Ia. is 13 years old and disappeared on Aug. 12, 1984. He is 5 feet tall, 105 pounds, thin, with dark brown hair, brown eyes and a dark complexion. He was wearing blue jeans, a gray midriff shirt with white stripes and red sleeves, and blue Trax tennis shoes with white diagonal stripes.

$94,000 REWARD

$25,000 offered by The Des Moines Register for information leading to the recovery of either of these missing persons.
(Additional reward money being offered by businesses, friends and relatives.)

WHY JOHNNY CAN'T COME HOME!

Ken Wooden researched and wrote this guide as an outgrowth of his work as an investigative reporter for ABC News 20/20 and as the founder of the National Coalition for Children's Justice and the National Child Victim Computerized Network. The information is based on interviews with convicted child molesters and murderers—the experts.

Ken Wooden has authored three books which center on the injustices suffered by children. *Weeping in the Playtime of Others,* a best-seller, served as the basis for three "Sixty Minutes" segments. *The Children of Jonestown* is the culmination of his investigative work for *NBC News* and the *Chicago Sun-Times;* it garnered a Pulitzer Prize nomination. His third book, soon to be published, *Prey-Missing and Murdered Children,* is the result of five years of investigative work.

Wooden's articles and books have prompted Congressional inquiries and legislation dealing with interstate commerce of children, the child pornography industry, foster care reform and, most currently, the problem of missing and murdered children.

THEY HAVE NO CRIME.... I HAVE NO SON!!!!

HAPPY DAYS JOHNNY, ME AND NEPHEW

SURVIVAL.... A WAY OF LIFE FOR NOREEN

I had the benefit of growing up in a home filled with love and being instilled with the "right stuff" from the beginning. I was the oldest of six children, growing up on a farm with my five brothers, we learned about the simple pleasures of life as well as the "work ethic". I never heard a harsh word spoken between my mother and father. They were the most loving and devoted couple/ parents I have ever seen to this day. When I was fifteen my father died of cancer. He suffered tremendously and was bed ridden for many months. During this time, we cared for him at home, while pulling together as a family to with the tremendous job of running the farm.

At my high school prom, a young man, who had just returned from the Air Force, a former graduate of our school, came just to see all the decorations in the gym that night. He came to the school with his younger brother and my younger brother, who were friends. As they were sitting in the bleachers, he saw me on the dance floor with my date and asked his brother; "Who is that girl in the pink dress?" My brother replied, "that is my sister, Noreen.". Later that night when he went home, he told his mother "I have just seen the girl I am going to marry". I am sure his mother was a little shocked to hear such a revelation.

SURVIVAL.... A WAY OF LIFE FOR NOREEN

I was graduating from high school at seventeen, it was only about a week later that Bob came to my home to see me and asked me for a date. I had never dated anyone that much older than myself.... He seemed nice and I was impressed by the fact that he was interested in me. We did start dating... within a year Bob asked me to marry him and gave me a diamond. All caught up in the whirlwind of planning a wedding, it seemed that time stood still and flew by all at the same time. Soon we were married and settled in our home.

The following year, I was expecting our first child. It was only a few months after she was born that Bob became ill, he went to the doctor, and they ran some tests. Surgery was recommended.... The verdict came back cancer...... colon cancer. He was operated on at the University of Iowa Hospitals in Iowa City. It was 1963 and there was very little they could do other than surgery. Bob recuperated quickly and returned to work. I was both surprised but pleased a few months later to discover I was expecting our second child. Towards the end of my pregnancy, Bob returned to Iowa City Medical center for a checkup. When he got home, he told me they discovered a reoccurrence of the cancer, and he would have to go through more surgery.

I was terrified for him, our little family and me. Our second child was born within a few weeks and then leaving both children with my mother, we went back to Iowa City for more surgery. The day of surgery, I was told by hospital staff that Bob would be in surgery and recovery for many hours; that it would do me good to take a break from the hospital and to come back later. I did as they suggested and went to visit my sister-in-law in a nearby town. While there I took a nap before going back to the hospital. I had a dream while resting, in my dream, *I was driving into the hospital parking lot and there was a parking space right as I turned the corner. (Extremely rare at that hospital) I went into the hospital, got on the elevator. When the doors opened, I was greeted by an orderly who said" Please come with me, Dr Crowley wants to see you right away". I followed him to a long, narrow room, with green walls and white furniture. Dr. Crowley walked in and took my hands and said "I am sorry, but we had to close your husband back us, there is nothing we can do for him. He is infected with cancer and will not live much longer.*

I woke up with a start, telling my sister-in-law about the dream, she said "just take it easy, you have been under a great deal of stress, just had a new baby and haven't fully recuperated yourself yet". So, I thanked her and headed back to the hospital. As I pulled into the parking lot.... *I saw the parking space right there (just as my dream), I took it, went into the hospital.... Got on the elevator... when the doors opened, there was the same orderly as in my dream, asking me to go with him to meet Dr. Crowley I followed him to a long, narrow room with green walls and white furniture.* I knew what was about to come. The doctor entered the room and took my hands and then told me *"I am sorry, but we had to close your husband back up, there is nothing we can do for him.... he is full of cancer and will not live, much longer."*

I couldn't believe my ears and yet, I knew he was telling the truth. I had been given the information hours earlier to prepare me for this shock. I was alone, just nineteen, and I didn't know what to do. Bob was still in recovery, and I couldn't see him. I made a phone call to my sister-in-law; she had three young children at home and said her husband would come to the hospital.

Before he arrived, I was permitted to see Bob, as I walked towards his bed, I saw all the tubes he was hooked to but something looked strange, one tube was bright red. I pushed the button for the nurse, and she came, I showed her what the tube looked like, she pushed me out of the way, yelled for help and told me my husband was bleeding to death. It was all too much for me and I fainted. When I woke up, I was in a hospital bed, my husband was in the other bed in a private room, with my brother-in-law sitting on a chair. He had been told what took place. He had also donated blood for Bob as they were the same blood type.

Bob pulled through and was sent home, he did recover somewhat for a short time from the effects of the surgery.... And he didn't LOOK SICK.... That was the part that amazed everyone, he looked at the picture of health and yet he was dying. The months went very quickly and he began to go downhill very rapidly .. It seems that once there was the surgery the cancer began to spread like wildfire.

The doctors told me he would never feel "good again" but they would do everything they could to make him comfortable. Soon Bob was unable to work, he was too weak. We were living in a home on acreage close to his parents and mine. The baby was not quite a year old and his sister only two and a half, when our world exploded one night. Each day was a struggle, a worry, I tried to keep the spirits up for Bob, who was worried about leaving his family. It had been very hot, on September 21st, 1965; we went to bed that night trying to get some sleep.

During the night, I was awakened by what sounded like a freight train roaring overhead but yet right though our home, we did not live near a railroad track. Everything was black, except for occasional lightning outside with tremendous thunder. The whole house was shaking, I tried to get up to make my way to our sleeping children, down the hall in their room. When I got up, I was hit in the ribs and in the face with the dresser drawers which came flying out .... I blacked out, when I awakened, I was laying in the field next to our home, rain hitting me, I got up and had searing pain in my chest and face. I started digging through the rubble to locate my babies. I found my daughter, unconscious, lying face down in broken glass. I picked her up, just then she started to scream, I kept telling her I was there, and everything would be okay…while I looked for my baby son. I pulled one of the doors up from the house and saw.

Through the lightning, rafters from the ceiling in the house had pierced through the end of the baby crib and into the mattress like harpoons. I looked all over and couldn't find him. He came crawling out from under some rubble, he looked to be just fine, scared and crying but not injured.

I began to look around only to discover that large sections of the house had landed on both cars and the roof of each car was flattened. I don't know how we managed but we got into the one car with over half the roof flattened with no windshield and drove to Bob's parents' home. We were lucky to be alive. We suspected and it was later confirmed that it had been a tornado. It destroyed our home and both cars. We all went to the hospital emergency room. Both kids checked out okay, but Bob and I were injured. I had broken ribs and had spears of glass embedded in my face. I was fortunate I still had my eyesight. Bob, in his weakened state was banged up badly after being tossed around in the storm, his condition only worsened after that storm.

Within days there were insurance adjusters to work with as our home was a total loss as well as both cars. They were very kind and did help us speed up the process. We continued to stay with Bob's parents until we had another home we could move to. Most all our belongings were either destroyed or blown away. The kids' toys such as teddy bears and plastic toys all had to be thrown away because they were riddled with glass. Clothing and shoes had to be thrown away as the tremendous force of the wind drove the glass spears through the fibers of the clothing and the shoes. I had never seen such destruction in my life.

I got us moved into another home, Bob was so sick and weak, he laughed when he walked in carrying his box of pills/medication, saying that is all he had the strength to carry. Within a short time, his health had taken a turn for the worse. He was in so much pain. Both children were still so frightened from what they experienced in the storm they couldn't sleep at night. The days were exhausting but so were the nights, I rarely got more than three hours sleep. The doctor gave me Morphine. The visiting nurse taught me how to give the injections to Bob for pain. There was no money for us to place Bob in a hospital, as he waited for the cancer to take him. He also wanted to be near the children for as long as possible.

Bob made the statement; he was going to "live long enough to see his son walk". Approximately ten days later, the baby pulled himself up and walked from the coffee table to the couch… that night, I had to call for an ambulance. Bob lapsed into a coma and was taken to the hospital, where he died a few hours later. We had only been married three years, three months and two days.

Bob died about thirty days after the tornado destroyed our home, took everything we had. I was just 22 years old, with two children and had to learn how to start completely from scratch.

I felt so grateful that my children were alive, they could have been killed in that terrible storm. I knew we would make it…. We had each other. I watched as everything I owned was destroyed and taken from me, I had to borrow a dress for his funeral, as I no clothing to wear, it had all been destroyed or blown away but realized at that young age how important, precious and fragile "LIFE" is….

I learned how to be a survivor from this experience. I learned how to start over with nothing. I viewed life much differently than any of my family or friends after the twin disasters…. destruction and death. Little did I know. …these terrible events would prepare me for what was to lie ahead in the years to come.

By this time, I was faced with raising two children, no husband and no job. I thought it couldn't get any worse, but it did. One day shortly after Bob's funeral, a little man knocked on my door. He identified himself as being with our insurance company. I let him in…. he sat down and began to explain that "unfortunately because Bob died just four days short of the waiting period for cancer patients, that I would not receive any of the insurance benefit." He was sorry but also said "it is too bad you couldn't have kept him a life a little longer." Gads, the things people will say sometimes.

I realized that I had to go to "Plan B", unfortunately I didn't have one yet. I needed a job, so I began to scour the ads for job opportunities. I found one, applied and got the job, it was in an insurance agency. My mother agreed to watch the children while I worked. I really liked my new job, and it was all working out.

Two months after my husband's death, I was in the bedroom of our home, I heard someone knocking at the door. Before I could get there my little daughter of two and a half, opened the door, thinking it was her grandfather. Instead, it was a stalker, a man was standing in my living room,

I had no idea who he was. He told me he saw my name in the obituaries… and thought we ought to date. I quickly told him I was very busy that night, but could I have his phone number and I would call him later. I wanted him out of the house and away from my children without incident. He was satisfied with that and left. Within a few minutes, a friend of ours stopped… I immediately told of the "unusual visitor" who had just left. He immediately called his friend who was the Sheriff, giving him the man's name. We learned this man had preyed on "young widows" for years and was well known to the police and Sheriff's department. He was warned to stay away from me.

I didn't realize this man had been stalking/watching me for weeks.

He would follow me to work, sit across the street and watch my office, where I went to lunch, etc. Following the Sheriff warning him to leave me alone, he continued to position himself across the street and follow me to the restaurant at lunchtime. He did not approach me after that, but it took a few more weeks before he lost interest.

That winter I had everything from frozen pipes in my home to power outages. I was really looking forward to spring. When the beautiful weather arrived, so did tornado season again in Iowa. One day in June, the sky turned black, the wind started to blow, I knew another tornado was coming, I piled my children and dog into the car and drove to my mother's. I pulled into their driveway, lawn chairs, tree branches and debris were blowing everywhere. I stopped the car, put it in park, just then my Stepfather John came running out of the house and yelled "Get the hell out of there". I shoved the car into drive, stepped on the gas, just in time to miss a building blowing over on that spot. This was one night I would have been safer at home.

Nearly a year had passed since Bob's death. My dear friend Peggy, called me saying "why don't you come to dinner next week and this time leave the kids with a sitter." At first, I was offended, why didn't she want me to bring the kids? She knew I didn't go anywhere without them. (I was terrified to let them out of my sight after almost losing them in the tornado). But I reluctantly agreed to go to dinner. When I arrived at her house, I was wearing jeans, a shirt…. Looking very casual. When Peggy opened the door, she shrieked "my God, look at you, we have a man coming here to meet you tonight… get in this house and hurry we have to do you over before he gets here." I said "what you set up a blind date…. Why did you do that… I am not ready to date". She replied, "I knew you would say that, so I didn't tell you ahead of time."

She took me into her room, opened her closet and said, "pick out an outfit… I will do your hair, (she was a hairdresser)" I hurriedly selected a different outfit, she did my hair and within minutes the doorbell rang. There stood her husband, Jim, and a friend of his named John Gosch. They had served in the Marine Corp. together and this was my "blind date".

We all managed to get through a nice dinner, the food was good, and conversation kept light. After a few hours, I said I needed to get home, so I prepared to go to my car. John asked to walk me to the car. Once we got outside, he asked me for a date the following evening. I looked at him and said "look, I am a widow with two young children, if that scares you… you had better pass". He smiled and said "I already know you are a widow with two small children, Jim and Peg told me. Now would you like to go to dinner with me tomorrow night?" I accepted and that is how my life with John Gosch began.

We dated for over a year and were married in 1967, Johnny was born in 1969. We had built a new home; John had a good job, and we had a wonderful little family. I thought we had a happy life, but I learned many years later, John had been unfaithful to me multiple numbers of times, while he traveled the country as a salesman.

Only weeks before Johnny's kidnapping, John Gosch phoned me from North Carolina, while on a business trip. He told me he was going to commit suicide. Obviously, he did not but from then on things were never the same…. (see John Gosch chapter)

Living with the stress and grief of Johnny's kidnapping, coupled with the increasingly bizarre behavior of my husband. My weight dropped from 115 to 89 pounds. I looked like a walking skeleton. I had to keep going, no matter what.... Johnny's life depended upon it. There was no time to sleep, eat or rest. I was holding down my job, the speaking engagements, fund raisers, public appearances for the coming years. I sometimes wonder where I received the strength to go on. I know the support and prayers of many people had to help but there was also a little voice inside of me telling me.... "don't sit on a pity pot.... Keep moving... you are not the victim... your son is! "

THE SPEAKING TOUR

During the eighteen years Johnny has been missing, I gave over seven hundred speeches to all types of groups, churches, schools, big companies, police departments, open to the public, and private groups. The name of my program was "In Defense of Children", it was an awareness program which gave the "profile of a pedophile". The program explained to both parent and child information to recognize those in our society who would molest a child.

All of the programs were rewarding but there are two which stand out in my mind.

One night, I was traveling very late from a speaking engagement in Boone, Iowa to Minneapolis. I had to be in Minneapolis early the next morning, I got as far as Mason City and decided to take a break. I pulled in at Hardee's, it was about eleven p.m. The place was packed; it must have been after a game, as the place had loads of kids. I went to the lady's room before ordering food, as I went in there were two teen-age girls putting on their lipstick in the mirror. They glanced at me and went back to primping. I was using the "facilities" when I heard them leave the restroom... just moments later I heard "HEY EVERYONE, GUESS WHO IS IN ON THE TOILET.... NOREEN GOSCH!" I thought ... "Oh God, what am I going to do now… there is no back door". I waited a few minutes, collected myself and walked out with my head held high and said, "hello folks, how is the food here?"

Sometimes people stare, point or take the time to talk to me. It is something that I had to become accustomed to "living in a fishbowl" due to the enormous press coverage Johnny's case received. I knew it came with the territory but at times it has been uncomfortable. I had given my word to Ken Wooden, I would continue to speak out publicly, as an advocate for the protection of children.

I know the work I have done has made a difference; many people have contacted me thanking me for the information I have shared from all the stages. It helped to prevent kidnappings and some sexual abuses to children. Due to my programs the parents and children knew what to look for and what to do, if the child found themselves in a bad situation. Hearing that made it all worth it.

In Garner Iowa, there was a full auditorium, nearly 1,000 people. The crowd was very receptive to the information; I was talking about the need to "hug your child every day". As I talked I noticed a little boy with big brown eyes in the second row watching every move I made. He had a chocolate bar he was munching; he was about four years old.

After the program, a crowd gathered around me to talk, and this little boy made his way through the crowd to me and wrapped his arms around my legs. He looked up at me and wanted me to pick him up. When I reached down and scooped him up had chocolate on his face…. He threw his arms around me and said, "he knew I didn't have my little boy at home any more to hug me", I was covered with chocolate and didn't care. I just smiled through my tears…. Realizing that this little boy heard what I said and understood… Johnny was gone from our home, let me know I was reaching the little ones. God often speaks through the mouths of babes.

WHY JOHNNY CAN'T COME HOME!

"OWLS" vs. "TIGERS"

HELP FIND JOHNNY GOSCH →

Benefit Basketball Battle

See the
WHO "OWLS"
take on the
VALLEY "TIGERS" STAFF

Valley High School Fieldhouse
Tuesday, January 4
7:30 P.M.

ADMISSION: ONLY $1.00!!!!!!

Johnny Gosch did not spend his 13th birthday at home with his family; he didn't get to celebrate Christmas at home, either....because early on the morning of Sunday, September 5, 1982, as he began deliveries on his newspaper route, he was abducted by some person or persons unknown. No trace of him has been found since that time.

HELP FIND JOHNNY GOSCH, INC....
...is an organization formed by relatives, friends and concerned citizens to raise funds to pay for the services of private detectives working on this case. None of the money raised goes to the family; it is all used by the HELP FIND JOHNNY GOSCH, INC. organization to finance the search for Johnny. Everyone involved is grateful for the support of people in the area - but more is needed to help "Bring Johnny Home"

SURVIVAL.... A WAY OF LIFE FOR NOREEN

TIMES-REPUBLICAN, Marshalltown, Iowa, Saturday, April 7, 1984

Central Iowans Turn Out To Hear Gosch Story

By ROSE KODET
(T-R Correspondent)

CONRAD — Approximately 400 men, women and children crowded into the BCL High School's 300-seat auditorium Thursday night to hear Noreen Gosch tell about the Sept. 5, 1982, abduction of her son Johnny and explain to both parents and children how they could avoid a similar experience.

The Gosches have been speaking to capacity crowds throughout the Central Iowa area in the past few weeks. Earlier this week, she spoke in Marshalltown and has made other appearances in Hubbard, Zearing, Ackley and Alden.

Future appearances in the area include Nevada on Monday, Ames on April 16 and in New Providence on April 27.

Gosch stated that the type of person who abducts and/or molests children is "not the dirty old man on the corner with a bag of candy. This is 1984 and it's much more sophisticated than that."

With television camera lights blazing and all eyes glued on Gosch, she recounted what she and her

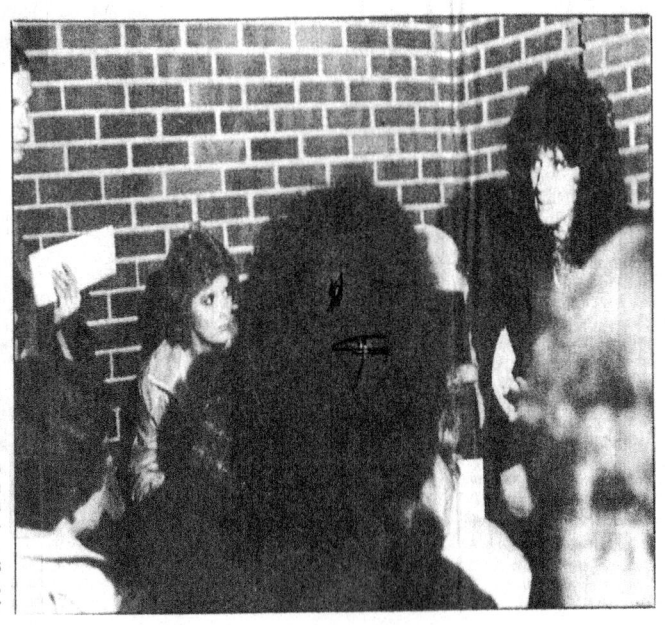

Noreen speaking to a group in Conrad, Iowa

WHY JOHNNY CAN'T COME HOME!

USA TODAY

NOREEN GOSCH
Guest columnist

10/14/82

'Forget our son? How dare they?'

WEST DES MOINES, Ia. — Johnny Gosch got up as usual at 5:30 a.m. on Sept. 5, 1982, to deliver his Sunday newspapers. On his way to the paper drop, a man in a car stopped him to ask directions.

Minutes later, a second man on foot approached Johnny from out of the shadows and walked him down the block. A short while later a car door was heard to slam, and a car was seen running a stop sign.

By 6:05 a.m. Johnny was gone. My husand and I were awakened by people who had not received their newspapers. It was then our entire world shattered. Our son was gone — kidnapped. Four witnesses reported the events to us and the police. We found Johnny's wagon full of newspapers on a corner two blocks from our home.

We immediately called the police. Our son was 12 years old. It was the policy of the police department to fill out a report and then wait up to 72 hours to see if the missing child was a runaway. We begged the police chief to act and to bring in extra assistance. He refused, saying he wanted to solve the case himself.

The chief had been investigated six months earlier for negligence and alcoholism on the job. We knew what we were up against. We contacted the media, did interviews, distributed Johnny's picture, posted a reward and called surrounding police departments to be sure they knew about Johnny — only to find that they knew nothing. Our police department had not told them.

We then hired a private investigator. To pay for it we sold candy bars and had garage sales and benefit dances. They say money isn't everything, but it becomes everything when your child is kidnapped.

In this country we have foundations to save baby seals, whales and battleships. But there's no help for missing children and their parents. It is the burden of the parents alone.

Johnny had been entered into the computer as "missing." We struggled for a year to have him reclassified as "abducted" — a vital difference, since it changes the way police pursue leads. Not until another newsboy in our area vanished under the same circumstances was our demand finally granted.

Noreen Gosch is a secretary, yoga teacher and mother of three.

> **"**
> We have foundations to save baby seals ... But there's no help for missing children
> **"**

But it should have been automatic. We should not have had to beg. The police were negligent. We filed a complaint with the U.S. Justice Department, only to be informed that due to the age of our son, the way police respond is a judgment call; they presume the child is a runaway.

Our son is a victim of a very sick crime. Yet one law enforcement officer had the gall to say to us, "Why don't you have another baby and forget about this whole thing?"

Forget about our son? Forget about finding him? How dare they. He may be alive. For many weeks the police told us, "We have no crime." But we still have no son.

83

SURVIVAL.... A WAY OF LIFE FOR NOREEN

9-10-85

Gosch filmed for Japanese documentary

by Mary McLain

A Japanese film crew was in the West Des Moines area last weekend filming the Gosch and Martin families who have each had a teenager kidnapped while delivering newspapers.

The two men are from Nippon A-V Productions in Tokyo, Japan and are accompanied by an interpreter from California since neither of the men speak English.

The television documentary will be entitled "America's Missing Children" and while in the area this weekend, the film crew interviewed and photographed both the Gosch and Martin families in their homes. They had earlier filmed a family on the east coast who also has a missing child and before returning to Japan will film a west coast family whose child is missing.

Through the interpreter, Kunio Kurita said Japan does not have the same problem with kidnapped children as does the United States. In Japan few children are kidnapped and those that are come from wealthy families where they are taken for ransom. They do have problem cases of run away children and children taken in divorce custody cases, a does the United States.

A Japanese film crew paid a visit to the John and Noreen Gosch home last weekend to film part of a television documentary they are making entitled "America's Missing Children." Seated on the left of the couch is Noreen Gosch, mother of missing newspaper boy Johnny Gosch, being interviewed by interpreter Chris Carriglia of California and Kinio Kurita of Nippon A-V Productions, Tokyo, Japan. In the foreground is the Japanese photographer photographing the interview for the

WHY JOHNNY CAN'T COME HOME!

Help for missing children. Illinois State Representative Lane Evans (left), Illinois Congressman Paul Simon (center) and Noreen Gosch of West Des Moines, mother of missing newspaper boy Johnny Gosch, held a press conference last week to announce a new legislative effort to help find missing and abducted children.

SURVIVAL.... A WAY OF LIFE FOR NOREEN

Noreen speaks to over 2,000 people in Alden, Iowa

WHY JOHNNY CAN'T COME HOME!

Noreen Gosch — In Defense of Children

A crowd estimated at over 1,000 people — part of which is shown in the photo above — packed into the Nevada Junior High Fieldhouse Monday night to hear Noreen Gosch, mother of missing paperboy Johnny Gosch, give a program entitled "In Defense of Children." Gosch told of efforts to strengthen laws concerning missing children, and also gave tips on ways to prevent child abductions. The photo at right shows Gosch talking to interested parents after the program concluded. The Nevada chapters of Beta Sigma Phi sponsored the program. Journal photos by Brad Williams

CENTRAL INTELLIGENCE AGENCY ON THE SCENE–1983

From being a working mother, I was suddenly immersed into the world of James Bond. Before Johnny was kidnapped, I'd never heard the word **pedophile**, now I use the word many times a day. A year after my son's disappearance, I was a **CIA ASSET**.

Within six months of the kidnapping, a young man calling himself Paul Bishop contacted me by phone. He began to tell me that an international kidnapping/pornography ring had taken my son. I asked, "How do you know that to be true, can you prove it!" He replied, "I work for a government agency which is investigating pedophile organizations. And there are indicators in your case that suggest your son was taken by such an organization. We feel he is being used for pornography and prostitution." All clues were pointing to the kidnapping being organized and not that of a "lone criminal". I found it difficult to believe and accept that my son could have been targeted by such an organization. It was only in later years that I was to learn the possible reason Johnny was selected.

I didn't know there was an organization like North American Man Boy Love Association or the Rene'Guyeon Society. The first targets little boys, the second little girls. Now most Americans realize that highly connected businessmen, lawyers, judges, politicians and police are involved in pedophile activities. We have only to look at newspapers in our local area to find teachers, clergy, scout leaders, coaches, arrested and charged with child molestation. What we do not see is the **important politician**, judges etc. charged with similar crimes. These **important individuals** seem to be above the law. Children who make claims against important people are either dismissed as liars or imprisoned for perjury.

We maintained telephone communication for months, in April of 1983; Paul made the trip to Des Moines. He called me when he arrived and asked that I meet him at Shakey's Pizza Parlor on Hickman Road at noon. Shakey's was an extremely popular restaurant at the time. I arrived at eleven forty-five and found only two cars in the parking lot. Strange, I thought to myself.... This lot should have been filled.

As I stepped inside, I was as nervous as hell, there sat one young man in a booth, he rose to shake my hand and said, "I am Paul Bishop", he stood about six foot three, dark brown eyes, medium brown hair, well built, very handsome face.

I would never have thought that this man would one day call me "Mom". He could not have been more than twenty-three years of age at the time. We sat down; he lifted to the table a large very worn, brown leather briefcase. I noticed a three-ring binder type of book all enclosed by a zipper. To the left of the booth, stood a man, approximately forty years old, looking as though he were standing "at attention" in some type of military pose with his hands clasped behind his back. He didn't speak, nor acknowledge me at all. It felt strained and almost eerie at first because we were the only people in the establishment. I wondered what I walked into! Who had the clout to take over a popular restaurant and turn away all its regular noontime customers? Why hadn't they chosen a quieter or isolated setting? They must be very powerful people and wanted me to recognize that fact.

Paul began talking about my son, telling me an international kidnapping/pornography ring took Johnny and that my son was very much alive. He claimed Johnny was being used in pornography, prostitution and perversion. I kept asking him how he knew this, just as I did many times over the months of phone communication, prior to his visit to Des Moines.

It was not until then that Paul Bishop revealed himself as being with the CIA, he claimed he worked as an **"Agency Asset"**, he opened his wallet, producing a government identification card with his photo but it did not say CIA. I looked at it and said, "anyone could have one of those made". I told him I had never heard of an Agency Asset. He then began to explain that they are put into situations to gather information, affect certain types of action and they are chosen carefully. He told me he was also known as Robert LaVeck. I remarked that he looked so young and how could he be in that kind of position. He then explained, Assets are people who will blend in to achieve a certain goal. So, the Agency will use many people in different walks of life. Today we know the CIA has used clergy, doctors, journalists, and housewives as **Agency Assets.** I didn't realize that I was about to become one of those assets.

As I sat there listening to all of this, my mind was spinning, so many thoughts were going through my head, how could I trust this person? Who is he really and what was he doing in Des Moines Iowa, talking about my son's case? I just sat there half numb for a long time, trying to gather as much information so I could ask intelligent questions.

He stated, "We wanted your help." I asked, "how can I help you? What does the CIA want with me?" He replied, "We need one stable parent in this situation to act, when directed to speak out to the public as to what happened to your son".

I doubted who he was, I could not grasp why they would want me. To convince me, he carefully unzipped the three-ring binder laying on the table. Slowly he rotated it and pushed it across the table to me. It was a complete dossier of my entire family, including those who have died. Noticeably absent was any reference to Johnny's father.... John Gosch. He allowed me to read through these pages, I was amazed and shocked that anyone would or could amass so much information on any one individual and here were pages of it involving my whole family. There were things I had not thought of in twenty years, which were detailed in these documents. I was not only shocked but frightened!

I realized this young man was part of a powerful organization, which has the ability to gather extremely detailed intelligence data on ordinary people. So, I listened intently to what he was proposing. He explained that I would be asked to supply information, give frequent press conferences to keep Johnny's story alive, so they could continue to pursue the investigation (supposedly?) He asked me to travel, give presentations about the case and sharing information from private investigative reports. How ironic the local police and the FBI were not interested but the CIA was. He claimed the CIA was in the process of investigating a very large organization, responsible for kidnapping children in our country and internationally (See the Finders). I agreed to assist but wasn't sure what I agreed to at that point. However, this seemed to be the only game in town.

Paul came to my neighborhood and asked questions of many people in the area, writing everything down in a notebook. After spending several days, Paul had concluded his initial assessment and prepared to leave Des Moines. He told me that he had a code name of "Firefox", I was given a phone number to reach him. I later learned the number was at Langley Air Force Base, CIA Headquarters.

For months we continued to be in daily contact by phone, I would telephone him when there would be developments on the case and to report information supplied by our private investigators. Other times, he would call me with directions to release certain information to the media.

All the information was regarding leads being investigated in the case. Many times, I wondered, what is this all for? What purpose is it to share information with the media? He would explain that there was a need to keep Johnny's case alive in the media, otherwise people would forget about it and the case would be buried forever.

Paul began to give me names of people he suspected as being involved in the kidnapping. Some were unfamiliar to me but then he gave names of people living right here in Des Moines— some of them extremely wealthy members of this community. Hearing of local involvement didn't surprise me, I asked him what we were going to do about it, the police were still not willing to explore any aspects of the case. He said he would make another trip to Des Moines in a couple months.

I followed all that I was required to do, many times not really understanding the need. However, each time there was a burst of publicity, more leads would come to us. Everything from "sightings of Johnny" to information about possible suspects. As they would come pouring in, I would in turn give them to our private investigator. Time and money were very necessary to properly follow up on each bit of information. I exhausted myself trying to find ways to raise funds. Parents of a missing child cannot afford the luxury of not checking out everything, one never knows when a piece of information might be the piece of the puzzle which would lead to solving the case.

I had been kept very busy doing speaking engagements, people all over the country wanted to hear the Johnny Gosch Story. My audience ranged from several hundred people to over three thousand. I traveled every evening of the week, telling the story and sharing safety tips with parents and children. When I began this there was no awareness that children were not safe in their own front yard. But today despite the tremendous awareness of kidnapping children continues to disappear.

Sam Soda, the local private investigator called me claiming he had valuable information for me and wanted to meet as soon as possible. He said it concerned "a second kidnapping in Des Moines." I made arrangements to meet him at his office on June 13, 1984. I brought a tape recorder along and placed it on the table.

During this meeting, he shared information that there would be a "second kidnapping in Des Moines". He claimed this came from an *informant.* The kidnapping was to occur on the second weekend in August, on the South Side of Des Moines and that it would be another paper carrier. I thought it was strange that he would be telling me this and not the police. When I questioned him on this point, he claimed that I should be the one to take the information to the Des Moines Police, as it would be their jurisdiction. I thanked him for the information and left. This was to begin an association with Mr. Soda, which lasted a few years. Years later, Paul Bonacci who participated in the kidnapping of Johnny identified Sam Soda as the man who brought pictures of Johnny to the kidnappers, in a motel room in West Des Moines, on September 4, 1982, the night before the kidnapping.

I did go to the Des Moines Police Dept., asking if I could play the tape of the meeting with Mr. Soda for them. The person at the desk would not allow me to talk to a Detective, he kept saying if they "felt my information was of importance they would call me". Repeatedly, I told him that I had a tape recording and in a couple of months there would be another paperboy kidnapped. They treated me as though I had lost my mind and they didn't want to be bothered with me.

When I left the Police Dept., I decided to at least talk to the TV station program managers. I did contact each of them and relayed the information, telling them I also had a tape recording of this conversation. *I was shocked to find out that even though they listened to me, no one wanted to listen to the tape.* I was very uneasy about the whole situation and felt that Mr. Soda had given me important information. I also called Frank Santiago, Des Moines Register reporter who had been assigned to Johnny's story since the beginning. He was the only one who listened to the tape. He verified my story when a police detective lied about my ever bringing the tape in to the police.

I received a call from Karen Burnes, a producer with ABC's 20/20 in July of 1984, asking to present Johnny's story. Plans were made with Karen Burnes for Johnny's Story by 20/20 to be filmed on the second weekend in August.

Paul Bishop returned to Des Moines, July 31, 1984. It was at this time, he gave me the name of the man who was the "spotter" ….in Johnny's kidnapping. Paul explained that a spotter is the person who secures a photo of a victim prior to a kidnapping.

When I heard the name, I said "Paul, you need to listen to this tape recording". He listened…I then told him of my attempts to share the information with the police department and media. Paul was not shocked at what he heard on the tape and paid a visit to Sam Soda, questioning him concerning the source of the information on a second kidnapping. Sam was not too cooperative, became annoyed with Bishop, asking him to leave his office.

Before Paul left, he created a very intricate map of the crime scene, indicating time sequence of each aspect of the kidnapping. Paul dated and initialed the map using GPB (George Paul Bishop)

After Paul flew back to Washington, I began to hear from Sam Soda on a regular basis. He wanted to be the investigator for Johnny's case. He asked for a bank account to be set up for him to draw upon for a salary. I explained to him we already had a private investigator and could not afford another. He continued to attempt to be involved in any way he could in the case. I think that this suggests how intricate the manipulations of those involved in the kidnapping and exploitation of children like Johnny.

I had been working with Senator Grassley from Iowa, he had been particularly helpful in dealing with the FBI. Many times, Paul Bishop would call me from Senator Grassley's office, when finished speaking with me he would hand the phone to one of Grassley's aides who I was familiar with. She informed me there was a Senate Hearing scheduled in August 1984 and I would be invited to testify. A short time later I received my invitation to testify in Washington D.C. before Senator Arlan Specter's Hearing on Organized Crime and its Relationship to Kidnapping.

I was instructed by Senator Grassley's office to Federal Express a copy of my testimony and to carry a copy on the plane when I flew to Washington

D.C. In testifying before Congress or State Legislature, you are required to prepare a written presentation of your testimony. Paul Bishop met the plane and escorted me to the hotel. I checked in and then he took me on a tour of Washington, followed by showing me some of the blighted places in D.C. where children as young as ten years old hang out on the streets late at night. Today it is not safe even on the White House Mall at night.

Later that evening, we spent time going over every word of my testimony. I wanted to be sure that when I presented my information the following morning that it was clear to the committee, "an Organized Pedophile Group" took my son. Again and again, I have met with denial on the part of individuals and organizations that any such groups could exist in this country. Paul not only approved of what I had written but was to back me up during the hearing. For my protection two men were posted outside of my hotel room door all night.

Paul Bishop, accompanied by two young men arrived at the hotel the next morning to drive me to the Capitol for the Hearing. As I entered the room, I noticed there were reporters everywhere, television, radio, newspaper and magazine. I recognized Ken Lanning of the FBI, I walked towards him, saying, "Hello, I am Noreen Gosch", extending my hand to shake his. He pulled back and said, "We know who you are". With that statement there was a definite chill in the air. It was as though the FBI resented me being asked to testify.

Paul sat beside me at the table as I testified to my knowledge of the slave auctions in the U.S. During my testimony, Senator Specter asked a number of questions about my son's kidnapping and the investigation. I explained the FBI refused to enter the case, because they wanted me to prove my son's life was in danger, the lack of response from the local authorities and the need for private investigators.

Senator Specter asked Paul Bishop of his relationship to the case and to me and did he know this to be true. Paul indicated he was an investigator and that every word of my testimony was accurate. At no time did Paul ever identify himself as CIA during the hearing and afterward during the interviews with the Washington Press. He withdrew from the view of the cameras. All attempts on my part to obtain photos from the hearing were unsuccessful.

Following the hearing, I requested from one of the staff members a copy of Mr.Lannings testimony and the pedophile material that was displayed on the table, including the catalog. She asked, " Mrs. Gosch would like a copy of the material presented by Mr. Lanning" she was told by an FBI Agent " This is the property of the FBI and it was acquired from a pedophiles lair, it cannot be given to anyone".

I was appalled with all this material in the hands of the FBI, presented by Ken Lanning to Senator Specters committee and examined by the National media, that there is ever any question today in the year 2000, about the existence of national and international kidnap organizations. Children are a commodity used in TV commercials and magazine ads in a sexually provocative manner. Is it any wonder that children are no longer safe in our schools because the pedophiles have managed to become their teachers, coaches, and mentoring programs.

It has now been sixteen years since Senator Arlen Specter has been given these materials. To my knowledge, no major report was given to Congress about the growing and influential pedophiles operating throughout the United States. What happened to the new media who immediately surrounded me following the hearing anxious for more details about Johnny? They had the same access to that catalog that I did. Why hasn't it become a major national story? I testified that slave auctions were being held in the U.S. the catalog clearly confirmed my testimony.

I flew back to Des Moines to meet with the crew from ABC 20/20. The following day Karen Burnes and the film crew from 20/20 arrived in town. It was a Saturday and the second weekend in August. They filmed locations around Des Moines and West Des Moines, including the site where Johnny was kidnapped. Later when we arrived back at our home. I decided to share the information regarding a second kidnapping, supposed to occur the following day. I played the tape recording for Karen and shared how I had been to the Des Moines Police Dept., hoping they would at least patrol the paper drop areas on the South Side of Des Moines. I also told her that I had given the information to the News Directors at the local TV stations. She showed great interest in the information.

We finished filming for the day, the crew went to the airport and flew back to New York. Karen announced she was staying over another night.... wanting to see if the "prediction of the second kidnapping" would take place.

The shock of the phone ringing early the next morning with a reporter at the local ABC TV station, telling me "The second kidnapping had just taken place" was like reliving Johnny's kidnapping.

He kept saying "It happened just as you said it would Mrs. Gosch". He also informed me the police were calling it a kidnapping immediately and the FBI were bringing in agents from Quantico, VA to assist in the investigation and search.

The young boy kidnapped was Eugene Martin, a newspaper carrier, preparing to deliver his papers on the South Side of Des Moines. He had only had his paper route three weeks.

In Johnny's case, the FBI refused to enter the case, the reason they verbally gave me in my home was that "they had no crime, and it was my responsibility to prove my son's life was in danger". Why now with Eugene Martin's kidnapping under identical circumstances was the FBI coming forward with a bevy of FBI agents.

Based on this phone call alone, I called Karen at the hotel and told her the "second kidnapping had just happened", exactly as Sam Soda had predicted on June 13, 1984. She immediately contacted her network and arranging for a film crew to come back to Des Moines, when the crew arrived, they went to the Des Moines police department.

The police department was in a state of confusion; Karen asked the police chief. Are you bringing in FBI Agents for this case. They didn't for

Johnny Gosch? Are you going to use canine search teams? They didn't for Johnny Gosch. Will you do an aerial search? They wouldn't for Johnny Gosch.

The police chief had no comment about the Johnny Gosch case and stated the department would do everything in their power to solve the Martin kidnapping. The police went all out using FBI, SWAT Teams, Canine Searches, and aerial searches but like Johnny, Eugene Martin was probably quickly taken out of the immediate search area. This case was a duplicate of Johnny's kidnapping.

Karen decided to stay in Des Moines for several days, interviewing and gathering information on this latest tragedy. The story about Eugene Martin and Johnny appeared immediately on ABC news, a tremendous advantage for any victim of kidnapping.

After the Martin kidnapping, I expected the Des Moines Police Dept, to contact me and want to discuss the information I received from Sam Soda. Even though my information proved valid the police never asked to listen to the tape.

Instead, I was warned not to talk about it to the press and certainly not the Martin family. It was difficult for me to understand how they had the opportunity to prevent the second kidnapping, due to the advanced information and chose to ignore it and me. Instead of listening to the information I tried to give them, I was treated like a "nut" and dismissed. If the newspaper drop points been patrolled Eugene Martin might not have been taken. If the local media had acted, the police might have been forced to act. It seems that where the kidnapping of children is concerned neither media or police show much interest. I can understand how at first someone might think, the information

wasn't accurate but when there is a possibility of a child's life at stake. I feel it calls for investigation. I felt terrible that this kidnapping had taken place ... I tried to get the attention of the people here, but no one would listen. I took the responsibility and went to the authorities despite the fact I was treated like a nut.

To this day, there are some who refuse to admit that I brought the information. The parties I shared it with... know I am telling the truth and played the tape for them. As for the rest, may God forgive them for ignoring this and allowing another child to be taken from our community.

A few days later, NBC Today Show contacted me, asking if I could get in touch with the Martins, as they had been unsuccessful. It seems the FBI had set up a command post in their home and calls were being screened.

The Today show wanted to interview both the Martins and us the following day. I called the Martin home, an FBI Agent answered the phone, I told him I was Don's sister and wanted to speak to him. The agent handed the phone to Don, Eugene's father. I said "Don, this is not your sister... it is Noreen Gosch....The Today Show wants us tomorrow.... can you do it." We then made plans to do the Today show from the local WHOTV studio in Des Moines, the NBC affiliate.

Sam Soda, in a total reversal began to contact the Des Moines Police telling them that Paul Bishop (my CIA contact) had been in Des Moines a short time before the Martin kidnapping and was somehow involved.

Sam must have bent the ear of some influential people because shortly afterward a Federal Grand Jury Hearing was scheduled, and Paul Bishop was subpoenaed to testify. He returned one last time to Des Moines. Paul was detained at the hearing for hours. Following the hearing Paul took a taxi to my home. While he was sharing the details of the hearing, the phone rang several times. It was Sam Soda each time wanting to know if Paul Bishop was there. He became very angry and agitated when I told him Paul was not there. He claimed he was looking for him and could not find him. We felt it best for Paul to change his travel plans. I decided with friends for Paul to stay the night at their home. He flew back to Washington D.C. a couple of days later. That was the last time I saw or spoke with Paul.

Shortly after that visit, Paul Bishop or Robert LaVeck vanished without a trace. Suddenly, the phone number at Langley was no longer working. We have never been able to discover what happened to Paul Bishop.

For some reason Paul always called me "Mom." He was a young person in his twenties, and I sometimes wonder if he had been one of the boys we now know as "lost". Had he been used in some manner by the very element that took my son? Was he sent here to share with me the threads of truth, which would unfold later? Paul gave me the first pieces of this puzzle. He knew things about this case which were revealed and documented years later in 1992. Below is the last communication I had with Paul Bishop, in a letter dated August 3, 1985.

WHY JOHNNY CAN'T COME HOME!

JOHNNY IN 1984-1985...
SKETCH SUPPLIED BY PAUL BISHOP
OPPOSITE PAGE:
MAP OF THE KIDNAP/CRIME SCENE PREPARED
BY: G. PAUL BISHOP (SEE INITIALS)

CENTRAL INTELLIGENCE AGENCY ON THE SCENE 1983

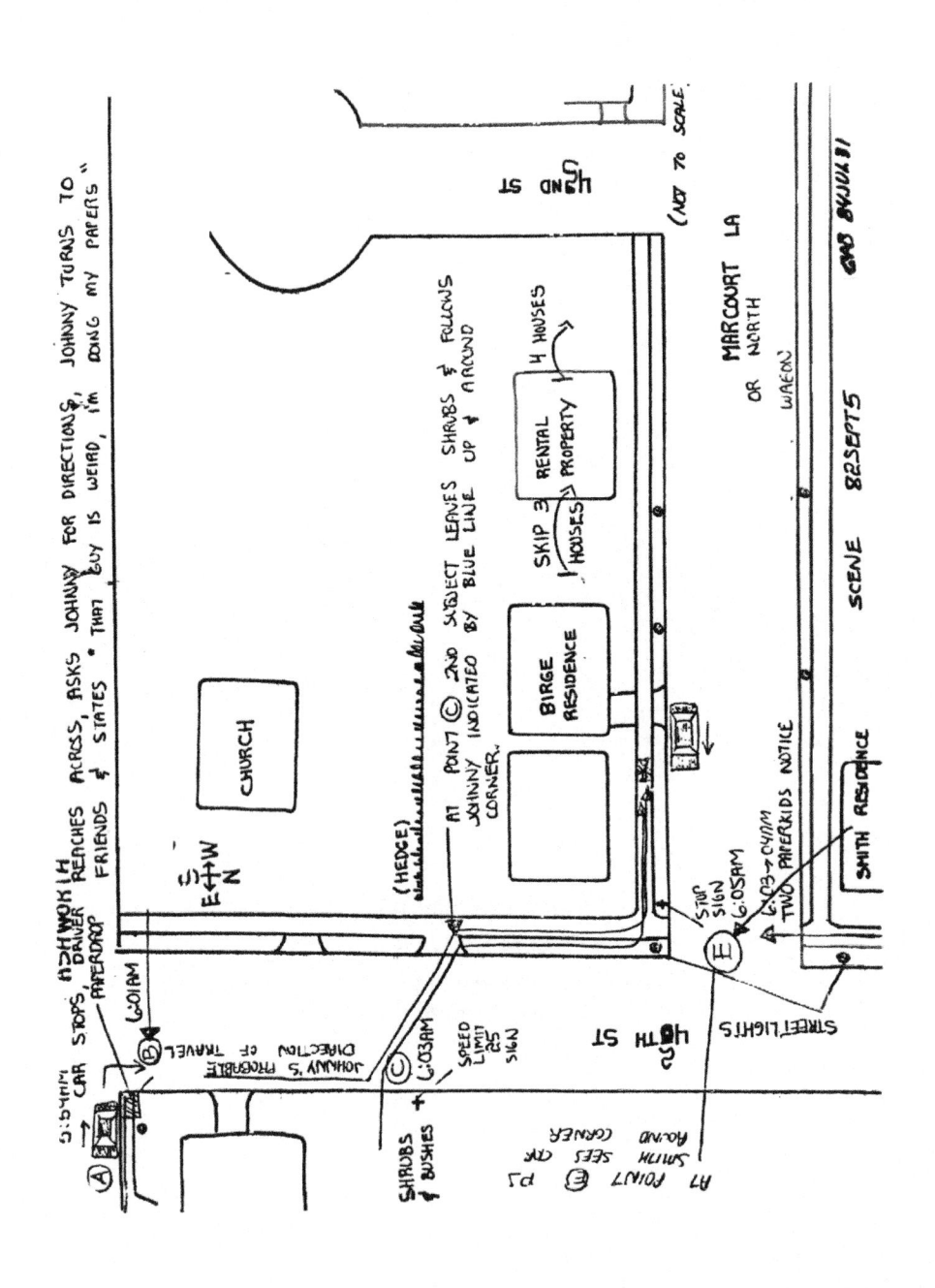

JOHN GOSCH...
JOHNNY'S FATHER

I was married to Johnny's father for twenty-six years... In all that time most people think they would know everything about their partner in life. That wasn't the case with... John, he was very silent about a lot of things in his growing up years.

John grew up on a farm in Northwest Iowa; he has thirteen brothers and sisters. In school, John was football jock, the whole nine yards.... He was suddenly whisked off to a Seminary to complete his senior year of school. The Crosier Fathers Seminary in Hastings, Nebraska for his senior year.

John claimed to have been thrown out of the seminary somewhere near the end of the senior year... for what I have no clue...but showed up at home one night at dinnertime. His sister told me ... "Mom and Dad were very upset to see him come home." Approximately a week later he was off into the Marine corp.

After he returned from the Marine Corp in 1966, I met him through some friends. Nearly a year had passed since the death of my first husband. I was alone raising two small children.

My dear friend Peggy called me saying "why don't you come to dinner next week and this time leave the kids with a sitter." At first, I was offended,

JOHN GOSCH...JOHNNY'S FATHER

why didn't she want me to bring the kids? She knew I didn't go anywhere without them. But I reluctantly agreed to go to dinner. When I arrived at her house, I was wearing jeans, a shirt.... Looking very casual. When Peggy opened the door....

she shrieked "my God, look at you, we have a man coming here to meet you tonight... get in this house and hurry we must do you over before he gets here." I said "WHAT... you set up a blind date? Why did you do that? I am not ready to date". She replied "I knew you would say that so ...I didn't tell you ahead of time."

She took me into her room, opened her closet and said, "Pick an outfit... I will do your hair, (she was a hairdresser)". I hurriedly selected a different outfit; she did my hair and within minutes the doorbell rang. Her husband, Jim answered the door, there stood a friend of his named John Gosch. They had served in the Marine Corp. together and this was my "blind date".

We all managed to get through a nice dinner; the food was good, and conversation kept light. After a few hours, I said I needed to get home, so I prepared to go to my car. John asked to walk me to the car. Once we got outside, he asked me for a date the following evening. I looked at him and said, "look, I am a widow with two young children, if that scares you... you had better pass". He smiled and said, "I already know you are a widow with two small children, Jim and Peg told me. Now would you like to go to dinner with me tomorrow night?" I accepted and this began my life with John Gosch.

John and I dated about a year then got married. We built a home in Eldridge, Iowa. Most things in our life seemed very normal, just like other people down the block in anywhere USA. We were thrilled when we found out a year later that I was expecting a baby. Everyone was adjusting to our new life together.

Johnny was born on November 12, 1969; he was such a good little guy, just like the other kids were as infants. It was a time of happiness in our lives. Within two years, a job transfer came through for John and we moved our family to Albert Lea, Minnesota. It was a beautiful little town, and we loved our home there. We lived close to the lake, and it was a very peaceful time in our lives. John's job required some travel, so we adjusted to the new schedule.

Several years later, the company John worked for transferred us to Des Moines. It was a big adjustment for all the kids, they had started to form close friendships in Minnesota. But everyone adjusted, liked their new schools and found new friends. For years life was calm and normal for the Gosch's. Nothing earth shattering took place. Not until early in 1982…

BEFORE THE KIDNAPPING

A great many strange things began to happen in the months prior to Johnny's kidnapping. John, my husband at that time had never been really a close father to the children, but his treatment of them became not only unfair but also cruel many times. He seemed to have a hatred, which was boiling over into our family life, and he would take it out on the kids. He began to treat my older son with unkindness and ridicule daily. He was a good kid and had not done anything to deserve this treatment. The same was true with our daughter and Johnny.

June of 1982, John wanted to take our son's Joe and John on a fishing trip, to Lake of the Ozarks in Missouri. He explained, "it might be his last or only opportunity to do so", I thought it was a strange remark. They did go on the trip, and it was uneventful. Although after returning from the trip the boys said his depression was really becoming apparent, as though he was operating with another personality, I couldn't understand what was happening to him.

In July of 1982, John left on a business trip to North Carolina, he called me from Raleigh, N.C., one evening and said, "I am going to kill myself, I can no longer live with it", then hung up the phone. I was home with the kids in West Des Moines. I had no way to reach him; whenever he traveled, he did not give me any kind of itinerary or a way to reach him in the event of an emergency. I telephoned the Raleigh N.C., police department and told them of what had just happened, that he would be staying close to the airport, as he had reservations going out the next morning to return home and that he was driving a rental car. The police located him in a motel and made him phone home to let me know he was fine. When he returned home, he gave no explanation of his words or actions. But rather became very agitated and angry when I asked questions.

August 1982, John insisted on taking Johnny with him on a business trip, they went to Omaha, NE. One of the places they toured was Offutt Air Force Base, which was a highlight for Johnny, as he loved planes. He was so excited as he talked about it when he returned home. It was strange as Johnny described their trip he could only remember parts of the days he was gone with his father. I attributed it to a young boy only remembering the highlights, which were the airplanes.

Following this business trip, we began to receive phone calls every night, usually about one a.m. or two a.m. John always answered the phone; it was located on his nightstand.

One evening in August, John was late coming home from work. When he arrived, he began to rant and rave that "he was dying and had a terminal illness", he named the doctor who had told him. I called the doctor the following day only to be told that John had not even been in for an appointment, he was not even a patient. When I asked him about it, he denied ever telling me that he was dying. He had said this in front of all three children, they looked at each other and at me … all of us were puzzled. Again, I couldn't understand what was going on or producing this unusual behavior.

The end of August came, and the kids started school Johnny was enrolled at Indian Hills Junior H.S. It would be his first year there. The first week of school was a short week, as Labor Day Weekend was the first holiday. It was Friday night, the first football game of the season. John, Johnny and I went to the Valley High School Football game. During the game, Johnny asked if he could go to the concession stand to get something to drink. I said "okay" but to come back to the seat afterwards. I waited for a while, and he didn't come back; so, John went down to investigate. He was under the bleachers talking to a man in a police uniform. John called him to come back, and he did so. After the game was over, we were walking out of the stadium and the same police officer was standing there, Johnny waved to him and then said to me "Mom, I think I would like to be a policeman when I grow up". We then went home.

The following day, Saturday, Johnny went to a movie in the afternoon with his friend Mark. That evening, my daughter and her boyfriend came from college, and I fixed a nice dinner for all. It was so nice to have all of them home at the same time for dinner. After they ate, the kids all were laughing and having such a good time visiting. Johnny jumped up and said, "I need to get to bed". He wanted to get up early the next morning, to do his paper route. Johnny had a paper route for the Des Moines Register on Sundays and delivered the evening paper on weeknights. He had been doing the route for a year and had a perfect service award for each month. A record he was proud of... it meant that he had always been on time with deliveries since he took over the route. The night before the kidnapping, our whole family was home for dinner, which I now call **"The Last Supper"**, we had a wonderful time together. Johnny got up from the table, looked at the clock and said he had to get to bed. He had to get up early the following morning to do his paper route. Before he left the kitchen Johnny said, "Dad, why don't you stay home tomorrow, I can do the route alone"! John said, "Well I guess it would be okay!" It worried me, as it was so dark at that hour of the morning, they had to start deliveries. So I said, "no, John, our agreement is that you would go with him on Sunday mornings. John finally said, "No, Johnny, wake me in the morning and we will do the route together".

Johnny gave everyone a hug and went upstairs to bed. A few moments later, he was back in the kitchen standing next to me as I was cleaning up after dinner. He gave me a hug again and said "Mom, I will always love you.... You are the best!" He went to the stairs, looked at me, smiled and then went up to bed. Little did I know at that moment... It would be the last time; I would see my son for nearly fifteen years.

JOHN GOSCH...JOHNNY'S FATHER

We received a phone call at 1:30 a.m., every Sunday morning from the beginning of August, until September 5th, the morning, Johnny was kidnapped. My husband, John would pick up the phone and say, "You've got the wrong number", and hang up. On the morning of the kidnapping, Sept. 5, 1982, at 1:35 am, the phone rang, he answered, I woke up to hear him saying "alright…alright…okay, "then he hung up. I questioned him about the call and he just kept insisting it was a wrong number. He seemed nervous at the time, but it was late, and I drifted back to sleep, not realizing the worst was about to happen.

The next morning our world was blown apart by the phone ringing … neighbors were complaining they hadn't received their newspapers. I leaped out of bed, ran down to Johnny's room, he was gone. I assumed he was out working on the route and was running late. I thought it strange John was still asleep in bed, as he had told Johnny he would go with him that morning. John got up and said he would go help Johnny. Moments later he returned to the house, his face was ashen… yelling, "call the police, Johnny is gone, his wagon is full of papers at the corner, something has happened to him.

It is said that everyone reacts differently to any situation. I believe that but what I experienced following Johnny's kidnapping…. I was not prepared for it at all. Of course, the kidnapping was a tragic blow to all of us that knew and loved Johnny. Personalities are changed by the events that happen in our lives.

Following the kidnapping, there was unbelievable turmoil and chaos at our home. The phone was ringing every ten minutes, our home was transformed into a command post for the searches which were taking place daily. So, I guess, I didn't interpret the subtle changes taking place as "red flags". We were all stressed to the max and to just function each day became an "art form".

John began to take issue and argue with every decision which had to be made concerning the case. It was almost as if he was trying to place obstacles before me and I didn't understand why. Stress, pain and worry seemed the logical answer at first.

Within ten days after the kidnapping, we both had to return to our jobs, taking turns manning the phones at home so that it would be answered 24 hours a day. Life had to return to some kind of normal.

John's job involved travel over several states. So much of the time, he was on the road. When I would ask him for an itinerary… phone numbers, motels where he would stay… he told me "No". I certainly didn't understand this at all. We had a kidnapped child, and I was left to handle every decision.

I was not able to reach him when things happened, and decisions had to be made. Unfortunately, that also placed me before the public doing a "solo act". Soon the rumors and normal talk took place in the city…most of it attacking me for demanding answers on the case. There should have been a more aggressive investigation from day one. Instead, the West Des Moines Police classified Johnny as a "runaway" for several months. I tried and tried to get John to stand with me and go to the police to make changes. He simply would not. Instead, he would say he had to go out of town. I then took over and did what had to be done.

I used to hear things like…. Poor John, his son was kidnapped but Noreen is such a "bitch". This used to hurt me tremendously; I couldn't understand why people would make such judgments when I was trying to fight for my son's life.

John began to change very rapidly, he would get up in the middle of the night and prowl… the neighborhood… walking, walking, walking. One day, I received a call from a neighbor telling me to "keep my husband at home". The neighbor went on to say "they had been away from home the previous evening, leaving their seventeen-year-old daughter home alone. John stopped at their home, ringing the doorbell around one

a.m. The girl answered the door, he asked if he could come in. She let him in … feeling sorry for him, thinking he just needed to talk. Once inside the door, John began telling her how much he needed some hugs and kisses. The girl became very upset, irate and told him to leave, or she would call her parents. He took off and walked home". My neighbor was furious but said in view of the tragic loss they would not press any charges against him and cause me any further pain. I talked to John about this when he returned home the next day. His comment was "the girl is a slut'. This girl isn't, wasn't and never will be a "slut". She is a wonderful person and I could understand how the mother felt. She had been a friend of mine but that quickly ended the friendship and within three months the family moved from the neighborhood.

After this incident, John was very quiet for a couple days. One morning, I was on my way to work, I had this terrible feeling come over me and knew I needed to go back home. I made a "U-turn" in the middle of Woodland Ave. and drove home as quickly as possible. I walked in through the garage door being very quiet. When I opened the door to the kitchen … John was seated at the kitchen table loading a pistol. I walked in and asked him if he was "going hunting". He replied, "I can't live with this any longer, the stress is too great, I am going to kill myself today". I thought carefully because I felt he meant it and was going to do it. (I knew if I could make him angry, he would momentarily take his focus off the gun) I looked at him and said **"Well for the love of God don't shoot yourself in the house and leave the mess for me to clean us…go somewhere else and do it".** He said, "you are sure mean, telling me to do it somewhere else". He put the gun down and stood up, walking away from the table. I made a dive for the gun and got it…. Asking him to sit down while I called someone, to talk to him. He surprisingly did as I asked. I called the police department and asked if there was someone who could come over to assist me by talking to him. They did send a detective. Later the detective told me "John needs counseling".

Later, after things had calmed down, I told him to survive this we should go to trauma counseling together. He refused, saying he didn't need it. I did seek out a trauma counselor to talk over the things, which were happening. I had one child missing and two other children to think about. One of us had to remain stable and I guess that was me.

Everything and everyone increasingly agitated John. He was cruel to our other children, telling them, he wished the kidnapper had chosen them instead of Johnny. He was horrible to the private investigators, who were working very hard to give us the answers we so desperately needed. Again, I attributed it to stress. **WRONG!**

There was the obvious need to raise money to pay investigators. It was suggested we sell "Worlds Finest Candy Bars" and I should accept speaking engagements. John threw a fit about the candy bars, although it is a legitimate fundraiser. When I would leave home to travel to speech, he would throw things at me, yelling…. Calling me filthy names. I would think, why wouldn't he help instead of trying to destroy every avenue of progress. I again thought stress was causing him to change so drastically but something else was emerging. John's entire personality would switch…. much like I witnessed years later with Paul Bonacci. Paul suffered from MPD (Multiple Personality Disorder).

Nearly eighteen months had passed, I was still working my job, teaching my Yoga classes, and accepting every speaking engagement offered to me. It was August of 1984, approximately a week after the Eugene Martin kidnapping. We were invited to attend a dinner. We were staying at a motel in Davenport, Iowa, not far from my family home. Things were going well but then someone asked how the case was going and if we had any other children. I looked over at John, he was suddenly playing with his food, looking all around, like a five-year-old. His whole facial expression had changed again.

I knew we had to get out of there and quick before there was an incident. Each time I had seen that expression on John's face previously, he had caused a scene in our home. I didn't want one in this restaurant. We got outside, were in the car and driving out of the parking lot. Suddenly, he doubled up his fist and began hitting me in the face. I tried to jump from the car to get help, he threw the automatic locks on the car and sped away from the parking lot. Over the course of the next two hours, I thought I was going to die. He drove me around for two hours, stopping the car to beat on me, then speeding up again and driving like a wild man. Finally, I could see a familiar area, I quickly pushed the automatic locks forward, unlocking the doors and jumped from the moving car, rolling into a ditch filled with mud and water. I laid there in the darkness until I heard his car leave the area.

My foot was hurting badly, as I climbed up on the street from the ditch, I had lost one of my shoes. As I was standing alone by the side of the road, a dark colored van pulled up, the door opened and a man took a snapshot of me, using a flash on his camera. They too sped away.

I could see the motel in the distance, so I began walking, by now my foot was hurting so badly I knew it had to be broken. When I got to the motel, I walked into the lobby, the desk clerk looked at me strangely, I asked him for the key to my room. He handed it to me; I hobbled down the hall, going into my room. Once inside, I looked in the mirror, I was covered with mud, blood, my face was swollen, my jaw wouldn't come together, and it appeared to be dislocated. I looked down at my foot it was swollen twice its size and turning blue. I knew I needed some medical attention.

I called my brother, telling him that John had snapped, beat me and I was hurt. He said he would be right over. He arrived with my sister-in-law and Sam Raley, Scott Country Sheriff's Deputy (now retired). They began asking me lots of questions; within a few minutes there was a knock on the door. Three more of my brothers were standing there, (I have a big family… nine brothers and two sisters), they all came to help me. It was decided I needed medical attention, but they didn't want to take me to the emergency room due to publicity. The reporters would be on it immediately. They contacted a doctor in the area, and he agreed to come to the motel to treat my injuries.

The detective stayed for a long-time asking questions, made some phone calls to other law enforcement. They caught up with John driving around in the area. I kept telling everyone there that John seemed like he had "snapped into a different personality without warning and he began beating on me". I didn't understand it. (please see the Sheriff's Deputy report later in this chapter)

It was August 1984, just after the kidnapping of Eugene Martin. The publicity was raging about Eugene Martin and Johnny's case. I decided not to add any fuel to it by pressing charges against John. Instead, I contacted my attorney, he talked to John telling him he would have to move out of the house and leave me alone for a time or I would press charges. He did take up residence for a time at a nearby motel. He could only use the house while I was gone. I had my attorney draw up divorce papers, he did so but also warned me that this was the worst possible time to proceed with such an action. That I should try to wait till the publicity died down, thinking it would be better later. My attorney gave the advice he thought was best, but it was the wrong choice for me.... I should have filed for divorce at that time.

John was eventually allowed to return to the house and lived there..He traveled most of the time, away most of the week. He would only come home to repack his suitcase. Most people thought I was divorced years before I filed, because they always saw me alone.

My nine brothers also took him aside and told him to "never hurt their sister again or there would be dire consequences." From that time on John ignored life, our marriage and me. There was no life together. I realized in 1984 the marriage was over.

John became very secretive and made many trips to Lincoln and Omaha Nebraska, spending a lot of time there. Here again, no phone numbers or itinerary were ever furnished to me. I had no way to reach him when he traveled if there was an emergency or anything urgent in Johnny's case.

I was working many hours, still on the speaking circuit, so I tried not to notice his absence. I felt it was probably better in the long run. It wasn't long before, I would get phone calls from men in town, saying, "Keep your husband away from my girlfriend or wife". I received many of them. John had his own life separate and apart from mine.

Johnny's case had come to a very quiet period, not too many leads coming in, my speaking schedule was still very active. Network TV shows

JOHN GOSCH...JOHNNY'S FATHER

continued to invite me to go on and tell Johnny's story. I was doing everything I could to keep the story alive.

I was at work in July of 1991, when a friend called me to say, "there is a young man who has confessed to kidnapping Johnny", it is all over the news. I had known about Bonacci for only about a week. I had been told to keep it quiet by Private Investigator Roy Stephens from Omaha, Nebraska. So, I was surprised it was all over the news. All the TV stations were reporting it… The FBI came marching through the door of my office to question me. I told them I didn't have much more information than they did, and they should check with Mr. Bonacci's attorney, John Decamp, whom I had never met. It was upsetting to have it released to the media in this way.

And the FBI charging into my office. I was anxious to talk to John when he got home from work. He didn't come home that night. Finally, around five a.m. he came walking in the door. When I asked, "Where were you all night"? He replied, "It is none of your business." I asked if he had heard the news about Paul Bonacci? He said "Hell yes, I knew about Bonacci… for over two years and didn't tell you"! This was a shock; I had no idea he had been keeping all of this information from me or WHY. Why would a man, a father keep something so important from the mother of their son? I had a thousand questions, which were not being answered. Not by John anyway! I knew in time I would find the answers and that became my focus.

The press went crazy with the news of Bonacci, some believed him, some thought he was a nut. I didn't know what to think because I had never met him. It was several months later, when I was able to go to the prison to interview him myself. I contacted WHO TV and asked them to go along and record it all on film, so there would be a recording of anything Bonacci told me.

I asked John to go with me to the prison…. HE REFUSED, SAYING HE WAS TOO BUSY! At the time I thought this most odd, strange and it disappointed me…this was about our son.

WHY JOHNNY CAN'T COME HOME!

All the publicity was seen and heard nationally; within a few weeks a call came from America's Most Wanted. They wanted to do Johnny's story and include all the information about Paul Bonacci.

In 1992, America's Most Wanted filmed Johnny's story, this unleashed a great deal of publicity, the case seemed more active than ever before. The hundreds of calls which were generated, brought us many good leads and information.

There was a very strange outcome of one of the leads, involving John Gosch. The lead was about a man near Sioux City, Iowa, which Paul Bonacci had identified as "Charlie" and a being part of the kidnapping. It seemed Charlie owned the house on a farm, where they took Johnny after he was kidnapped. It was there he was molested repeatedly on film. Charlie's house was a "safe house" so to speak, a "way station" for the kidnapped children. Before they were sold off to their "pedophile buyer/ owners". Many kids had been brought there over the years. Who would suspect in a small town, on a farm?

I worked with the Country Attorney in that part of the state. Surveillance was set up to watch this man. The County Attorney felt they had enough evidence to arrest Charlie. He told me the day they were to make the arrest. During conversation in our home, I told John about the call from the County Attorney and the date for the arrest. I told no one else.

On the day scheduled for the arrest, the County Attorney called me, he was "livid", he was screaming over the phone, "why would your husband deliberately sabotage 10 months of police surveillance work?" I had no answer for him. I asked what he was talking about. He reported "the officers and detectives were in place ready to move into make the arrest, when John drove up, went to the front door, knocked.... Charlie answered the door, John said, "I am Johnny Gosch's father, I want to talk to you" Discussion followed between John and the man. John then went inside Charlie's mobile home he kept on the property. Apparently, the police had a listening device because they reported to me the conversation between John and Charlie.

This was the only warning Charlie needed and the cover of the investigation was "blown". After John left his home, Charlie packed a bag and took off in his truck for weeks.

I couldn't blame the County Attorney, he had a right to be angry. I was angry too. Why would the father of a kidnapped son, jeopardize, sabotage the only possible arrest we had the opportunity to make in years on this case? At that point in time, it made no sense to me. Needless to say, the County Attorney washed his hands of it and stopped all investigation. Who could blame him on this one? He had been so very kind to me throughout the whole thing.

At that point, I knew I could no longer stay married to a man, who would deliberately sabotage the investigation. Nothing made sense about the behavior that John was exhibiting. It seemed he wanted to stop the investigation at any cost. I began making my plans to file for divorce.

In 1993, I filed for divorce; never dreaming it would take so long or be so disruptive. The decision to leave was one I thought about for a long time. It is never easy to end a long relationship, partly because of shared memories and living in a routine of life, fear of the unknown. But our life together had deteriorated to the point that it was not a marriage. I could no longer overlook the secrecy, infidelities, beating and finally the sabotage of Johnny's case. I guess that was the last straw for me. None of it made any sense until a few years later.

The divorce was not final until 1995; I continued to work and struggle with Johnny's case, doing it alone as I had for so many years prior, I was just doing it from a different residence. The search and investigation went much slower due to the change in income. I worked extra jobs whenever possible in addition to my regular daytime job in order to have the money to continue the search for Johnny.

I was subjected to more than normal harassment during and following the divorce from John. For a man who didn't want to be a part of the marriage, I couldn't understand why he didn't just "let it and me go". My divorce attorney told me he had never seen anyone try "to destroy another human being with such vengeance in all his years as an attorney." That made me feel great… but he was right. It was during the divorce, all my video tapes and many records on Johnny's case were taken by John out of spite.

Johnny's case had gone for another 10 months without any solid leads of information. I prayed one night that I would be able to know one way or the other if my son was alive or dead. If he was alive, I would find the energy and the money to continue, if he was dead, I wanted to know.

I was invited to go to California to the Leeza Gibbons show, I told them I didn't think I could make the trip this time due to my heavy work schedule, and it was almost Christmas time. They pleaded with me to come back on the show because of the tremendous response there had been when I was on two months earlier. So, I agreed. During that show, Leeza asked me to give a special message to Johnny. I looked at the camera and said "Johnny, I know you are alive, contact me, I will help you. I still live in West Des Moines in an apartment. I no longer live in our old house, I am divorced from your father"!

The Leeza Show was about well-known psychics; Dorothy Allison and Cheri Mancuso who work on kidnap cases with police departments. While I was on stage, they were able to give some very accurate predictions about the case. Both ladies were very talented and extremely kind in the way they shared information. Things, which were about to be discovered. Dorothy Allison asked to see me in the dressing room privately. After the show, I met with her and she reported to me "To believe a young man who had confessed in the case, because he was telling the truth, and it would later be proven in court. She also warned me to be very careful, because there was a woman "impersonating me" making public appearances. She then told me … Johnny is alive and will appear at your door when you least expect it"!

I flew home after the show, taking the late flight out of California, thinking about the experience, wondering if Johnny heard my message. I accepted what the psychics told me on this show but had my doubts about the "imposter". Little did I know what was ahead for me.

I remember the night as though it were yesterday. I had just come home from a family reunion and unpacked the car; it was March 18, 1997. I had gone to sleep early that night but was awakened by a persistent knocking at the door. When I went to the door and looked out the security glass, I saw him.... It was Johnny. I asked who it was, and he answered, "it is me Mom, it is Johnny." At first, I thought this...isn't real but as I looked through the glass, I knew it was my son. I opened the door; he came in and gave me a big hug. Johnny told me he saw me on the "Leeza Show" and knew he could come to me, and I would help him. (Please see the detailed account of Johnny's visit in "Why Johnny Can't Come Home)

Life changed drastically after Johnny's visit home. I had to find a way to help him bring out this story and at the same time protect him. You will see as you progress in the book the legal steps, I took to protect my son and myself.

Within months, I did some more network TV shows. One of them was Inside Edition, they did a fine story, and this led to ABC 20/20 calling me to do another update of the story. My longtime friend Karen Burnes, a producer for 20/20 was the one to do the show.

After meetings with her in New York, we decided on a film schedule and dates to begin in November of 1997. The ABC crew arrived in Des Moines to begin filming. One of the things they wanted on film was a meeting with John DeCamp, Bonacci's attorney and me. I had never met John DeCamp.

Karen, the producer, the film crew, George and I all met at John DeCamp's office in Lincoln, Nebraska. As we walked in, John DeCamp took my hand and said "Noreen, it is so good to see you again"! I looked him rather puzzled and said," I have never been here before, I have never met you." Silence fell like a rock.... Everyone looked at one another not knowing what to say. Then everyone looked at me like I had lost my mind.

DeCamp said "well sure you have been here, with your husband, John in 1989, we went out to the prison together to see Paul Bonacci". I repeated that I had never been there. He finally called in his assistant and office manager, Jan, saying to her "Jan, didn't John Gosch come here in 1989 and introduce his wife to us, then we went to the prison?" Jan said "yes you sure did but it wasn't this woman (as she pointed towards me)". Needless to say, we were all dumbfounded. None of us knew what to do or say.

Jan, Decamp's assistant, immediately went to get records they had of all phone calls which came in she kept them by year.... She looked through them and found many entries of a woman also telephoned asking for records on Bonacci, saying it was Noreen Gosch.

Decamp and Jan also remembered John Gosch giving them a phone number in Des Moines for them to use but they were instructed to "NEVER CALL THE GOSCH HOME AND DISTURB NOREEN".

This was just the beginning of the unraveling of yet another part of the mystery of Johnny's kidnapping. Why would John Gosch have an imposter ... posing as me? Why would he introduce her as me, take her to the prison, to speeches in Colorado and numerous other public appearances? These were questions none of us could answer.

Reverend Morrow of Lincoln, Nebraska and part of the Nebraska Leadership Foundation did the same thing when introduced to me. He shook my hand saying it "was good to see me again". I had to explain to him I had never met him before.

In a conversation by phone with Dr. Judienne Denson Gerber concerning Bonacci, I said to her " I hope one day we can meet in person". She responded, "Noreen, we did meet in 1989 in Nebraska, you were there with your husband many times. You were in court during the Bonacci hearings years ago". I then had to explain to her that there had been an imposter. She was as shocked as I was when it was discovered.

I was so afraid to meet anyone new, because I thought they would tell me they had met me before. To date there are twenty-five people of importance on Johnny's case and the Franklin Investigation, who all dealt with the "other Noreen Gosch... thinking it was me".

Early on a Sunday morning, I received a phone call from a woman in Omaha Nebraska, saying, "Did you know you have a double"? There had been an article in the Omaha World Herald that morning about Johnny's case and it had my picture. This was my stroke of luck; the woman knew the name of this woman but did not have any idea she was impersonating me.

Once she told me the name of the woman, I began investigating, I found out she had been a private investigator for a short time. I telephoned her former boss and gathered some more information. Another coincidence (or was it), this woman knew and had worked with a man, John Gosch had secured to interview Paul Bonacci concerning his information about Johnny.

I kept hearing she looked like me from so many people. John DeCamp suggested I call the Secretary of State's office, a friend of John's, and explain the situation. I did... the man was so patient on the phone, he put me in touch with the Private Detective department, where I related the whole story once again. That man told me "this is your lucky day, we keep photographs of everyone who has ever applied for or gotten a license". I will search for it in our archives. If I find it.... I will send it. In about a week, in the mail came a package containing the photo.

Yep...you guessed it! She did look like me. Her hair was styled very similar to the way I wore mine in 1989....she looked enough like me to pass for me.

I kept hearing reports about the woman appearing in Colorado giving a speech with John ... posing as me. I did a little more digging and eventually found someone who had taken a photo of them together. I am not releasing this woman's name at this point, as it might be very important at later date, if I decide to take legal action. I am placing the pictures in this section of the book.

It was brought to my attention that John had telephoned ABC, Karen Burnes assistant, and told her not to telephone me any longer because I wasn't able to take the stress. Nothing was farther from the truth, it appeared he wanted to prevent me from discussing the case with the media.

As this all unfolded, I remembered the predictions of the psychic, Dorothy Allison on the Leeza Show, telling me "Someone has been impersonating you during this case." Dorothy was right about many things but most certainly about the impersonator.

Other than the absurdity of this whole situation the questions should be asked: Why would anyone impersonate me? What possible reason could there be? What benefit to anyone to have this imposter?

I have not seen John Gosch since the divorce was final… We had attended a friend's wedding. He came over to me and said, "I wish I could be more like you". I said, "Why would you want to be like me, you were so mean to me". He replied "You aren't bitter and hateful to people. I know it hurt you when Johnny was taken but you didn't treat other people badly because of it. I did and have destroyed every relationship I ever had". I said to him… "It isn't too late for you to get counseling … you can still have a life."

In this chapter, it was important to relate certain facts surrounding the case, John and our life together. I have no feelings of bitterness towards him or anyone else. Elements within this chapter are very important to this case. I have spent forty one years of my life putting the pieces together on this case. It is time for it to come out. Johnny deserves that much consideration.

JOHN GOSCH...JOHNNY'S FATHER

May 9, 1999

To Whom It May Concern:

My name is Sam L. Raley, I live at 948 Cimaron Drive 52804, Davenport, Iowa. I am a friend of Ron Hesse of davenport, Iowa, the brother of Noreen Gosch. The following is the events of August 17, 1984.

At about 7:45 p.m. Ron Hesse called me at my home and stated the following: Ron's Sister Noreen Gosch had just called him from a motel and was crying and wanted Ron to come right away. She stated that she was at the Ramada Inn on Brady St. in Davenport. Ron knowing I was a law enforcement officer called and asked me to go with him. I asked Ron if his sister had called the police and he said she had. I then said, I would go with him.

Ron picked me up at about 8:00 p.m. and we drove to the motel. At the motel, this is what we found. We went into Noreen's room and she was crying and in a mess, the right side of her face was marked, her right eye was turning black. She had finger bruises on her arms and neck. Her face was bloody, hair messed up. She had blood all over her clothes and many other marks on her body. There was a girl who worked at the motel there with her, her name was not known to me.

Ron asked her who had done this and she stated her husband, John Gosch. By the time we got there, as far as I know, he had left the area. She stated that " he began beating her in the car on the interstate". When he pulled off the interstate, she jumped from the car and landed in the ditch ... then walked back to the Ramada Inn on Brady Street in Davenport and called her brother, Ron.

At approximately 9:00 p.m. the Davenport police arrived. Officer Mike Wyatt Davenport P.D. stated to us they had been busy and therefore there was a delay in responding to the call. The officer took her statement. We left the motel shortly after the Davenport PD arrived, as two other brothers arrived to help her.

Sam L. Raley

Sam L. Raley
Scott County Sheriff Deputy
Retired officer

WHY JOHNNY CAN'T COME HOME!

Will the "REAL" Noreen Gosch please stand up....

JOHN GOSCH...JOHNNY'S FATHER

KIDNAPPED
JOHN DAVID GOSCH

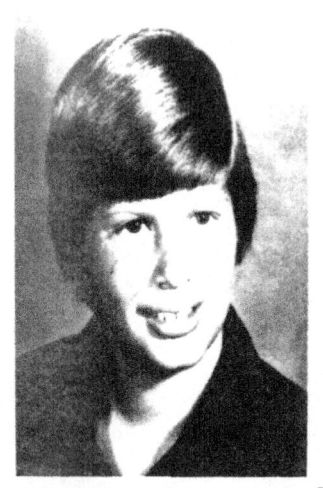

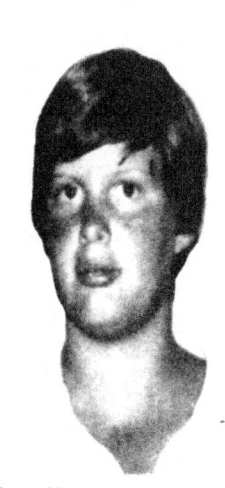

Taken 81/82 School Year

Fair Photo '82

Composite Of Suspect
5'9", 175 lbs., dark eyes, black eyebrows, older, early to mid 40's, black hair, combed back, full in back, black mustache, heavy beard or unshaven appearance, Latin appearance.
This man may be driving a two tone blue car, real dark top and light blue bottom -mid size - 79 to 81 model -clean inside and outside - no vinyl top -plush interior -Iowa plate.

DESCRIPTION: Age: 13 years old, D.O.B.: Nov. 12, 1969, Ht.: 5'7" Wt.: 145 lbs. Hair: light brown, Eyes: blue, Complexion: medium Teeth: gaps between front teeth, Shoe Size: 9½-10, Marks/Scars: freckles, large birthmark upper left chest, horseshoe shaped scar on tongue, large lower lip. Stature: At 13 years old, John has the physical appearance of a boy 15 or older.

JOHNNY DOESN'T LIVE HERE ANYMORE

November 12, 1985, it is my son Johnny's sixteenth birthday. My thoughts of him is stronger on special days. Where is he? What is happening to him? He always loved the excitement of birthdays in the family, especially his own. He would have requested his favorite "German Chocolate Cake... triple layer of course". And always those "relighting candles", that produce so much smoke, it would set off the smoke detector in the hallway.

Just like any young boy today, he would want his drivers license and begin to use the family car just as his friends were doing. Each passing birthday is another reminder of how much of his family's life is missing. What kind of pain and suffering is he going through at the hands of his kidnappers? Would he even know it is his birthday today? I would buy a little gift and card, putting it in his room; in hopes that one-day he would be home with us again.

We kept his room just as he left it with his electronic game sat on the night stand, his bulletin board had all of the perfect service awards from each month he had the paper route. He had thirteen awards in all. On the other side of the room sat all of the models of rockets that he so carefully built.

Each time he would earn a little extra money, he would ask to be driven to the hobby shop at the mall, where he would purchase more "rocket supplies". He was very interested in the space program and would buy anything connected to it. With the change he would receive at the store, he would run upstairs to the floral shop and buy a single rose for me. They would wrap it for him and he would have it all tucked behind his back, out of sight, when I would meet him to drive home. Then he would whip it out with a big smile on his face and say, " this is for you, Mom".

From the time Johnny was five years old he would tell everyone that he wanted to be an "architect". People would smile because he was barely able to pronounce it properly and most little children that age didn't know what an architect was or did. He continued with that dream, asking for a drafting table and supplies for Christmas this coming year.

Passing by Johnny's room had both a comforting and painful effect upon me. At times it would be so painful I would have to keep the door closed. Yet at other times, I would go in there and sit quietly praying for inspiration to keep the story alive, not knowing what to do next to try and save his life. I never for one moment believed that Johnny was dead. I felt his presence.

At first we didn't allow anyone in Johnny's room, thinking the police department would want to dust for fingerprints. However, the police chief, Orval Cooney said that they would not be taking prints because it "makes a hell of a mess in the house"! Later, when reporters would ask if they could photograph his room, we then allowed them in for a short time. Many of them would walk out saying they felt something in that room, almost as if they were connected to him in some way. I was not the only one to feel his presence in his room.

I will never forget the reporter who came out of Johnny's room. His face was as white as a sheet; he asked me " Have you noticed anything unusual in that room?" I replied "Like what "? He stammered then said " Electrical shocks were hitting my face and body as I stood in the middle of the room,

I have never experienced anything like this before"! That was the first time I knew I was not the only one that felt something in that room.

I had talked to other parents of missing children who were reunited with them. They shared how important it was to buy the gifts and cards so the child would see they were never forgotten on birthdays and holidays. In 1985, the Ankeny Press Citizen newspaper asked me to write a letter to Johnny for his birthday and they would print it. So their readers would be able to understand what it is like to not know where your child is, whether he is alive or dead and face another birthday without him.

I was about to leave the house for an appointment in the afternoon, when the phone rang; it was a woman by the name of Donna Chapel. She is a long time Country Western and Gospel singer. Donna at that time had recorded three albums in Nashville and was planning the release of her fourth album. From her life on the road as a singer, to the dark side of Nashville, to life on the farm, to love of a mother for her child, Donna explained that she expresses her emotions in music just as her family had done for generations. In 1936 Donna's three aunts, the Amburgey Sisters, were pioneers in the country and gospel field with the first all female string bands in history. From the coalfields of Kentucky they rivaled the famed Carter family.

In October of 1985, Donna had made an appearance in Washington D.C. at the Farm Aid program. As she was walking through the airport, she saw a huge picture of Johnny hanging on the wall. It really began to bother her, wondering how she would feel if someone would take her son, almost Johnny's age. After she boarded the plane, she was inspired to write another song, "Johnny Doesn't Live Here Anymore" in tribute to my son Johnny. The song serves as a memorial for all parents who have lost a child and suffered this pain in their lives. She then decided it was time to call and talk to me about the song.

We hit it off immediately on the phone, as she explained how her thoughts and prayers had been with me and how seeing my son's picture in the Washington D.C. airport affected her. She asked, "Could I meet her at one of her performances to hear the song". I made arrangements to meet Donna on November 23, 1985 in Sioux City, Iowa (ironically I learned five years later that this is where Johnny was taken within hours of the kidnapping). She wanted me to hear it before she sang it at the show; this was to be the first time the song was sung publicly. We took a few private moments for her to sing it for me. As I sat listening to the words, I felt heartbreak and comfort. It is difficult to describe how both emotions can be felt at the same time. Donna had captured the feeling of emptiness in our home. He was no longer would coming home after school, saying "Mom what's for supper. No longer bringing me a rose and all the normal things we take for granted on a day-to-day basis.

I knew that in a short time the song would be sung again. This time before hundreds of people and it would be difficult to keep my composure. I was touched by the words in the song and also by the love and kindness of Donna. Who was moved to write a tribute to my son. To have people you do not know remember him and do something extraordinary such as this made me feel so very thankful. That night was the beginning of a loving friendship, which has lasted for many years between Donna Chapel and myself.

Since that night, when we met for the first time, Donna has continued to sing Johnny's song at each and every performance throughout the United States. Donna requested a picture of Johnny; I furnished her with a very large framed picture of him. On stage with her at all times is the picture of Johnny on the first day of his paper route. When people see this picture and hear the words to the song there is not a dry eye in the audiences. The song brings a great deal of heartfelt emotion from everyone. Many people can identify with the words and how they might feel if their son or daughter would be taken from them.

The first day of his paper route, we took a picture of Johnny. He of course like most children, did not want his picture taken. Little did we know that this photo would become the "publicity picture" used by all forms of media for years and years following the kidnapping?

As I look at this photo today, I realize that more than half his life has been away from his family and friends. If I had it to do over again, I would have never allowed him to carry the Des Moines Register.

We discussed recording this song in Nashville, how soon the song could be released, as well as the remaining details. This was an area so new to me. Donna made all the arrangements for the recording and traveled to Nashville early in 1986. We kept in touch by phone and letter as to the progress of the recording. We made a decision to present the song in a meeting with our Iowa Governor Terry Branstad, on April 29th, 1986, the release date for the song nationally. Country radio stations all over the country were sent copies; it was received well by the public.

As I travel around the country for speaking engagements, TV and radio interviews I would play this song before each event. It always gave me an uplifting feeling and strength of my resolve to let every man; woman and child know what was happening to the millions of Johnny Gosch's around the world.

Johnny Doesn't Live Here Anymore... a song written by a friend for Johnny.

Johnny Doesn't Live Here Anymore

v.1: He'd get up before sun-up, throw the news by the door, and that day was no different-like many times before, and his pillow still showed the print of where he laid his head, but now Johnny won't be sleeping in his bed.

v.2: His life had just begun, he had everything to live for, he was slowly turning into a man, his smile would brighten up my day, now that's all taken away, and I know Johnny doesn't live here anymore.

CHORUS: He doesn't live here anymore. He won't walk right Through that door, and say "Mom, what's for supper", and throw His books down on the floor. And the hardest part of all, I don't know Where, I don't know why. We didn't even have the chance to say goodbye.

v.3: As time goes by, I miss him more. Things aren't like they were before. We send our love up to the stars, for they must know just where you are. We'll always wait and love you more, and keep the light on by the door, but now, Johnny doesn't live here anymore. I know my Johnny doesn't live here anymore.

WHY JOHNNY CAN'T COME HOME!

Dear Friend
—DONNA CHAPEL

DEAR FRIEND	(2:57)
MY LOVE IS WITH YOU	(2:50)
FILLED WITH HIS SPIRIT	(4:42)
TAKE ME AWAY	(3:56)
ON THE ROAD	(4:07)
IMITATE THE MAN	(2:36)
TOO OLD TO DIE YOUNG	(3:04)
BARNEY JOHN	(3:45)
COUNTRY MAN	(2:56)
JOHNNY DOESN'T LIVE HERE ANY MORE	(3:22)
CAREN'S SONG	(3:57)
MUSIC CITY MADNESS	(3:22)

All Songs Written by Donna Chapel and published with Metro Country Music Publishing, BMI, with the exception of "Too Old To Die Young."
"Too Old To Die Young" written by John Hadley, Kevin Welch, Scott Dooley. Sony ATV LLC DBA Tree Pub. BMI; Sony Tunes LLC DBA Cross Keys ASCAPP.

Recorded at Bitten Moon Studio
Produced by Donna Chapel and Lana Chapel
DONNA CHAPEL – acoustic guitar, harmony and vocals
LANA CHAPEL – guitar, bass, mandolin, harmonica and harmony vocal assist

To Order: Donna Chapel Productions, PO Box 30, Bridgewater, SD 57319 or www.donnachapel.com

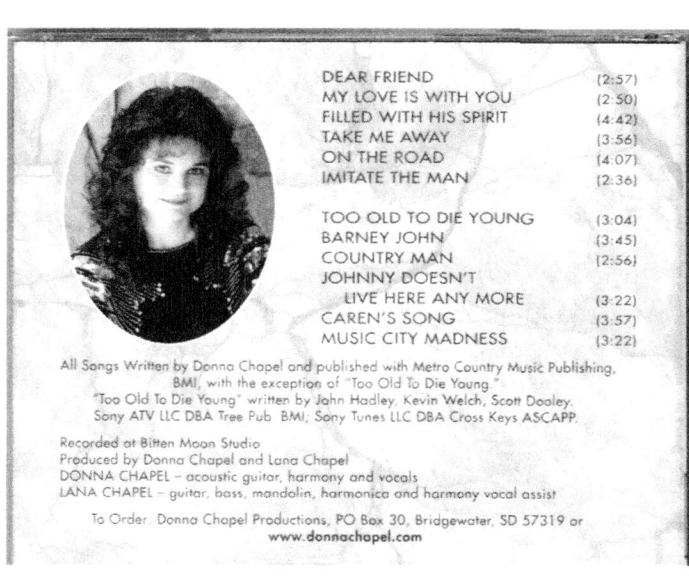

DONNA, ME AND GOVERNOR BRANSTAD APRIL 29, 1986

Donna Chapel presented the first copy of the song "Johnny Doesn't Live Here" to Governor Branstad. She was inspired to write the song after seeing Johnny's picture at the Washington D.C. airport. Donna still sings Johnny's song at ever performance while holding a large picture of him.

Check www.donnachapel.com to see the story of Johnny and a link to www.johnnygosch.com

WHY JOHNNY CAN'T COME HOME!

The Cedar Rapids Gazette: Tues., Nov. 20, 1984

Branstad to seek tougher laws child abuse, kidnapping

By Judy Daubenmier
Gazette Des Moines Bureau

DES MOINES — Strengthening laws to prevent exploitation of children will be a priority of Gov. Terry Branstad during the upcoming legislative session, the governor said Monday.

Branstad said reports of sexually abused or missing children are increasing and must be stemmed.

"These sorts of things are happening all across the country," he said.

"They're happening too often. I believe we need to respond," he said

Branstad told reporters he is looking at proposals to require background checks of people working in jobs dealing with children, such as in day-care centers.

Branstad also said he is considering legislation to allow the Iowa Department of Public Safety to disseminate information about missing children.

The department is now involved in a lawsuit over its refusal to give the news media names of children who are missing.

Branstad also said he may propose tougher legislation regarding the use of children in pornographic movies.

Gov. Terry Branstad
'We need to respond'

"There's a great deal of concern about children," Branstad said.

"We've had a 100 percent increase in the sexual abuse of children over the last three years in this state. We have two newspaper carriers that are missing and presumed to have been kidnapped. There is great concern about the exploitation of children.

" . . . I intend to make dealing with this issue one of my personal priorities, and one of my recommendations to the Legislature will deal with substantial changes in our state laws to be more effective in improving the safety and security of our children in this state."

The governor said he hoped sympathy for missing Des Moines newspaper carriers Johnny Gosch

The kidnapping of Johnny Gosch is still an unsolved crime. Thanks to the courage and tenacity of his mother, Noreen Gosch, dramatic changes have been made in Iowa law and federal law to help missing and exploited children and their families. It took the "chutzpah" of a Noreen Gosch to accomplish these dramatic changes in public policy. This book tells her story!

Terry E Branstad

.... BILL

My Mother told me "When things get so bad.... they must get better." I would ask her "what time will that happen, Mom?" She was amazing through the kidnapping of Johnny, always a positive support for me. Helping to keep me bolstered with the principles I was raised with my whole life. My Aunt Rita would call me on a regular basis ... telling me *"No situation merits a disturbed attitude... you can handle anything that comes to you..."* Meaning .... No matter what happens keep a cool head, keep calm, think before acting or speaking. It is true, no matter what situation happens in our life, the situation will always remain the same... it is how we happen to IT that makes the difference".

Trying to live that... is a tall order when your son is kidnapped, and you begin to see how the system doesn't work. There were many times when I felt things just couldn't get any worse. Then something would happen which would renew my hope of finding Johnny and getting answers.

In October 1982, a tall man walked into my office, He resembled the actor, Clint Eastwood. I didn't know this man and thought he was there to talk to my employer. Instead, he pulled out a business card, handed it to me and said, "When you get tired of what the police are NOT doing, give me a call, I can help you!" He then turned and walked out of the office. I wasn't exactly sure of what just took place, but I put his card in my wallet.

As with a roller coaster ride, the ups and downs come at you fast…. They did in Johnny's case too. I felt I was at the end of my rope one day; the private investigators we hired were trying to do their job. Each time they would be working on a lead, not causing any problems to or for the police. The West Des Moines Police would arrest them which would put a temporary stop to the investigation. It appeared to me that it was deliberate. But who am I… just the mom seeing it all through my eyes.

I finally decided to call this man who offered his help. I had no idea what kind of help or how, but I thought "what the heck, I can't lose anything". I called him …he said, "let's have a cup of coffee". I met him after I got off work that day. He was a very kind man, seemed caring and interested in the case. I was so nervous, not knowing what to expect. He started by explaining "there is a lot you don't know about the kidnapping of your son. He was taken by an organized group, who kidnaps kids for sex and profit. I have a friend, whom I have known for years in business, he is a very powerful man and has offered to help you. "I asked "in what way can he help"? He responded, "You will only be allowed to contact him through me, I will then reach him, relaying to him any request you may have at the time. Unfortunately, we cannot return your son to you, they have him so hidden and we cannot get close to him. What I can offer at this time is information at any time you need it. Protection for you and your family should it be necessary."

I told him I was afraid and didn't have anything in which to give them in return for their help. He then smiled and said, "we know that we know you are struggling, we also know you are getting a bum deal, it is time you had a break." I finally said, "Okay I will be most grateful for any help you can give me." He told me to call him whenever I had a request for information or protection, and he would do his best to have an answer for me within twenty-four hours. If I have information for you in the meantime, he would call me and say, "Let's have a cup of coffee".

I call him "Bill", I have never revealed his real name to anyone and never will. I was given help above and beyond my expectations at the time of our first meeting. When I needed information concerning a suspect in Johnny's case I would receive it within a very short time. It seemed they could locate almost anyone.

One time, I needed information on a particular suspect, I had given it to the Police as well. Bill called me back within two hours; it took almost two weeks from the police. One of the detectives from the police department said in front of me "I wish I had her connections and could get information that quickly". I didn't want to know how they got the info so quickly, I just appreciated getting it.

It might sound small to some people but when the chips were down and there wasn't an ongoing investigation with the Police, I had to take charge using private investigators and use any means possible to get the truth.

Bill's men provided protection for family members and me a number of times when there were death threats made against us. If it hadn't been for their help, I know for certain I would have lost another loved one. I was up against powerful people in this kidnapping, and they did not like it that I was pushing for an answer on the case. Most of the time, my family was unaware that I had men posted near them round the clock until situations were stabilized.

I do not know to this day the identity of Bill's friend. Bill once mentioned he was the head of a powerful "family"!

As we progressed through years on the case, I had to call upon Bill many times, each time, I would think… "Well maybe he is getting tired of this and will say …not this time." But not once was I ever told "no". Instead, I was met with as much cooperation as possible. When Paul Bonacci surfaced in the news… July 1991…Bill called me and said, "Lets have a cup of coffee". We met… "he told me Paul Bonacci was telling the truth about Johnny's kidnapping, the pedophile/ porn ring and people Bonacci named."

Bill also named several men from Des Moines involved with the same ring." He warned me to be very careful what I would say publicly concerning Bonacci or local involvement. He then said, "there is a woman who has impersonated you... I want you to wait several months before going to the prison to meet Bonacci." I didn't totally understand his reasoning on that one, but I agreed to trust him, as he had been accurate with everything since we first met.

Bill was always there when I needed him, but there were periods of time when the case was dormant. As the Bonacci story faded only to be revived by America's Most Wanted, there were times I called Bill to check out pieces of information. Leads coming in from the show.

The one thing Bill kept telling me was.... Johnny is still alive. He has not been killed. He also provided support and strength because there were times the information, he had to give me was not exactly pleasant.

On the personal side, a man living in Des Moines got the wild idea to harass me, which he did quite thoroughly. He broke into my apartment, would telephone me up to 40 times a day, keyed my car on 4 occasions. It didn't matter where I parked it. He would find it. The man was a "nut ball" who was operating without any sense of moral judgment. It was finally through "surveillance" which Bill provided ... that I learned the identity of the man. Once I knew who he was, I could give the information to the police, and they could do something about it.

It took another year before there was enough evidence for an arrest.

In 1997, After Johnny had been here to see me, I told no one Johnny had been here, not even Bill. I couldn't keep my promise to my son. I knew he was living on an Indian reservation but there are hundreds in the U.S. and Canada. I had been to the Indian College in Lawrence Kansas to get the list. I had planned on contacting each one personally but thought there might be a better way. I called Bill asked him to meet me... I told him Johnny was alive, but I didn't know where he was living. Bill suggested I go to WHO TV in Des Moines, ask them to do a "PSA (public service announcement) taped interview" speaking directly to Johnny, to broadcast regionally in the United States. WHO was very helpful, did the promo tape and began broadcasting in the area Bill suggested. Within 48 hours we had a phone call, people recognized Johnny's picture. Bill sent his men in.... Johnny had lived there for a time, worked but moved on to another location... the people either didn't know or wouldn't say.

We then broadcast in the second regional area.... Bingo... we got another call; someone recognized his picture. I called Bill and he sent his men right away. Then the day came.... September 18, 1997... Bill called me and said, "Let's have a cup of coffee". His voice sounded different than ever before, I asked, "do you have good news" he replied, "yes I do".

I could hardly wait until it was time to meet him... when I got to the coffee shop, I sat down and said, "well what do you have", he smiled and said, "we found him, he is okay, safe and working", Bill gave me the name of the Indian reservation where he was living. I told him I wanted to go right away... he cautioned me to wait a little while then we would plan it a bit more carefully. Meanwhile, I would receive a weekly report on Johnny, where he went, who he was with, the times he was at the trading post buying his groceries, I knew my boy was at least safe for the moment.

When It was finally decided that I would go to the reservation and would be meeting Karen Burnes of 20/20, Bill told me to guard what I said to the Police Chief Willie Strong, because he was somehow connected to criminal activity. When I arrived at my hotel, the cell phone rang, it was Bill, saying he was glad my trip was safe, and he gave me the name of the hotel. If I had ever doubted his ability to watch someone it was removed with that phone call. The visit to the reservation is detailed in other chapters in the book.

I returned home from the trip, Bill agreed to continue a weekly report to me on Johnny's activities. A couple of months later, Karen Burnes and the P.I. ABC hired went to the reservation on their own. Bill called demanding to know "Why are they there without you? Why didn't You go with them? Johnny heard some strangers came to the reservation and talked to the Indian Council, he is afraid, he took off. He is on the run now, looking for another safe place to live." This was a "misstep" on the part of ABC to go there without me. It caused Johnny to bolt for safety.

Within a day or two Bonacci called me to tell me the same thing, Johnny was again running for a safe place to live. The best of intentions went wrong. It was certain both Bill and Bonacci were in their own separate ways able to know Johnny's movements.

It was only a short time later; Police Chief Willie Strong was removed concerning drug charges being filed against him. He was very helpful to me when I was there.

Bill became ill and has died recently, I will be forever grateful to this man who walked into my office … handing me his card and saying, "call me I can help you." Without his help, I would not have had some of the pieces to this puzzle.

When one prays for help… you never know what in what "form" it might be. I have been blessed in many ways during the investigation…. Just the right person at the right time.

ON THE AUCTION BLOCK

Two months after my son was kidnapped, Dennis Whalen, our private detective called, asked me to meet him in a public place. I met him at the Village Inn restaurant, in West Des Moines.

Whalen began by telling me that he had "contacts on both sides of the law!" I knew what he meant and didn't ask any further questions. He explained that he received a call indicating there was to be an auction of children. I was shocked this could be happening … in America. The thought of children being sold on the auction block made me feel sick. As the years passed, I heard again and again that auctions of kidnapped children were being held in many major cities across the country.

I knew from what had already taken place, that my son's kidnapping was not a random act but one of an organized pedophile ring. I later learned that they were international in scope. You will find a chapter in this book called "The Finders" all evidence we have obtained indicates this group is run from Washington D.C. under the sponsorship of the CIA.

I asked Dennis Whalen how he could smuggle himself into such a slave auction without detection. He explained "his underworld contacts were able to get him as a perspective buyer."

My private investigators took great personal risks to try and find out what had happened to Johnny. The preparations to attend this auction were very intricate.

Whalen was told to drive to the old Kansas City Airport, park his vehicle and then walk to the end of one of the runways. He was instructed to wait in the darkness until a small aircraft would land, pick him up and they would be on their way. Whalen wanted to know how much he could bid for Johnny. In other words, how much money could I raise in a hurry. I told him $50,000. He told me he would do his best and be in touch with me. I was instructed not to talk to anyone about it. If we were able to recover Johnny, I would only be able to report to authorities and media, that I paid a ransom demand without the assistance of law enforcement.

Whalen drove to Kansas City; I waited nervously for several days until I heard from him again. Finally, one night he came to the house, he reported the following to me:

He boarded a twin-engine turbo prop airplane. He was blindfolded immediately even before takeoff. He knew only that they were in the air for a long time, approximately two and a half hours. He had no idea what direction they were flying until he overheard the control tower giving landing clearance to the pilot. At that point, he knew they were approaching Houston, Texas. Gunderson has also indicated Houston; Texas is one of the locations where slave auctions are held.

He was taken from the plane, put into a car and driven approximately forty-five minutes. When they stopped and his blindfold was taken off, he was outside the warehouse type building. He commented it looked like an "industrial park" housing lots of buildings for business and storage. He could see the lights of the city in the distance.

Once inside, he saw several men, some looked to be foreign buyers, they were wearing turbans. Soon the children were paraded out on to a stage. The auction began. He looked at the children, noticing how dazed they looked. Each boy was wearing a thin rope around his neck suspending a "number". They were only wearing underwear. All the boys seemed to be between the ages of ten to thirteen years old. Johnny was not among them. I later learned from Paul Bonacci, The Col. had purchased Johnny, directly from his kidnappers within two weeks after he was taken.

As Whalen described the auction, I felt sick for several reasons:

1. How horrific this was to auction children.
2. That Johnny wasn't among them.
3. Wishing Johnny had been, so he could have been "bought back."

Whalen's contact told him the auctions take place all over the country; they move them, so as not to be detected. He also reported that a "blue eyed blond 13-year-old boy could sell for as high as $50,000". Whalen was not able to go to any more auctions. They had discovered he was not a "real buyer". His cover was blown.

Once I had all of this information, I documented it, but who was I going to tell? I knew that in December of 1982, no one would believe me. I knew at some time in the future all the information I was storing would become very important. I knew that others would eventually stand up to help confirm what was happening to the children.

Ted Gunderson, FBI, who has spent more than 20 years investigating crimes against children, at great risk to his own life. He has multiple verifications of the existence of such auctions. He names Las Vegas and Toronto Canada as two other locations for these auctions. He suggested they take place in most major cities in this country.

Dr. Julienne Denson Gerber, Psychiatrist and expert witness on child abuse, also states auctions of this type take place in Baltimore MD. Paul Bonacci has personally attended many such auctions.

October 13, 1990

Report by Robert Hansel to Franklin Credit Union/Investigation

This investigator took over following the mysterious death of Gary Canadore, July 11, 1990.

"At approximately 2:00 PM, this writer proceeded to Donna Owens, (Alisha Owen's mother) residence, at which time, we discussed information regarding Paul Bonacci's diary. It is a synopsis of incidents that occurred to him. One incident took place in September of 1982, an account of a man named Amelio (Emilio), who took Paul to a farmhouse in Iowa, and he saw two boys that were locked in a room with no windows and only one door which was bolted shut. One of the boys was approximately nine years old, 4 feet tall, 80 pounds, blonde hair, and one blue eye and one brown eye. He also had a scar on his left leg approximately nine inches long. He also had a mole on his chest. He cried for his mother a lot and according to Paul his name was Mark.

The other boy was approximately 5'5" in height, 130 pounds, blue eyes, and brown hair. The boy was wearing black jogging pants and had a dirty shirt on that had the name of Kim's Academy on it. At that time, Mr. Bonacci asked if this was Kim's Karate, which he never did get an answer. The boy was approximately 13 years of age and he found out later that his name was Johnny, and he couldn't recall his last name. The boy was from Des Moines, Iowa. The other boy was from some town in Minnesota possibly.

This information had been circulated around Nebraska, two years before I learned about Bonacci. Caradori learned about Johnny as early as 1989, he called our home and once again John Gosch took the call and didn't tell me. According to the records, I learned Caradori was trying to share information concerning Johnny… they thought it odd that Johnny's mother didn't respond, since I had been so active on the case.

It was simple…. I had not been told.

Bonacci declined to go on with some of the kidnappings but his (forensically authenticated) diary of 1982-83 indicated that such kidnappings were routine for Emilio. He describes going to another farmhouse in Nebraska where several boys were being held, one night two men came and bought two boys.

ON THE AUCTION BLOCK

In the chapter, called the Finders the customs investigator describes finding on the computer an evacuation order to move the children from safe house to safe house before the arrival of investigators. Paul states that warning usually comes from "friendly" informants in law enforcement. July 17, 1991, Ted Gunderson on the Jan Michaelson show over WHO Talk Radio Des Moines described it the same way.

There is no way Paul Bonacci writing in 1982-83 could have known that a customs officer would find the same information on a computer in 1986. We know about it only because Gunderson salvaged reports that were ordered to be destroyed.

Bonacci told me, that in October 1989, he received a letter from "Mike" ... telling that Emilio and "Charlie" had gone to "Minnesota to get another kid", It was just a week later Jacob Wetterling was kidnapped. After learning this, I telephoned Patty Wetterling to give her this information. I felt she would want to know and thought it might be something they would want to investigate. She was gracious but wasn't interested in this information at all. I left no stone unturned in Johnny's case. No matter what information came to me, I investigated it. Remembering in my mind the words of a very wise detective who told me... "Just because you don't believe something doesn't mean .... It isn't true".

Repeatedly women have surfaced claiming they were "mind control slaves "of celebrities, politicians and VIP's. Sue Ford, in writing her book "Thanks for the Memories" under the name Brice Taylor, states "Elitists in the market for mind control slaves, attended auctions that appeared at first like children's fashion shows and then progressed to strip tease acts. At this show where Bob Hope bought me, there were lots and lots of little girls and boys competing. They said these children were what they called "sponsored", if they were chosen. They said it was better to be chosen early because the sponsors (owners) could mold you the way they wanted you. There was a modeling ramp where all of us children were displayed. I modeled casual clothes, then sophisticated evening clothes, and then sensual/sexual attire and finally appeared totally naked.

I won first place at this show and was sold to Bob Hope on the open market. They put a white cape around my naked body and Bob Hope came up and stood with me, while everyone in the audience cheered."

How many thousands of children writing their stories will it take before we believe?

Perhaps the man, who has heard more sad stories from children, Father Bruce Ritter, founder of Covenant House in New York. A refuge for street kids. Covenant House began as a one-man operation in 1972 and continues yet today with branches all over the country. In his book, "Sometimes God Has a Kid's Face", Ritter describes a young man who hitchhiked across the country to tell him that he, "Mark", had been sold to a "Fortune Five Hundred Company."

Mark described how at fourteen he was a throwaway kid. "I ran away when I was fourteen, my mother and father were alcoholics. I met this guy he gave me a lot of affection and a place to live. I needed the affection bad. He taught me a lot about sex, and I guess, he put me to work. I was young and pretty, so he sent me out to my customers dressed like a girl – transvestite. I lived with fourteen other boys in this big house. We were all young and scared; he made us all watch; a kid get beaten with a wire hanger. It was bad. That is what happened when you tried to leave. The next time you are dead.

When I turned seventeen and got some muscles, and my beard began to grow, I went butch… they made me join another group … Man–toMan… It was a "call service," high-class customers.

Then the Fortune Five Hundred Company bought him. Ritter states, "You would recognize the name."

Mark continued, "I had a company car and an apartment and took care of corporate clients. They would fly me all over the country. The Corporation had a representative that would take a portfolio of the kids in their stable, both boys and girls, to their clients. We didn't have any clothes on in the photographs. The clients could pick anyone they wanted."

Mark told Ritter that he had hitchhiked halfway across the country so he couldn't be traced. The next morning, he had disappeared.

Ritter comments in his book, that there was a club near Time Square, where children could be bought anytime for drugs, for guns or for money. In Readers Digest, October 1993, an article titled "Asia's Shock-

ing Secrets" describes how men who want to have sex with children while traveling in foreign countries.... Are facilitated by top NAMBLA members in deciding to have a little boy or girl for their pleasure. NAMBLA was making the same arrangements within the United States for pedophiles but at a much higher price.

Johnny was considered the "Golden Boy or Celebrity Boy" due to all the publicity which circulated about him. This unfortunate title given to him meant his captors could get more money for his services but it was also a reason to keep him alive.

UNESCO in recent reports sites AIDS, as a major contributor to the increasing number of children who are being sold into slavery worldwide for sexual purposes. The molesters of children consider them to be safer than prostitutes on the streets, since they would have little or no sexual experience prior to being kidnapped into slavery.

WHY JOHNNY CAN'T COME HOME!

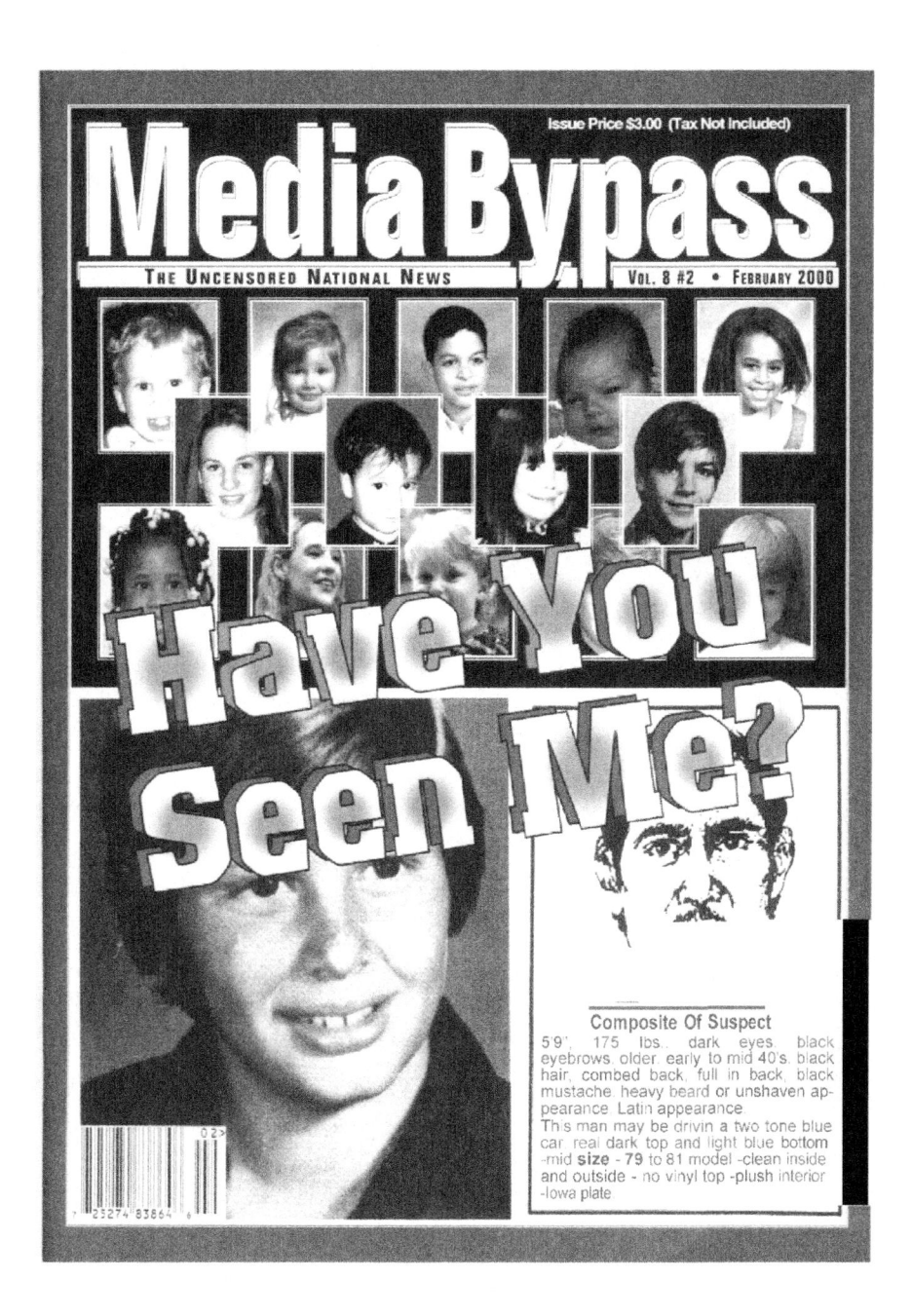

ON THE AUCTION BLOCK

Above: Noreen and Roy Stephens Faith Daniels Show Below: John DeCamp and Noreen Leeza Show Why do parents have to plead for investigations of their missing children on talk shows?

148

SECTION TWO

THE FRANKLIN COVER-UP

On Jan 10, 1989, the Nebraska State Legislature created the Franklin Investigative Committee. Its chairman is Senator Loran Schmit, good friend of John De Camp, who was to play a major role in the Franklin Investigation.

As fellow Republicans, they had worked together in the Legislature, after DeCamp left; he became Loren Schmit's lawyer, business partner in developing and selling farmland around Lincoln. Schmit had earlier closed his ears to stories (rumors really about children being abused). It didn't fall within the purview of his investigations.

It turned out to be more than a simple investigation of another mismanaged savings and loan. In the end there would be evidence of Iran/Contra Money Laundering and an organization called the North American Man Boy Love Association, who put five million in the credit union as the nonprofit Church of the Beloved Disciple.

In early February 1989, Senator Schmit, received an intimidating phone call from Omaha Chief of Police Robert Wadman saying, "I've got something on all of you," less than a month after the committee was formed. He states other phone calls followed all suggesting he shut down the committee,

When Schmit met with King on February 19th, 1989, King seemed more interested in warning Schmit he had powerful friends than discussing the failed credit union. King said "Harold Anderson, publisher of the Omaha World Herald called him all the time." He stated: "A large number of blacks in the Omaha Police Department and the FBI are related to him. And that Omaha Chief of Police Wadman was "a dear friend", whom he had offered the use of his Washington D.C. house. Wadman later denied knowing King Loren Schmit said when he first heard the allegations of child sexual abuse connected to the Franklin Credit Union, he dismissed them. "My job is to follow the money!" he declared, dismissing the other matters. His job, he said was to find out for members of the black community in Omaha, what happened to their money and their credit union, which Larry King ran.

His early statements about following the money were misinterpreted by Foster Care, other organizations and individuals as a declaration that he was abandoning the children. It raised a firestorm of protest, and he went to see John DeCamp. They both were to be discredited in a relentless campaign by the news media.

Schmit is an old-time farmer and crop duster who came late in life to the Legislature and served 21 years before he was unceremoniously dumped. On Aug 21, 1989, he hired Gary Caradori, as Chief Investigator for the Franklin Committee. Because of his decision Schmit was once more threatened and within a short time the deaths began.

On November 4, 1989, Kathleen Sorensen died in a car accident on the way home from filming the second episode of two Cable Access programs that dealt with her uncovering the satanic abuse of her foster children. Although Geraldo Riviera did a two-part series on Satanism in America. The program singled out the Omaha area as one of the centers for Satanism. Sorensen was one of the guests on Geraldo's program. Geraldo has since refused to do any further programs on Satanism.

A few courageous individuals like Kathleen Sorensen took their complaints to Foster Care, which were being ignored by the Attorney General Robert Spire. Foster Care Director, Carol Stitt, stated in

"Conspiracy of Silence" that she put a "foot high pile of documents before the Attorney General".

An informant later claimed that the car accident, which killed Sorensen, had been pre-arranged with a satanic suicide driver. (See Gunderson Chapter). It is almost impossible to prove an auto accident was deliberately caused yet it offers often a sure-fire way of getting rid of the problem. (See Rusty Chapter)

A little more than a month, after the death of Kathleen Sorenson, Caradori began the first of a series of interviews with kids regarding sexual abuse on the part of Larry King and others. Sexual abuse and satanic activity were intimately involved as was the military and the FBI.

On December 27, 1989, videotaped testimony was given to the Attorney General Robert Spire and U.S. Attorney Ron Lahners. On the same day, John De Camp accompanied Loren Scmit, at Schmit's insistence to the office of the FBI.

From "The Franklin Cover-up" DeCamp says; "**I agreed to go, but on the condition that he first meet one-on-one with the regional head of the FBI, Nick O'Hara.**

He did meet with O'Hara for about one hour. Then I was called into the room. It was only at that time, through discussion, that I learned that the individual in question was former Omaha, Police Chief Robert Wadman.

In brutal language and with the most somber demeanor possible, O'Hara made it clear that probably his closest friend in the world was Police Chief Robert Wadman, and anyone who would dare to accuse Robert Wadman of impropriety had better realize that in accusing Wadman, they were effectively taking on Nick O'Hara and the FBI.

When we left the FBI offices, I said to Senator Schmit "Wow, did I make a mistake. Anybody who dares to investigate this is going to get him or her buried by the FBI, if they start making any accusations against Wadman or anybody associated with him. "

I had no idea how prophetic those words were (Curator's death is linked to the FBI). See Rusty Chapter

On January 18, 1990, Decamp wrote a memo to World Herald Reporter Bob Dorr. In it, he mentions the papers Publisher Harold Anderson, Larry King, former Omaha Police Chief Robert Wadman, OWH Reporter Peter Citron, and Alan Baer as central figures in the Franklin Investigation.

Schmit found that the tapes Caradori had made which were given to the FBI had been leaked to the News Media. Pam Vuchetich, attorney for Alisha Owens one of the witness on the tapes turns confidential information over to the FBI, and compromises her client's position by making statements to the press. It was reported, she was having an affair with FBI Agent Mickey Mott.

The FBI Agent in charge claimed, "Stories of Child Abuse do not stand up to our scrutiny".

Less than a month later, a U.S. Magistrate Richard Kopf orders a "mental evaluation" of Lawrence E. King Jr. On March 29,1990, King is ruled incompetent to stand trial.

The next day, the media carried a story that two of the male victim witnesses failed a FBI lie detector test. No tests were ever taken by them. The following month, Troy Boner openly recants his testimony. On April 22, 1990, a World Herald article talks about the young people manufacturing "a carefully crafted hoax".

On May 15, 1990, former Omaha World Herald Entertainment Columnist, Peter Citron, found guilty on two counts of sexual assault of a child. Less than a month, before Omaha Mayor Morgan testified before a Douglas County Grand Jury that he was "outraged" at accusations that he had attended parties.

FBI begins harassment of Senator Loren Schmit's eighty-eight year old blind mother, Accuses Schmit of having mob connections. From "The Franklin Cover-up"

"It was only after Caradori's first tapes had been turned over to law enforcement agencies, that leaks of what was on them began reaching the public and became the subject of widespread discussion. Articles began to appear in the Omaha World Herald aimed to discredit the witnesses and intimidate any other potential child victim-witnesses from testifying or coming forward with information.

As the stories proliferated, Gary Caradori expressed to Senator Schmit his concern for the safety of the victim-witnesses who allowed them to be taped. Schmidt sought DeCamp's legal advice again."

Schmit stated: "These kids need protection or they are going to end up dead, or become afraid to continue to tell the truth. The committee has to do something to guarantee their protection."

The Legislature failed in protecting children that came to them to plead for help in prosecuting their sexual abusers. Alisha Owens, who would not back down on the sexual abuse charges, received up to 25 years in prison on nine counts of perjury. Former Senator DeCamp made it clear that this was a gross violation of her constitutional rights.

The Legislative report agreed that indeed Satanism did exist in Nebraska and yes, they did use and abuse children and adults. In the satanic chapter it states that 100% of those involved in Satanism were also involved in drugs.

The Franklin report states: The most frightening thing about cult (satanic) abuse is the tendency to pass perversions, aberrations, and other psychic and physical injuries on to the children."

The report quotes an opinion of the US Court of Appeals for the Fifth Circuit, in upholding a drug dealer's life sentence without parole.

> **Except in rare cases, the murderer's red hand falls on one victim. Only, however grim the blow: but the foul hand of the drug dealer. Blights life after life and like the vampire of fable, creates others in its owner's evil image—others who creates others still, across the land and down our generations, sparing not even the unborn. Terrebone v. Butler, 848 F.2d 500, 504 (5th Cir. 1988) (en banc),**

The report then launches into a discussion of Satanism, as it exists in the country "The purpose of this report is not to deny people the right to worship Satan if they so desire. The purpose of the report is to discuss some of the problems that may be concomitant with Satanism, some of the indicia of satanic abuse, and some of the dangers that may arise in connection with satanic worship. Law enforcement personnel frequently respond to homicides, child abuse, arson, and other criminal activities that are done in connection with satanic activities...." How very different is this from the report of Ken Lanning of the FBI Web site claiming there is no criminal activity associated with Satanism.. A comparison between his theories and the facts are to be found in the chapter on Satanism.

The sad result of this report is that there were none. Despite the recommendations of Dr Judianne Densen-Gerber, psychiatrist and lawyer, Lee Orr, Kansas City Homicide Detective and Ted Gunderson, FBI Retired . Despite the death of Gary Caradori, the Legislature's Chief Investigator and of Kathleen Sorenson, a foster parent, who testified to the satanic rituals and murders her children had been involved in. Nothing was done.

Dr. Desen Gerber admonished the Committee: "I know that there have been extraordinary pressures on both the Committee as a whole and on individuals. I know the type of power that has been brought to bear. So I am not here in any way criticize the Committee. I want to say one thing. I would not want the Committee to disband. I think that it is not in the best interests of the average Nebraska citizen ...I would also not want the material turned over to any other Committee, because it takes two to three years for the average person to get through the automatic denial that goes along with this kind of material.... I've got documents and I've got cases and I've got police that can tell you these are the things they've seen". She stated that Bonacci had witnessed or participated in five satanic sacrifices, four in Nebraska and one in California. That he had performed necrophilia by having sexual intercourse with a dead child on film. He said there were two doctors present, who worked with the cult. She warned of increasing AIDS especially in younger children and stated that Bonacci also belonged to a Nazi cult. All cult sites usually show some homage or salute to Hitler.

The Franklin Investigation came to an ignominious end. The report issued from this investigation indicated that much more could and should have been done. But those involved were too important to be brought down by the rape and in some cases murder of children.

The report is entitled **"Cult Abuse and the Safety of Children."** unfortunately, it went nowhere, not the FBI, not the Governor, not the Attorney General acted on its proven points. Information was given to various members of the Iowa Legislature, even while the investigation was going on. This information, including reports from the police and others, indicated the same things were going on in Iowa as well. All information was ignored, completely unacknowledged.

Franklin Investigation Final Report:

"The Franklin investigation proceeded in ways that were at times surprising to the Committee members and their counsel. From the outset, members of the Committee, and various people acting as counsel or investigator to the Committee, were often thwarted in our attempts to gain information directly from the principle parties involved in the Franklin failure. There were individuals who, on the advice of counsel, would not communicate with the Franklin Committee at all. There were various agencies of a fact gathering variety, who felt free to pick and choose among the Franklin files as to what they did or did not wish to use, or follow up on, but who determined that the flow of information would be so one-sided. **In view of these obstacles, it is perhaps surprising that the Franklin committee amassed the pure quantity of information that we did.**

Although the Legislature had given the Franklin Committee a broad mandate as to activities that were to be investigated, it was finally the public that largely determined our agenda.

There were many people in the State who believed that the Franklin Committee would provide their last resort, or perhaps their only opportunity, to discuss matters that concerned them.

It was, finally, citizens who came forward with the hope of giving or receiving assistance, which determined what, was and was not "Franklin related."

One of the issues that various citizens brought forward again and again was the matter of ritual abuse. People were concerned about cults, and the possible danger that could arise in connection with various cults. There were witnesses, who claimed to have been victimized by unlawful activity, and there were other witnesses, who were concerned about what appears to be the proliferation of harmful cult activity through-

out the country in general, and in Nebraska in particular.

The initial response to allegations regarding occult behavior is of course one of disbelief.

In a recent case in San Francisco, a pentagram had been carved in the victim's chest, and his body had partially been drained of blood during a ritual. Candle-wax dropping were found in his right eye. During closing arguments, prosecutor Paul Cummings described the proceeding as a "voyage into an underworld we don't want to admit exists in our society."

The report goes on to discuss a satanic cult uncovered in 1986 in Rulo, Nebraska. During the trial counsel brought in a witness named Priscilla Coates, from New York, who represented the Citizens Freedom Foundation, a support group of former cult members.

Continuing the report "She describes cults as destructive groups that are a problem on an international basis. She testified extensively about cults, and other destructive groups, (including Jonestown), in which children were constantly abused for purposes of cult discipline. She testified that she had information on cults encouraging people to commit numerous crimes ranging from prostitution to theft to selling drugs.

She stated that information regarding Rulo, in terms of forcing cult members to have sexual relations with their children and with each other, was not uncommon, and that bestiality (making people have sex with animals) was also not uncommon.

The members of the Committee are fully aware of the fact that people do not want to hear about cult activity and are fully aware of the fact that to discuss Satanists is to risk being the subject of ridicule and even hostility.

The various horrifying experiences of the people at Rulo need not be set forth in this report…

The main concern of people who have been in contact with the Committee has been ritualistic abuse of children. Child abuse is intolerable both from the standpoint of the law, and from the standpoint of society in general. The problem with ritualistic child abuse is that many times it is difficult for children to communicate what has happened to them….

Our society is admirably aware of the problems of sexual abuse of children, and frequently a parent or professional will be on the lookout for evidence of child sexual abuse, but ritual abuse is almost never suspected, and often becomes apparent only after children act out, and discuss bizarre activities. Children will sometimes speak of people in scary costumes, make references to body painting, or have unusual bruise patterns on their bodies. Such children often play in an aggressive, sadistic way, and are destructive and intent in hurting of other children. Abused children often act out mutilation on their toys, threaten other children in bizarre and shocking ways, engage in play that is not appropriate to their age or the normal experience of children that age.

Loren Schmit echoed the words of William Colby, former director of the CIA, when he said; **"Children have been harmed and even killed, but too many important people are involved and "My God, I think they are going to get away with it!"**

RECOMMENDATIONS FOR LEGISLATION

Sadly, the warnings given to Senator Loren Schmit would be carried out (See Conspiracy of Silence video transcript). The Committee was shut down literally around him. He was removed from posts on other committees that he had been on for years.

Even more sadly the deaths that occurred before, during and after the investigation would go unpunished. (The Report issued by the Legislature cited Dr Judienne Densen-Gerber, lawyer and psychiatrist who examined Paul Bonacci.) She reported the association of Satanism to multiple personalities, and Satanists who are involved with cannibalism.

It also states, "It is instructive to hear of some of Mr. Orr's experiences". (A Kansas City, Kansas homicide detective), who had been investigating satanic homicides around the Midwest. The report matter-of-factly states: "He once met the leader of a cult that believed that the power of everlasting life was gain by consuming the internal organs of dead people" This document that was never widely circulated…certainly not reported on by the Nebraska news media has a chilling effect because of the apathetic way it presents, human sacrifice, blood drink-

ing, cannibalism, mother, child, and baby sacrifice.

Dr Densen-Gerber told of the Antichrist cults, that are the more vicious because they contain breeder mothers, who have been "married to Satan", between the age of 8 and 13, and in which the young girl is tied to an altar, and a man dressed as the devil would rape the child, and there are numerous other disgusting practices such as bloodletting, and the fetal Eucharist.

Dr Densen-Gerber's recommended satanic investigative teams inside the police departments of Nebraska and the Nebraska State Troopers. To deal with child sexual abuse, child pornography, child trafficking (euphemism for kidnap/slavery), and the use of illegal drugs by underage persons."

Nothing in the report would indicate this abominable conduct was being done by important politicians, businessmen and military both in Nebraska and Washington D.C.

Nothing in this report was ever acted upon by the Nebraska Legislature, no law was passed.

Nebraska State Senator Loren Schmit Chairman
of the Franklin Credit Union Investigation

Paul Bonacci

PAUL BONACCI

If Paul Bonacci were your child, you would shrink in horror to hear what he has gone thru since the age of three. I can tell you that Johnny Gosch went thru some of the same tortures by the same men who tortured Paul.

If you have not seen that Hollywood movie 8 MM, then you cannot begin to understand what is going on in Iowa, America and the World. The movie is about a detective who is hired by the wife of a dead millionaire because his wife has found a film locked in his secret safe after his death. All she wants the detective to do is find out if the murder of a young girl is faked or real. Money is no object the widow says. He swims in the sewers of porno stores—pays $5,000 for a fake "snuff film" but eventually he finds the girls mother and the one who killed her. They kill his friend, burn the film and try to kill him. He escapes tells the widow it was real, she commits suicide and now he has no proof that the film exists, so in true Hollywood fashion he finds and kills the "snuff film" makers.

That was Hollywood and now the truth. The above film 8MM can be found in any video store, but so can "snuff films" There is a series of films called "Faces of Death." A part of the film was shown by Kansas City Homicide Detective E. Lee Orr at their meeting in Lincoln, Nebraska. A hundred and fifty members of the audience recoiled in horror at what they saw—a documentary of a Satanic cult from California who cuts open and eats the heart and liver of a young girl who has supposedly just committed suicide for the benefit of the ceremony.

This film was available in video store after video store all across America. According to Lee Orr this video documentary is a prime indicator that satanic activity is in the area. Orr spent the final five years of 25 years on the Kansas City police force investigating satanic homicides. He was amazed at how many satanic homicides he investigated that were later called drug related homicides.

You will learn here in these pages that Paul Bonacci participated in the making of snuff films in which the other child was killed. Paul Bonacci claims to have been with the head of the North American Man Boy Love Association in New York City and that he was sent frequently to Washington D.C. to warm Congressmen Barney Franks bed. He also participated in satanic cult human sacrifice, but refused to eat the eyes, according to Dr Judi-Anne Densen-Gerber, psychiatrist. Gerber specializes in NAMBLA and Satanism, and was brought to Nebraska by the Nebraska Legislature to determine if he was a Multiple Personality and if he was telling the truth. Densen-Gerber wrote a special report to the Nebraska Legislature in which she found him entirely credible and incapable of lying. She also stated that as a much-abused multiple personality he belonged in treatment not in jail. Yet her expert testimony and the effort of his lawyer John DeCamp did not succeed in getting him freed. It would be years before Paul Bonacci was finally released.

Paul Anthony Bonacci was born on August 3, 1967 to Marilyn May and John Angelo Bonacci. The father was of Italian descent. Bonacci's parents were divorced while he was but a baby. His father never claimed him until he was almost 19, Bonacci's mother remarried, but it didn't last long. She divorced soon afterwards because of physical abuse by her new husband. She then married Jack McCoy, who treated her with love, honor and respect. Paul loved his new stepfather, but was, mysteriously never able to tell him.

Bonacci remembers when he was four years old and his mother would go to work, he would try to follow to the bus stop. Bonacci recalled a couple up the street who gave him cookies. "A weird guy lived close to us who would take me home, too, but he started to harm me," Bonacci recalled. Down in the "weird neighbor's" basement Bonacci saw a wooden altar. Then Bonacci recalled a hideous, but vivid memory. "He had this little boy that was down there. He was probably about 2 years old, and I was about 4. He made me have sex with the boy. And as I was doing it, he started cutting the boy. He was telling me that he was putting the boy's spirit in me and then afterwards he told me that the boy wasn't really hurt, and that it was all just a game. That's how Alec was formed because Alec is only about two years old and doesn't talk or speak. He's a baby person. He kind of represents the boy that was killed.

When Paul speaks of Alec, he is describing only one of many "personalities" that live inside him. Paul Bonacci has been diagnosed as having multiple personality disorder.

Paul continued to recall the horrible tale: "He took the boy's skin off and then put it on me. That's why I want to take five or six showers per day. I'm washing my hands but I can't get the blood off. I always see it. It's right there!

When Bonacci was 5, he was molested by a baby sitter. When he was 6, he had a friend named Jeremy (a pseudonym) who was 13. Jeremy took Bonacci to his fort where they played a game called "truth or dare' (just like in the new Madonna movie). One thing led to another and they ended up performing fellatio on each other. At age 7, Jeremy introduced Bonacci to anal sex. Bonacci was small and Jeremy protected him from other boys, so Bonacci considered him like a big brother. Jeremy told Bonacci not to tell anyone and he didn't – not for a long time. He did finally ask his best friends mother about it, but she said it was normal and not to worry about it.

In the latter part of 1975, when he was 8, Bonacci started going with a friend after school to Sacred Heart Church. He recalls, "Even though I was not a Catholic, my friend introduced me to the priest. My friend only called him "Father."

In February of 1976, Bonacci went to the church around Valentines' Day. "The priest took me into a room where he began to play with me and said I was very pretty for a little boy. He kissed me on my cheeks and lips and told me it was a blessing to have a priest kiss you. He told me to come back the next day and he'd show me something real nice.,"

"The next day I came back again he took me into the room. As far as I could tell, he and I were the only ones in the church. He had a collection of football cards, which he said his father had given him as a kid. Most of the cards were real old. While looking at them, he came up behind my chair and put his arms around me. He then started undoing my pants. At first I told him not to do that. He told me I would go to hell if he didn't touch me and bless my whole body. I was scared and couldn't say anything. He picked me up out of the chair and began to pull down my pants and my underwear. He then laid me on the table and began to fondle my little penis. Then he kissed me and licked my penis, saying he was blessing me. I left when he finally let me go. I asked my friend if the priest ever did that to him. He told me the priest did it to him 10 times and that, " it's his way of blessing you!

"I was again molested by this priest who did the same thing to me on at least two dozen different meetings. This is the main reason for my dislike of the Catholic Church. I have been sexually molested by at least 10 other fathers or brothers in the Catholic Church.

"About July 4 of 1976, I met a man named Walter Carlson, while in Hanscom Park in Omaha. My family was having a picnic or reunion. I was by myself near the tires when he and two boys came over and began talking to me and asking questions. We played for a while and when he got ready to leave, he asked me if I'd like to come to his house sometime and play with his nephews. I said yes. I gave him my address and phone number."

"When I first went over, I played games with other boys who were there. This went on for several weeks,. All we'd do is play games or watch cartoons.

Some of the boys were sexual with each other and with me, which didn't bother me since we were all kids.

"After awhile he started showing regular movies to us. Then the movies started having men and women engaging in sexual activity. Within six months, it was movies with adult men and boys engaging in sex. It was then that Carlson began touching me, at first on the outside of my clothes, then he undid my pants and fondled me and put his mouth on my penis! He also had me perform oral sex on him. He had us performing anal sex on one another while he watched or took photos of us."

Bonacci's recollections continue, "It was through Walter Carlson I met about two dozen other adult men, many of whom I knew by first names although some only by nicknames. Carlson also asked me to perform sexual acts with other boys and men for several men, who filmed the sex and sold the photos as kiddie porn."

"I honestly never learned the last names of all the boys I was with. Most of them were older than me and had been involved for several years more than me. Carlson and several men referred to us as pets and used us any way they wanted to use us. I had oral sex with four men whose names were Todd, Albert, Joe and also a guy named Tank.

"In 1977, I met most of the men at parties either at the Carlson's home or at Joe Burke's house. (Bonacci had met Burke in December of 1976. He didn't like him because "he tried to get me to do disgusting things with him and others." In early 1977 he met Kent Bruner.)

"I had been forced to have oral sex with adult men including Carlson almost every week. There was a man who's name was Anderson who is not the Harry Anderson whom I also met at Carlson's home in 1978. I only had oral sex with that Anderson one time, unlike Harry Anderson.

"I traveled with Walter Carson and several boys to Adventureland in Des Moines in the summers of 1977, 1978 and 1980 I went with him to Worlds of Fun in Kansas City, Missouri. Mr Carlson was a pro and knew how to keep everyone quiet without a lot of threats.

"In 1979, I started going around with Carlson and the men connected with him much less and hung out on The Milk Run and around the old Diamond Bar and the Stagedoor and the Cave (all bars). About the only reason I went to Carlson's was to take part in parties or in kiddie porn movies which were filmed at several different places."

"Over the next few years I went out with Carlson less and less and then he vanished altogether for a while. I have seen him since then at the Leavenworth Café in September or October of 1989, though I didn't say anything to him. He's out now running around looking for more young boys to molest. He was with one the last time I saw him.

It is noteworthy to point out here that Walter Carlson and Joe Burke were among 13 men arrested in Omaha in connection with a large pornography/pedophile case. Joe Burke had a library of 2,000 videos and 10,000 photos, which were confiscated. Convicted in December of 1985, Carlson was paroled in February of 1989. This was referred to in a 12/20/85 article in the Omaha World Herald.

Noreen meets Paul Bonacci

I first learned about Paul when Private Investigator Roy Stephens from Omaha Nebraska called to tell me that a prison inmate had confessed to the kidnapping of Johnny. It was March 1991. Roy brought a dozen tape recordings from his meetings with Paul Bonacci. As we sat listening to them, I was annoyed at the reaction of John Gosch Sr. He seemed less than interested, almost bored. He finally fell asleep and slept through the remainder of the tapes.

Roy explained it was very important to not talk to anyone about Paul Bonacci, he wanted the opportunity to check out the information Paul had given him. So I agreed with him and did not talk about it to anyone. Roy stated he wanted me to go to the prison and talk with Bonacci. I told him I would but wanted to wait until I could go and not display any anger or frustration with him. Paul has Multiple Personality Disorder and information came out very fragmented as he changed from one personality to another. I knew that if I showed emotion in his presence that he would clam up. Roy said, "he was counting on the shock value of having Johnny's mother come to see him, thinking that it would cause Paul to release even more information about his part in the kidnapping." I told Roy I would let him know when I could go to the prison. Upon hearing all the details of the kidnapping and sexual abuse of my son, I wanted the time to process this information.

It was only a few weeks later that I received a phone call from a friend, telling me that WHO-TV our NBC station was running a story about "THE INMATE IN NEBRASKA WHO CONFESSED TO KIDNAPPING JOHNNY GOSCH". I couldn't believe it, no one had called me nor had I talked to any TV station. With in two hours of the TV news report, I received a visit from the FBI, two agents arrived to question me as to Paul Bonacci's claims of his helping to kidnap Johnny.

The FBI agents would not accept the fact that I did not have a great many details concerning Paul Bonacci. They went into their "MUTT AND JEFF" style questioning. No doubt, the FBI had already contacted the Omaha Field Office and knew exactly all of the details about Bonacci and their visit to me was simply to harass me. I finally told them to leave my office that I had no more information to give them and suggested they call John DeCamp, Bonacci's attorney and ask him questions. I had never met or spoken to John DeCamp.

Later I returned home to fix dinner. John did not come home that night. Finally around five a.m. the next morning, I heard him coming in the door. I went downstairs and asked "Where were you all night?" He didn't reply. I asked again "Where were you all night? Did you hear the news? Someone released the story about Bonacci! Did you know the FBI came to question me?" He turned around and with a smirk on his face he said "Hell, I knew about Bonacci for almost two years and kept it from you. I have been to the prison to interview him!" My mouth fell open, I could hardly believe what

I was hearing from John. Why would a father keep information so important about his son ….. From his mother? John would not say any more, I knew he was hiding something but he became almost withdrawn every time the name Bonacci was mentioned.

I didn't learn until 1997 that John Gosch did go to John DeCamp's office, bringing another woman who looked like me, he introduced her as his wife, Noreen Gosch. Together they all went to the prison to interview Bonacci for the first time. John Sr. felt that he was telling the truth and called in Roy Stephens a private investigator to begin the long process of questioning Paul Bonacci about the kidnapping of Johnny.

I called Roy Stephens to let him know that the TV coverage was everywhere concerning Bonacci. He decided to drive to Des Moines. When he arrived, I confronted him with the information I had just learned about Bonacci, John Gosch and the visit to the prison. Roy acted very "sheepish" and kept looking at John Sr. for an answer. I knew there had been some type of collusion between them but neither one of them would talk about it.

Meanwhile, there were many local and network TV stations covering the story. This appeared to be a big break in the Johnny Gosch Case and people were very happy for us. However, around the next corner came the big slap in the face, one I was not prepared for …..Law enforcement considered Paul Bonacci a NUT because he had Multiple Personality Disorder. The West Des Moines police refused to interview him, saying he was not credible. The FBI refused to talk with him. Every word of Paul's confession had been hand carried to the FBI Headquarters in Omaha Nebraska.

I wasn't sure what was going on but it was beginning to look like the FBI was covering up something. Their refusal to talk to Paul, coupled with their visit and harassment of me directly after the first news report of Bonacci's confession. We had problems with the FBI from the beginning of Johnny's kidnapping but I would have thought this was different… we had someone actually confessing and giving details of the kidnapping.

During the months, Roy Stephens continued to work on the Bonacci information he was able to confirm details of Bonacci's repeated connection to Johnny over the years. He also gave us the names of the other people who participated in kidnapping Johnny. How they took him. Where they took him. What they did to him after they arrived at their destination. Who purchased Johnny and where he was taken after the first two weeks captivity. For the first time in all these years, we knew "WHO… HOW….WHY Johnny was kidnapped! Our first decent break and **LAW ENFORCEMENT REFUSES TO TOUCH IT!**

I contacted Roy Stephens three months later and told him I was ready to go to the prison and to set up an appointment with the warden. I decided to call WHO-TV and ask Jim Strickland, a reporter who had covered Johnny's case extensively to go to the prison with me and record on video all of Paul Bonacci's statements. I wanted a video record of this meeting. I also asked John Gosch to go to the prison with me…. He refused saying he was much too busy and couldn't make it. Again, I thought this was very strange because it was also his son who was kidnapped and yet he seemed so disinterested in following up with Bonacci.

The morning came to drive to the prison; it is about a three-hour trip to Lincoln Nebraska. Jim Strickland and the camera crew were to meet me in Lincoln outside the prison. Roy wanted to meet me at the Denny's Restaurant, leave my car and ride with him to the prison. When I arrived at the restaurant, Roy was waiting for me. I hopped into his car and off we went to the prison. As we drove up, I thought to myself…. I wonder what it is like to be behind bars, unable to have any freedoms. It must be awful.

As we entered the lobby area of the prison office, we were told that we would have to walk through maximum security …. This was a very frightening experience; the male prisoners were lined up against the bars and would yell sexually explicit jeers at me. I guess it had been a while since they had seen a woman. Finally, all of the men in our group circled around me and I walked with them but inside of this protective circle, until we passed through the maximum-security area.

There was a very large room in which we were told to wait. Jim Strickland and his cameraman were busy setting up their equipment. I looked across the room and made eye contact with Paul Bonacci as the guards led him into the room in chains. At that moment, I knew for certain that I was about to hear exactly what happened to my son once again but this time the man would be sitting across from me at the table. I did something I have never done before throughout this case I

fainted…. collapsing on to the floor behind the table, the camera man saw me begin to faint and ran to cushion my fall so I would not hit my head against the concrete wall. Both he and Jim helped me on to a chair as I collected myself to meet Paul Bonacci. WHO TV was gracious not to show my collapsing when they aired this story on Paul.

The guards removed the chains and Paul was brought to the table. Roy Stephens introduced Paul to me by saying "Paul, this is Johnny's Mom". Paul immediately broke into tears saying, "I am sorry… I am so sorry". I told him that " I don't blame you, please tell me what happened to my son". At that point, Paul hesitated and stammered but slowly began to tell me how the kidnapping took place. He talked about a man named Emilio who was the driver of the car and also had identified a composite drawing done by an artist I had hired based on the statements from witnesses. Paul said Johnny had been photographed about two weeks before the kidnapping. Those photographs were brought to a motel the night before the kidnapping to show Emilio who they were going to kidnap the next morning. The man who brought the photo was identified as Sam Soda. Paul had earlier chosen Sam's picture in a photo line up of twenty-five pictures.

He explained he had been ordered to lay in the trunk of Emilio's car along with Mike another boy brought along to help with the kidnapping. After Emilio made his first contact with Johnny by asking for directions, then leaving the area, only to turn around and go back to where Johnny was sitting in his wagon, preparing to deliver his papers. Paul and Mike were told to get into the back seat, lie on the floor and cover up with a blanket and to wait until they heard Emilio begin to speak to Johnny again. They did as they were told. Paul said Emilio had placed the barrel of a gun in his mouth and told him he would shoot him if he did not do as he was told.

When they pulled up along side Johnny sitting in his wagon, Paul and Mike started to talk to him to lure him over to the car. They opened up the car door, Paul said a man named Tony had been told to come from behind Johnny and push him into the car. Paul and Mike held Johnny down and placed a cloth with chloroform over Johnny's face, as the Emilio ran the stop sign and turned left onto 42nd street and headed towards the Interstate 80.

There actually had been three vehicles in the area. The car Emilio drove, a van parked several blocks away and a green station wagon on the street north of the kidnap site. Sitting at a vantage point and being able to see the entire kidnapping. The green station wagon had the type of rear door which opened from the top and the side hinge. It was a Ford product, only available for certain years. After learning the description of the car, I telephoned the Motor Vehicles Dept. asking for a list of vehicles owned by "Sam", the man identified by Paul Bonacci. Bingo.... Motor Vehicles had the entire list of vechicles owned by "Sam" and one of them was a Ford station wagon, green with the type of rear dor which opened from the side or top.

The plan for the kidnapping was to grab Johnny, Emilio to meet with the driver of the van which was Tony and they would transfer Johnny's body to the van. Then all three vehicles would leave West Des Moines in different directions and rendezvous at a farmhouse just outside Sioux City Iowa. A man named Charlie Kerr owned the farmhouse.

Johnny was kept in a room in the basement. The room was long and narrow, it had a dirt floor in that part of the basement, windows were boarded up with only slits of light coming through. The walls were painted a very dull medium green shade. He was kept bound and gagged most of the time. They administered drugs to Johnny. Paul and Mike were instructed to have sex with Johnny while Emilio, Sam and Charlie stood by watching and snapping pictures.

Paul told me "he and Mike talked to Johnny telling him that if he behaved and did what they told him to do….. he would live." He reported Johnny was very upset and kept crying wanting to go home.

Paul said, "They worked on Johnny making him feel guilty for what had happened to him. Telling him his parents didn't want him. He would be killed if he tried to escape from them."

They kept Johnny there for nearly fourteen days. There were numerous occasions of sexual abuse during this time. After this period of time a man that Paul called "The Colonel " who paid Emilio (the driver of the car) $15,000 cash for Johnny. The "Col" took Johnny to Colorado. He no doubt ordered his kidnapping. Paul did not see Johnny again until 1983 and 1984 in London Ontario Canada at an "encampment" where they kept kids being used by this pornography/prostitution ring. Paul last saw Johnny in 1986 in Colorado at an orgy held at a ranch owned by the "Col". Johnny had been renamed "Mark" and his hair was dyed black. Johnny told Paul at that meeting "He tried to get away down the mountain but was tracked down by the men who were always at the compound/ranch and beaten then "branded with a hot branding iron". They often did this to kids who tried to get away. Telling them they would always be able to track them down due to the brand, which would always be on their body. Most of the boys were branded on their shoulder, hip, thigh or calf of the leg.

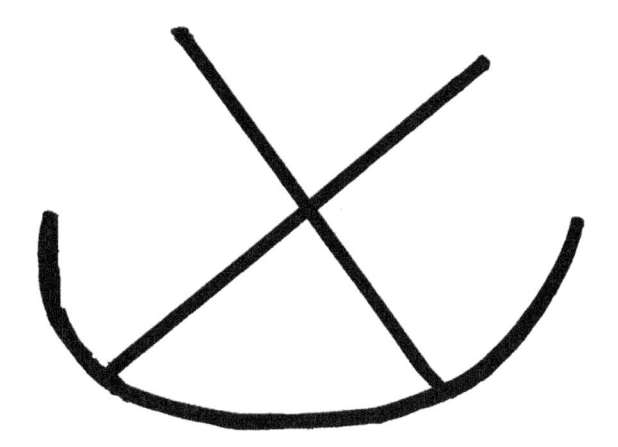

The Rocking "X" Brand

The brand used on Johnny and many other children. The brand was located as a Registered Brand in the state of Colorado by our Private Detectives. The Brand Registry Office would only tell us that the brand had been used but was not now in use by any ranchers in the area.

A number of years later, Paul received letters from two friends saying that Johnny had been taken to Mexico by "the Col." he had surgery and went back to being a blond.

The television coverage Jim Strickland did was in the form of a series on Paul Bonacci. This was fed to the networks; as a result we received a phone call from America's Most Wanted. They were interested in doing Johnny's story and of course wanted to include all the information about Paul Bonacci's confession. I had the first of many conversations with Paul Sparrow, the producer who came to Des Moines to do preliminary interviews and line up all the details for the filming of the show.

They were to come to Des Moines and spend days doing the reenactment of the kidnapping, using actors and actress's to do all the scenes, even a little dog like Johnny's was hired. The day they did the actual kidnap scene, it was necessary for the dog "to bark on cue". The lady who owned the dog stood off camera and turned on a "dust buster" which the dog was afraid of and would then bark on "cue".

Paul Sparrow contacted Sam Soda and they created a scene in which Sam was giving me the details of the second kidnapping which was to come. All Paul would say to me about his discussion with Sam was that .... Sam is an unusual guy. The following day I received a phone call from Sam, he was all upset and nervous. He was almost out of breath and kept saying "America's Most Wanted thinks I had something to do with Johnny's kidnapping." I thought it interesting to say the least, that this would unnerve Sam to the point that he would call me after all these years. It had been almost seven years since I had talked to him.

Paul Sparrow and all of the entourage of people who accompany America's Most Wanted, then left Des Moines and went to Omaha Nebraska to interview Paul Bonacci, John De Camp and Roy Stephens. They were in Nebraska several days, returned to Des Moines to do a little more follow up filming in the area. Paul Sparrow came to our home the night before he left to go back to Washington and said to me "is this whole story real or is it some CAREFULLY CRAFTED HOAX!" I was outraged and informed him I didn't have to take that kind of remark from anyone. He later apologized for his remark but that he wanted to see just how committed I really was to solving this case.

The Nebraska Leadership Conference had published a small book called "A Carefully Crafted Hoax"

The title was misleading, it told in very matter of fact detail about a cover up of child sexual abuse, child porn, Satanism, and murder, that was being investigated by the Nebraska Legislature. The book debunked the Omaha World Herald stories that portrayed the investigation as a carefully crafted hoax. It became obvious that people in high places can triumph over children who had the backing of the Nebraska Legislature.

The day came when America's Most Wanted were about to air the program. I received another call from Paul Sparrow saying "The FBI contacted them and told them to **KILL THE GOSCH STORY.**"

In other words, the FBI did not want Johnny's story aired by America's Most Wanted. John Walsh and Paul Sparrow stood up to the FBI and told them they were going ahead with our story no matter what they said or did. The FBI evidently backed down and didn't interfere any further because the show aired in November 1992. The show received more telephone calls from the public than any other show in its history. Leads were coming from all over the country concerning Emilio and Charlie.

One of the many leads, which came in from the program, was a letter addressed to "Johnny's family". It arrived at our home with no street address or zip code….. It just said "Johnny Gosch's Family… Des Moines, Iowa."

The letter was from a young man, calling himself Jimmy. He described being involved in a prostitution/pornography ring. This ring also kidnapped children. Jimmy had been a runaway and was grabbed after he had taken to the streets. His parents suffered through other runaway episodes with him and hadn't searched too hard for Jimmy this time. In his letter, he went on to say that he not only knew my son but had spent many years with him. He told me he, Johnny and another boy stole a car to get away from the people, who had held them captive for years.

Jimmy sounded pleading and pathetic in his letter, saying he wanted desperately to meet with me and he would be in touch soon. Within a few weeks, I had received four letters from him, no return address on any of the envelopes. The final letter indicated he would call me when he decided to come to Des Moines.

Late one night in January 1993, I received a phone call, when I answered a voice said, "well I am here". I looked at the clock it was almost one a.m. I responded by saying "you are where". He said, " this is Jimmy and I am at the train station in Osceola, Iowa… can you come and get me?" Then he said "oh by the way, do you have any warm clothing, someone my stole coat while I was sleeping on the train." I didn't bother to check the weather, temperature or road conditions… I just bolted for Osceola.

I got up, hurriedly got dressed, ran to the basement to get some warm sweaters, gloves, hat and coat. Off I went into the winter night. It was not only cold but snowing heavily. Osceola is nearly an hour's drive from Des Moines. When I got to the train station, there he stood on the platform, huddled with a blanket wrapped around him…. all alone. Jimmy was about five foot five, brown hair, square shaped face, brown eyes and slight build. He looked to be about 22 or 23.

I pulled up and he jumped in the car. He knew who I was due to television and he was the only one there in the middle of the night. I felt safe in assuming that he was "Jimmy." When he got in the car, he said he almost froze to death waiting for me to get there, because the train station was locked up and he had nowhere to go till I arrived. I suggested we go to the restaurant/truck stop on the edge of town and get something hot to eat and drink. That sounded pretty good to Jimmy as he was tired, cold and hungry.

As we sat there talking, he related to me how these boys had been used sexually, by wealthy, politically connected pedophiles in this country. He said they kidnapped many children throughout the years. He also had with him some maps of the United States. He had enlarged copies of Arizona, New Mexico, Colorado and Utah, he showed me the areas where they had "safe houses." Places in remote areas where the kids would be kept and it was too far to ever walk out. Some of the boys had tried and were dealt with severely, usually beatings and torture as an example to the others not, to try the same thing.

As I sat there listening, I thought to myself, I wonder if this kid is on the level, anyone could tell these stories. I asked him a few questions about Johnny. He then said, " I want to show you something"…. With that he leaned over and pulled up the pant leg of his jeans. When I looked over I was horrified to see a scar of a "brand" on his leg. It spanned approximately five inches in height and three inches in width. It was the same brand Paul Bonacci had shown me. The Rocking "X" Brand. He explained that most all the kids had the brand somewhere on their body. The men told the kids, this was one way they could always track them.

Jimmy went on to tell me, I had created an insurance policy for Johnny with all the publicity over the years. He was known as the "golden boy or celebrity boy and the perpetrators could get more money for his services, so it kept him alive." It wasn't what I wanted to hear! But it did tell me that all the efforts counted for something. It kept my boy alive until he could break free.

After they escaped, Jimmy said, "Johnny and the other boy had gone with him to his parent's home and stayed for several days." Jimmy's parents gave them food, some warm clothing and a place to stay. After a few days, Johnny and the other boy left, saying they were going to live somewhere and would be in touch with Jimmy soon.

Jimmy later learned an Indian tribe had taken them in and given them shelter on a reservation. He explained there was no way any of the boys would contact their parents nor go to the police, they were too afraid. I asked why Jimmy felt he could go home to his parents. He replied that his dad only thought he had run away, he had no idea anything worse happened to him. I accepted his answer because I didn't want to challenge him, while he was in the mood to talk.

Before I knew it.... The sun had come up and it was morning. I asked Jimmy if I could call a private detective to come and visit with him. He said it would be "okay". I telephoned Roy Stephens in Omaha, Nebraska; he said he would be there as soon as he could. Roy arrived a couple hours later; Jimmy repeated the whole story for Roy as well. Then he showed him the brand; Roy had seen this before on Paul Bonacci.

Jimmy agreed to stay in the area for a while, so we could sort out some of the information. It was decided, he would return to Omaha with Roy. He could find him a place to stay. Once there, Jimmy was introduced to Paul Bonacci, John DeCamp and others. Much of what Jimmy told us matched the information we had gotten from Paul, a couple years earlier.

Jimmy told me his father was a CPA in a nearby state and I could talk to him if I wanted to do so. When I did hear from Jimmy's father, he told me about the night the boys came to his home, they were cold, tired and hungry.

After the two boys left, it was then Jimmy's father saw the America's Most Wanted show and realized one of the boys he helped was Johnny Gosch. Jimmy's father said he felt so badly and urged Jimmy to write the letter to me so I could learn more about Johnny. Not knowing for sure whom I was talking to on the phone, I sent a private detective to that city to check out the man. We did verify that he had a CPA firm and was indeed Jimmy's father.

During the time Jimmy was in Omaha, America's Most Wanted followed up on the story and what leads we had received. When I told Producer Paul Sparrow of Jimmy, he said they wanted to fly back out to the Midwest and do another update of the story. Plans were made for them to come the following week. When they arrived in the area, they interviewed me, Paul Bonacci, Jimmy, Roy Stephens and John DeCamp. Jimmy and Paul kept telling everyone there was a safe house located in the mountains in Colorado and they could take the film crew to it.

They set off on a trip to Colorado, Jimmy, Paul, Paul Sparrow, Roy Stephens and the crew. Once in the mountains, Paul Bonacci led them to the house. In the basement were cages where the boys had been kept when the adults were away from the site, to prevent the boys from "wandering away". It was all filmed and shown on America's Most Wanted in the updated show, in February 1993.

I intended to show these pictures in this book and repeatedly requested copies from America's Most Wanted. At first, they said they would send me the copies. I have waited over six months, with repeated requests. THEY NEVER SENT THE PHOTOS. I am not sure, if it is merely an oversight or someone didn't want these pictures shown again in this country.... perhaps the FBI stepped in once again. Is someone afraid that showing pictures of cages where kidnapped children were kept would be too much for the American people?

Despite the fact the information appeared in the updated TV show, no action was taken by any law enforcement. The FBI works very closely with America's Most Wanted .... Why was there no action taken?

After returning from Colorado, Paul Sparrow and Roy Stephens reported to me that every time the crew passed by a phone booth, Jimmy would yell, " I need to stop and make a call." He would jump out of the vehicle and run to the phone booth, make his call, acting very secretive. If anyone walked near him he would stop talking immediately.

Jimmy did not have a pocket full of quarters, nor a phone card of any kind...We can only assume, he was calling someone collect. He appeard to be reporting the every move of this expedition to someone. Roy Stephens told me he felt Jimmy was definitely working for someone and was sent here for a purpose. to disrupt the investigation.

After three months, Jimmy left the area, returning to Wisconsin to live. Once there, he would call me "thirteen times a day", telling me that Johnny wanted to talk to me and would be showing up at my door unannounced, when I least expected it.

By spring of 1993, Jimmy faded from the scene. No one heard from him again. Only shawdowed pictures of him exist, he would never allow any other photo's to be taken. He insisted on having his face blacked out when he did the interview with America's Most Wanted.

"Jimmy"
The way he appeared in America's Most Wanted

BONACCI DOCUMENTS

When John DeCamp, former Nebraska State Senator, began to represent Paul Bonaci, he received from Paul, diaries and various written records. DeCamp then turned said documents over to the Nebraska Legislature. To avoid the allegation that they had been fabricated/written all at one time. They were sent for forensic studies, which determined that they were prepared over a period of time. The result of the forensic study confirmed various inks and papers could be dated back to the 1980's. Bonacci wrote these diaries in order to try to keep his multiple personalities straight. Imagine, a dozen people inside one body all trying to communicate with each other. One deliberately created to add confusion, one to cause destruction.

Monarch? When? How? Why?

"I chose to write this as a very separate account aside of all other issues involved. This is, I believe, the most accurate and detailed writing on my total involvement with Monarch and any of it's programs, I was directly involved with."

... Paul Bonacci

Project Monarch was an outgrowth of Operation Paperclip. It brought Nazi scientists into this country with all of the technology they developed, by experimenting on prisoners in the concentration camps. Monarch was one of 149 subprojects involving 23,000 victims in drug and mind control. It was the worst known misuse of governmental authority for illegal medical experiments to occur outside of the Nazi death camps...... Congressional Record

It all began to my best belief sometime in 1970. My family lived in South Omaha and my mother and father had divorced. My mother had also already gone through her second marriage. Sometime during this time period my mother had a girl baby-sit me and my brothers and sister. This girl whom I do not recall had an older man who was in the Air Force and lived close by and took me to his house when my mother was at work. This man had another man who had long dark hair and a beard and mustache do sexual things to me and to two other boys. I was about 3. The boys I believe named Gary or Greg and John were both about 8 to 10. This man would have anal sex with these two and have them have anal sex with me. These boys I discovered later were involved in the Monarch Program.

The man with the long hair would tell me he would kill me when he'd make me put his penis in my mouth. He was a very mean man and sometimes slapped me.

This man was also into Satanism and sacrificed a boy, I believe named Alec. This was I believe about Halloween time in 1970. I've told about this but since the last integration (Paul is speaking of communication with his alternate egos. He may have as many as 20) more things have become clear. So I'll write this and many events again simply to set things right.

That night I was taken to the house and was taken to the basement. The boys Gary or Greg who I'll refer to as simply Gary and John were both there.

Also the Airman who was wearing a red and black robe and a girl maybe 13 years old was also there. The boys Gary and John took me in a room, undressed me and put me in a red robe, with a a funny band around me with weird symbols on it. They also put on Red Robes and we had nothing on underneath them.

Bonacci goes on to describe in minute detail what was done to this child!

"This man then with my hands on the knife started stabbing the boy. He stabbed the boy in his stomach and both sides and then in the chest. When he did that the boy stopped moving altogether. He used my hands the whole time. After this they took me to the room again where I saw the men and girl eating the boys flesh. The man with long hair grabbed me and put the boys skin on me.

"At Offutt Air Base Monarch training was conducted. As an Air Force Historian, I knew this to be the number one Strategic Air Command Base in the Country. If The Soviet Union was to be bombed this is the Command Air Base that would launch major nuclear attack bombers against the Russians. Yet from the evidence of the treatment of children it would seem they were the one that should have been bombed. On such a base a civilian does not gain entry unless sponsored."

…..John Zielinski

At the Air Base we met the Doctor who was one of my commanders who I called Major. Both Gary and John were now about 11 or 12. This was during 1972 and 1973. Other kids I met there were Dave—Kelly—Matt—Brian—Jeremy-Tony-Bradley-John and –Cindy. There were total 10 boys in our group. Cindy was the one we were forced to beat up during our training.

During this time they would drug us and scare us with use of (demons-monsters) Men dressed in costumes most likely, they also had men have sex with us. When they would do different types of sex they would tell us a code and number.

The Doctor always came to protect us and he'd say that well for example Beta 1... etc. etc.

Gamma 107, which would have been for giving a guy b_job. **Almost every military alter was begun as a sexual one. This was to destroy any worth they could feel to fight off things they did not feel right in doing."**

This training that Bonaci and other boys were undergoing even took precedent over school. He describes how he would be picked up and the school notified that he would not be there that day. The reader should understand that this activity was taking place on a high security Air Force Base. Dozens if not hundred of airman had to be knowledgeable about what was going on. This kind of activity was still going on at least into the 1990s if not at present. It is possible to investigate the facts of "government ritual child abuse" records must exists—witnesses are available. What is lacking is the will on the part of "big government" to investigate itself. What happened to checks and balance? What happened to justice? . It is not something to be found in the America government today. Any attempt such as Bonacci to report they have participated in a government program results in the total dismissal of the witness by all levels of government, local, state and federal.

Bonacci recalls, "During a trip to the house which was on the Air Base, I saw a Black man whom I believe now was Larry King, (this was fifteen years before the Franklin Credit Union was closed) I heard many times while at the house, my commander say that some big shot from somewhere was coming and he wanted two blond boys about 10. Or a thing like the Senator likes girls about 12 and wants them clean and smooth, which was pre-pubescent, no chest and virgin if possible. And I heard him say he wants a group of boys between 5 and 15 and he'll have friends to join the party. I heard him refer to congressmen, Generals, Colonels, Senators, governors and big businessmen, the owner of Brandies was mention several times, bankers, even diplomats from other countries. We boys were never told anything about anyone. I do know the bedroom most of the sexual activities took place had hidden cameras and microphones in it since they would show us boys how to get the men into positions so they could film sexual activities better or clearly...

What follows is a description of sexual acts they were forced to perform on various men. Bonaci writes my commander, and sometimes my handler, our handler as he refers to those in control of him. "The training the Major did with us was in several areas. He and other trainers taught us to use sex as an instrument to gain control over others. We were taught that we were the greatest servants to our country by using our bodies to help gain control of the government in order for it to be strong. That we were hero's to give all we had. In other words they made us feel good about doing a disgusting job.

They used all kinds of codes and games to teach us things. They showed us how to make, bombs, traps, shelters. How to develop pictures and how to make gases and drug powders, weapons. How to use weapons, how to kill animals and showed us pressure points and karate. They never taught one alter very much, so they would use drugs or hypnosis which they taught us in order to create sub alters who were part of a more mature one but had separate functions which that alter did not know.

Writing as another of his alternate personalities Bonnaci said: They showed us how to build little bombs and how to make things to knock out people. Such as Chloroform." He was learning these things at Offutt Air Base, when he was five and six and seven years old. He was fourteen years when he placed chloroform over John Gosch's face. His techniques both sexual and violent, he learned at the top Air Force Base in the country.

"I also remember seeing Larry King at Offutt talking with my commander and other men, who worked with my commander, who I called or was told to call Major. I was never told his name and around us kids he never wore a tag. I learned pressure points and how to paralyze people.

The nature of the Bonnaci documents as explained by Paul Anthony Bonnaci present a thirteenand fourteen-year-old trained at Offutt AFB, SAC command trained as soldier and prostitute from the youngest age.

*Entry Log 10A300-61992 400-1600 Hrs PAB

This notebook's first section is to be used for Military information and information that West Lee will be providing. Some information may be spread out but all information will be relayed exactly as originally stated with only spelling word corrections. Entries will be done as neatly as possible and no waste of paper will be made.

End entry Paul Anthony Bonnaci 10A300

*Entry Log 10A301-61992-405-1600 hrs

The following information has been gathered thru several talks and from information provided from West Lee. In discussion with West Lee "I asked him the following questions 1. Why he was created and by whom? 2. Why he is needed to censor information 3. Why he has chose to disobey by protecting me.

His answers were direct and straight out. 1. He was created to block entry into a sensible store of information. Also to promote confusion and to jumble information. The person who created him was one of the men involved in Monarch. No name was ever given to him outside the code name. Alpha-Charlie-666-Delta. He also heard some men call him Gerry no last name available. 2. He was not to censor but more so keep certain sensitive information outside my realm of knowledge. He was to make reality-fiction 3. Because I had saved his life one time when he almost drowned when a man tried to drown him. He says I hit the guy with a board and helped him get away and run from the man.

The reader must understand that Paul and West Lee occupy the same body. West Lee was being conditioned when his main alter surfaced and hit the man with a board. Then together they ran.

West Lee then asked me to tell the following story about him. He is completely aware of all of my life as Paul or any other alter, who has lived in my outward appearing life. He has tried to help me thru Mikey, who when I thought we had integrated, he was actually helping Mikey get things put together: West Lee is very bright with a IQ of a Genius (unless he has to spell words). He can use most any object as a weapon and can create deadly or harmful chemicals out of common household chemicals.

He does not like to harm people but is trained in assassination skills and tactics.

West Lee then proceeds to tell Paul how to poison someone with a mushroom, how to use chloroform to disable a human, and how to make napalm using aluminum salt, laundry soap and gasoline, he lists poison after poison... such as uses for mustard gas. At the time this document was done Paul was around 14 to 15 years old. He had participated in satanic sacrifices, murders of a children, the kidnapping of Johnny Gosch and had received two special tours of the White House for his services. (See Conspiracy of Silence)

The Courier

Paul Bonnaci lived thru hell. In granting him a million-dollar judgment against an imprisoned Larry King. Judge Urbom declared, "He has suffered burns, broken fingers, beatings of the head and face and other indignities over a period of eight years. He gave up a desired military career and received threats on his life. He is a victim of multiple personality disorder, involving as many as fourteen distinct personalities.

Judge Urbom stated: "the plaintiff was subjected to repeated sexual assault, false imprisonment, infliction of extreme emotion distress, organized and directed satanic rituals, force the plaintiff to "scavenge" for children to be a part of the defendant King's sexual abuse and pornography ring, forced the plaintiff to engage in numerous sexual contacts with the defendant King and others and participate in deviate sexual games and masochistic orgies with other minor children".

This is a judgment for Paul Bonacci, Memorandum of Decision by United States District Court Judge Urbom on Feb 22, 1999. Note that he does say Bonacci participated in satanic rituals (many that resulted in the death of an adult or child). Remember Judge Urbom states Bonacci is truthful.

If Bonacci's statement concerning the kidnapping of Johnny Gosch is truth, and the satanic murders are truthful.... Why then has the West Des Moines Police, FBI and Governor Vilsack of Iowa chosen to ignore this information. Could it be Vilsack's close connection with former Governor Bob Kerrey of Nebraska? Could it be the WDMPD is protecting someone? Is the FBI negligent or criminally involved? This is clearly new evidence in the Johnny Gosch case and should have been investigated immediately following the ruling of Judge Urbom on February 22, 1999.

Bonacci telephoned me late one night, in March 1999, telling me that "Mike" one of the boys, who acted as "a courier", would be traveling through Omaha within 48 hours.... If I wanted to send a message to Johnny, I needed to overnight something the following day.

I did write a letter to Johnny and sent some family photos it was a few days later, Paul called me to tell me the message had been picked up at the drop point. He said it might take weeks before there would be a reply. Along with my letter, I had sent some family photos, thinking it might bring a response faster. I had also asked Johnny to designate a meeting place somewhere in the country and I would be there. It was at the time 20/20 was finishing their filming and they had pressured me to get him on film either through a video or photo... they felt it would be more compelling to have him tell a part of the story. It was explained that I could video him and yet not reveal his location.

I received a verbal response through Paul, telling me that they (the boys) had a meeting and it was decided they would all remain in hiding. They felt even though they could and would trust me, it was too much of a risk to their lives, as I would have no doubt been followed. There was then a statement ...commenting on something in one of the family photo's I had sent, which told me Johnny had seen the message and it was really him responding through Bonacci.

Paul Bonacci had the attributes of a leader. The other boys looked to him. Johnny Gosch and others communicated with and thru him. In one of the letters he had shown me, it said; J.G. had plastic surgery in Mexico and went back to being a blonde. What follows is a letter from one of those who escaped what we suspect is Project Monarch and has found refuge with Kansas City Satanists.

It is postmarked from Kansas City, Missouri Aug 20, 1992 and sent to Bonacci in Nebraska with no return address.

The post office stamped: "All mail must have a full name and return address Per DCS Rule, etc. It begins:

Dear Paul:

I wanted to let you know I am doing well. I am with friends here in Mizzou. They got Dicky and almost Lester, but Lester got away. Ricky is so doped he can't get away.

Our friends MC and MT both are well. They travel lots and so it's tough to spot them. Your nemesis Reme ask Jamy. Jamy is dying in some foreign hospital of aids. MT want's Jamy to get you his letter from a few years ago.

I know you as Paul, Pablo, Jamy and Mikey, or Poppy the Jungle Boy. Ask Mikey about Poppy (referring to one of Paul's alters ap parently)

That stuff I gave C was heavy to get all those cruds. They won't get me that's sure enough. I can't write my name or address since I'm moving around all the time.

We will come to you when it's safe. It's safe for you because they are more scared of you if you're killed. Strange, right!

You will have to ask Jamy to decode this letter since I use int. I work doing odd jobs and get paid under the table. I don't even exist to anyone. I as Jamy knows was raised to be sacrificed (see The Finders) Born in a house so if no one can trace me that's why. My parents are protected by the FBI who works inside the Church of California, LaVey's group. They are planning to get a child from the Chicago area in September for the fall Solstice. They will take anyone now, so it may end up a street boy. I am a victim and so is MT and MK. They tried to get a kid from Omaha for the summer solstice. They didn't though. They got one from someplace in the south. I think a couple gave up to the police, they wouldn't say it was a sacrifice thought I bet.

Well, I got to go for now. I will write more when I get something new.

Your Friend

P.S. Enclosed is a bad photo of me at 9. Bet you didn't know my hair was brown. A friend of mine got me this picture. The back was torn off, O, well. (Probably identification—many of these kids do not know who they are or where they came from)

At times Paul is able to send messages to Johnny Gosch and other communicate thru him. Note that his friend thinks the publicity is what has kept Paul alive.

WHY JOHNNY CAN'T COME HOME!

FEDERAL FORENSIC ASSOCIATES, INC.

Post Office Box 31567 · Raleigh, North Carolina 27612 · (919) 848-3696

January 14, 1991

Barbara J. Erickson
Handwriting Examiner
P.O. Box 1618
Scottsbluff, NE 69363-1618

RE: 1983 Appointment Book - Ink Examination

Exhibits

A   1983 Appointment Book with the months January and February removed and the printed numbers changed.

REPORT OF LABORATORY EXAMINATION

A chemical and physical examination was performed on the written entries of the referenced exhibit with the following results.

1. A total of five (5) different ink formulations were found in the exhibit. Three (3) blue ball pen, One (1) black ball pen and One (1) black Non-ball pen.

2. All of the above referenced ink formulations, except for the black non-ball pen, are similar to standard ink formulations which were available in 1983. The black non-ball pen ink formulation is similar to one manufactured by the Papermate Pen Co. and available as the Accupoint Pen. The first availability date of this instrument is being researched at this date, but is believed to be in the mid-1980's. For this reason the fact that the days in the exhibit have been altered to reflect the days of 1985 is significant. Results of this inquiry will be forwarded at the earliest possible moment.

3. A relative aging examination was performed between several entries of the exhibit and known dated writings of the same ink formulations maintained in this laboratory. Results of this examination were either inconclusive in nature or indicated that the exhibit was not prepared within the last 1.5 years. A more specific determination of preparation date could not be made.

Bonacci grieves for all the other children who were kidnapped, raped and abused for the Monarch program/MKUltra. He has done his best at great risk to right the wrongs.

A MAN CALLED RUSTY

It is hard to believe that even as we complete this book actions are being taken to silence those who have knowledge of the Franklin Affair and the kidnapping of Johnny. Phones are ringing, faxes are faxing. The Internet is alive with new information on Rusty Nelson?

If one picture is worth a thousand words, then Rusty is the man to turn to because he has been the chief photographer for Larry (Lawrence King). King ran a child prostitution and blackmail ring. King's connections are to the highest officials in this land and to Craig Spence identified by the newspaper "The Washington Times" as CIA connected. Spence dabbled in child kidnapping, to supply the needs of his many customers, which included CIA's once highly secret MK Ultra/Monarch Project. The July 29, 1989, The Washington Times front-page article screamed. "Call Boys Given Midnight Tour of White House"

The Times said all kinds of investigations were going on. The FBI, the Secret Service, and the Washington Metropolitan Police all were involved. Toward the end of the story, the paper stated: "It is suspected that children are being kidnapped off the streets of America and forced into prostitution and other perversions."

According to Paul Rodriguez who co-authored the above article, the paper eventually did sixty stories. "Rodriguez: We were able to do it through the mother lode provided us of credit cards receipts and cancelled checks. And then lists of the clients. The prosecutors had all this stuff... there were possibly 20,000 documents. They sealed the entire record by court order." All material gathered by all branches of law enforcement were also sealed. Rodriguez describes for the viewers of "Conspiracy of Silence" how this was done.

Here's how Ted L. Gunderson, former Senior Officer in Charge of FBI operations in California sees this situation. Since his retirement, he has been relentlessly tracking down those who abuse children whether in the name of Satan/CIA, the North American Man Boy Love Association, or like Larry King for fun profit and blackmail.

"Russell (Rusty) was a central character in the original Franklin Credit Union scandal, which occurred approximately ten years ago. Since then, he has had in his possession large amounts of physical evidence, including photographs, that implicate prominent law enforcement and political figures in crimes of child abuse, child pornography, and kidnapping, drug smuggling, money laundering, and illegal campaign financing. This also appear to be tied to the Iran Contra drugs for arms affair and illegal activities by the FBI and CIA. In Rusty Nelson 's statement of June 22, 2000, He also implicates some of the highest political figures in this country.

Over the years, much of his evidence has been confiscated from Rusty Nelson and never returned. Some of it remains hidden.

Rusty Nelson was on probation from Oregon and working in Nebraska since February 7, 1999, when he testified in Nebraska on behalf of Paul Bonacci in a civil suit against Larry King, a central figure/perpetrator in the above activities. (Bonacci was awarded 1 million in damages) In May 2000, Rusty Nelson was taken into custody for a "probation violation" with no explanation as to the nature of violation. On June 19, 2000, an extradition hearing was heard at Columbus, Nebraska. Neither the persecuting attorney nor the public defender were informed of the details of the probation violation. Rusty Nelson was not present during the hearing. John De Camp, Rusty's lawyer, reports that the hearing was initially scheduled for July 6,

2000, but it was moved up to June 19 without notifying interested parties. The outcome of the hearing was that Judge Frank Skorupa, Platte Count Court in Nebraska ordered Nelson returned to Oregon."

This was part of a report entitled "Russell Nelson…Waiting to Be Killed published on the World Wide Web. On June 28, 2000, while John DeCamp was out of the country when authorities shipped Rusty back to Oregon.

Larry King minced no words on those around him and told them he could have them killed and it would be declared a suicide. Both Alisha Owens and Troy Boner lost brother's to so called suicides after they spoke out too loudly of the sexual abuse the had endured and observed.

In the United States we never think of an individual as a "political prisoner". But Russell Nelson and a number of other witnesses connected to the Franklin Credit Union investigation certainly fit that category. It was significant that the officials chose to move Rusty while DeCamp was out of the country. DeCamp was the only defender for Rusty in Nebraska.

In 1988, John DeCamp, received a call from a detective in the Oregon State Patrol, who advised him they had arrested Rusty Nelson. Nelson, they said had in his possession thousands of pictures of children and other items, which the detective described as pornographic.

After several trips to Oregon and a great deal of paperwork, De Camp succeeded in arranging for Rusty to be placed on probation in Oregon, then permitted to return to Nebraska… where on February 5, 1999, he testified as an expert witness as to the involvement of Larry King with Paul Bonnaci.

The pictures taken by Rusty Nelson and obtained from authorities in Oregon were presented in evidence in the civil suit. The judge ruled that De Camp could view them, but that he could not make note of them in any way. The judge then placed a gag order on him…stating he could never reveal their contents under pain of disbarment. The judge stated the pictures could not be made public, as they would destroy the reputations of respectable citizens in the community. After they were reviewed by DeCamp they were permanently sealed by order of the court.

I hope the question is in the reader's mind. If these "respectable citizens" of Nebraska and Washington D.C. were caught in the act of having sex with children, are they indeed a "respectable citizen " who deserve every protection the court can give them. Or are they dirty perverts whose station in life renders them immune from prosecution no matter what their crimes"

Americans know little of the books that are censored due to "national security" or videos which are never broadcast as with "Conspiracy of Silence" or ABC 20/20...The Johnny Gosch Story.

In the Lincoln/Omaha area alone 80 children were identified as part of Larry King child prostitution ring. In Washington DC and other major cities in the country many children are involved in similar circumstances. On March 18, 1999, Rusty was featured on the Richard Boyden Talk show in Kansas City, Mo. KCXL 1140, a talk radio station. Here he discussed former Governor and now U.S., Senator Bob Kerrey's involvement and noted that King also ran a Day Care center in Washington D.C.

John De Camp reported that Rusty's testimony is consistent with that of Paul Bonacci. Bonacci had been used and abused since he was a small child, by priests, by Satanists and by politicians. He has admitted and detailed his participation in the kidnapping of Johnny Gosch in September of 1982. In the "Conspiracy of Silence" video Bonacci reveals that he was given a midnight tour of the White House once in 1981 and again after Johnny's kidnapping. It was arranged by Craig Spence, a so-called lobbyist, whose man service was furnishing young boys to anyone in Washington, who could pay with cash or his government expense account.

Rusty stated as a private photographer for Larry King, his duties included taking photographs surreptitiously of specific people. It was his job to make sure to photograph certain people if they" got together". In his testimony, John De Camp asked Rusty Nelson, "Who was at these parties?"

Nelson replied:" Politicians, dignitaries, wealthy business people... young people and Larry....

Nelson testified that he not only took pictures for King, but secretly kept rolls of film, which he mailed "home to himself. Rusty testified, he secretly also took other incriminating documents, including audiotapes, computer disks, and paper copies of documents including ledgers, without King's knowledge. He testified that he often mailed the documents back to his home, again secretly.

Rusty explains his attempt to retain these documents in his possession for years was insurance that he stayed alive. He testified that Larry King "flat out told me" that he had "taken out a man" named Charlie Rogers and made it look like a suicide; "This was another deal, I believe, through Wadman (then Omaha Chief of Police}" Nelson testified to one direct threat on his life by Larry King, and in the ensuing years, many threats conveyed with symbols that Larry King used to mean: "Drop it. Or you're going to get burned. He testified that he was shot at twice each time following the symbolic message. And in a statement from his cell, he indicated in writing on June 22, 2000, that he had been shot at for a third time.

Gunderson and DeCamp have made it clear that the extra legal maneuvers against Rusty were designed for only one thing... to put Rusty away before he can expose any more important figures in Washington D.C.

It was Rusty Nelson, who gave pictures and other documents to Gary Caradori July 11, 1990, the day of the fatal flight, which killed Caradori and his eight-year-old son A.J.

Caradori called Senator Loren Schmit and told him he had "the smoking gun." Caradori told the Senator he would fly home that night but his plane exploded in mid-air. The wreckage was spread over nearly a mile of cornfield, near the town of Aurora, Illinois. Coincidentally, Wadman, former Omaha Police Chief, had become the new Chief of Police.

A farmer witness said he saw a fireball then heard an explosion. Caradori's briefcase and the rear seat of the plane vanished, but according to Sandy Caradori, her son's backpack came thru virtually intact. She said "the FBI seized the backpack, containing A.J.'s camera, finally after weeks, it was returned to her. The FBI had gotten the pictures developed from the camera " They apparently wanted to verify A.J.'s camera had not been used to take any incriminating photos.

A sheriff's deputy on site began picking up photographs given to Caradori by Rusty…. reportedly of recognizable politicians with children. It was reported there were "porn pictures scattered in the field". The deputy stated the FBI, who told him to leave, snatched the photos from his hands and to keep his mouth shut. The deputy left but did not keep his mouth shut. Less than a year later, he was severely injured in a car crash that killed his wife. He can no longer work. He is not inclined to talk.

The wreckage of the plane was examined on a military base rather than at a location under the control of civilian personnel. The crash was ruled an "accident" by government officials and not an act of sabotage.

June 30th, 2000, Ted Gunderson received a phone call from Pam Purdie, Rusty Nelson's fiancée, acting as John DeCamp's assistant, received daily reports from Rusty by phone. He was only allowed to phone his lawyer, or someone associated with is lawyer. Rusty was transported from Columbus Nebraska to Omaha, Nebraska on June 29th. In route from Columbus to Omaha, his record sheet for taking medication disappeared and authorities were giving him the wrong epileptic medicine at the wrong time.

Purdie reports, he had an epileptic seizure the night of the 29th and injured himself quite seriously but was ignored by authorities. He stated they refused to give him a clean towel to clean up the blood. Rusty believes they transferred him to Omaha because he refused to take a Tuberculosis test. John DeCamp, an attorney assisting Rusty had advised him not to submit to any medical tests or shots. DeCamp feared Rusty might be poisoned or infected.

Pam Purdie stated that Rusty told her his bed was not even five feet long, (Rusty is over six foot tall), he was fed lunch meat that evening which was green. He was fed pancakes with a white powder on top, he was told it was powdered sugar, but when he ate it, he began vomiting repeatedly and not able to even keep water in his stomach. Gunderson suggested in his report that he may have been given a substance, which is a "slow acting poison". I suspect that even dogs were being fed better than Russell Nelson.

Rusty, who suffers from epilepsy was subjected to "sleep deprivation techniques", a bed, which was too small, and the guard knocked on the door every 30 minutes, so his sleep was constantly disturbed. Any interruption or change in routine in addition to medication being withdrawn can bring on epileptic seizures.

July 3rd, Pam Purdie informed Ted Gunderson that Rusty had suddenly been moved from a cell with a five-foot bed to a cell with an eightfoot bed and his meals were much better. They were providing him with his proper medication on schedule. Rusty asked Pam "What is going on…what happened to make this difference in my treatment? All hell broke loose here, all the guards are talking about this case".

Pam Purdie explained to Rusty that… "On July 2nd, Noreen Gosch drove from Des Moines Iowa to Omaha, Nebraska and hand delivered a 53-page report to the Douglas County Detention Center, informing them they were in violation of Rusty Nelson's Civil Rights. The report was prepared by Ted Gunderson." This formal complaint was sent to the White House and to Attorney General Janet Reno, FBI Office Washington, and any other concerned law officer or civil rights advocate, as well as the press and other concerned citizens. In each cover letter to the concerned citizens of this country, we urged them to send this report on to as many people as possible to begin a huge "letter writing campaign" to help keep Rusty alive.

Within 48 hours Rusty Nelson was moved from Omaha, Nebraska to the Correctional Corp. of America, Leavenworth Kansas. Immediately upon hearing of the transfer, Ted Gunderson, contacted Warden Stolc and informed him of the situation. Warden Stolc requested a copy of the 53-page report, it was emailed to him. The Warden specified that Ted should telephone him at seven a.m. Central time in Kansas, which meant Ted had to be up at five a.m. to place the call Pacific time in California. Warden Stolc, reported to Ted Gunderson, that he was shocked at this whole story and assured Ted that Rusty would be watched over and no harm would come to him. Warden Stolc paid a visit to Rusty's cell and assured him of the same. Within a few short days, the treatment of Rusty had once more deteriorated.

Pam Purdie reported that Rusty had been given fermented oatmeal, which bubbled like beer, and he was once again being deprived of his medication to control epileptic seizures. He began to suffer seizures, which lasted twenty minutes each, several times a day. He was running a very high fever and vomiting. Rusty believes these seizures occurred because his medication had been changed for an unknown reason. He is being given Dilantin for his epilepsy of Neurontin, the medicine prescribed by his personal physician, Dr. Anderson, of Columbus, Nebraska. During these seizures, July 10th, he fell to the floor, injured himself and was bleeding. He said a nurse came and checked him and was kind to him. Since his medications were changed, Russell Nelson reports hearing a highpitched sound in his ears and that he can barely see and cannot focus his eyes. These conditions continued at this facility until he was transferred and moved to Oregon on July 13th.

On Saturday July 15th, 2000, John Zielinski made a visit to the facility where Rusty was being held. When he arrived, he was confronted by the head of security, James Perry, showing him a folder with Rusty's name and ID# CCA16582047 ... US Marshall ID#64659065 and asking for Russell Nelson. He was told there was no such prisoner there... they had never heard of him. When he presented his Media ByPass Photo ID, they immediately changed the story to: He was here but he is gone now, therefore we cannot talk about him. Gunderson stated this is standard procedure.

Days went by with no contact or word from Russell "Rusty" Nelson. Ted Gunderson said that in his experience, as an FBI agent it was highly unusual to transport a non-violent, low risk prisoner by car halfway across the United States to Oregon. It was as if they wanted to make sure that Rusty didn't contaminate any other prisoners with his information.

I sent letters to everyone from the President to the Pope stating, Russell Nelson is a key witness Franklin Cover Up and my son's (Johnny Gosch) kidnapping case. Due to the information, he possesses… his life is danger within the prison system of this country. What is happening to Russell is both tragedy and a travesty of justice as was explained in the report by Ted Gunderson.

In his July 12th, Urgent Report on Russell Nelson; Gunderson states these matters need to be brought to the attention to anyone in authority who might be able to assure that Russell Nelson receives proper medical treatment and to prevent him being suspiciously killed through seizures, poisoning, ill ness caused from neglect, bad food, "accident", "suicide" or otherwise. If Russell Nelson dies of suspicious circumstances, these letters from concerned citizens will be evident that the appropriate authorities were notified and their level of response well documented.

It is only through the efforts of concerned citizens that we can preserve our freedom.

The Shadow Knows—Russell Nelson Lawrence E. King, President of the Franklin Credit Union of Omaha, Nebraska was a man of importance. Not just in Omaha, not just in Nebraska but also across America from sea to shining sea.

But Larry King knew how to hustle, soon he was laundering money for the CIA's Iran-Contra operation and by furnishing plenty of boys to NAMBLA, who forked over $5,000,000 to the credit union. Such glorious activity could not go unrecorded so when Larry King met an aspiring young photographer, he immediately made Rusty Nelson his shadow. Where Larry King went…Rusty with camera in hand also went. A four foot photo of Larry King with President Ronald Regan graced the entrance to the Franklin Credit Union.

A MAN CALLED RUSTY

What do you need Senator, Congressmen, Governor, Judge. A little boy? Nebraska Boy's Town provides an ample supply for the discerning pedophile. Coke, Heroin, Speed Balls. Or perhaps a little girl?

His parties were the talk of Washington D.C. He rented a $5,000 a month mansion on embassy row where Rusty had his own room…. a room that allowed him to photograph all activities. Rusty was 23, when he was introduced to King, but he was more than that as he explained in the testimony of Feb 5, 1999 "I was taking pictures at a bar called The Max on 79th Street, in Omaha Nebraska. After a drag show, I had gotten to know pretty much everybody who were regulars like Ron. I was having some financial problems and you know, I needed to find a decent job… Ron goes…I know somebody who could use a good photographer.

…Suddenly here's Larry King, I had no idea who he was, this, that and the next thing. I went and next thing I know I'm on a private jet to Washington, D.C. I sat in Larry's office at the credit union, sat in the meetings he'd have with the people. Seen him make payoffs to people. I watched as King handed over a briefcase full of bearer bonds to Col. Michael Aquino…. in a motel suite… The Ritz in Minneapolis, Minn (Iran Contra Payments) Very quietly.

"I went out and took pictures at his mansion on Embassy Row, where he held the parties" …He wanted me to do porn, kiddie porn and gay porn. (Alisha Owens identified Larry King as the photographer when she was being sexually abused.) I wanted no part of it. And he went to the extent of insisting on my wearing certain clothes, my hair had to be a certain way. They went as far as to take me out, supposedly it was Nancy Reagan's hairdresser doing my hair. It was permed, everything, totally changed my appearance.

Now Rusty goes on to describe another man, who was also a photographer, Larry shorter. He added: "It was just a fluke that I saw him." He went on to say this other man was passing himself off at times as Rusty Nelson, whose appearance was almost identical to his except he was shorter.

Nelson: Yes, I was told to disappear!

DeCamp: Who told you that he was three to four inches shorter. DeCamp asked him: Are you aware of the fact that in testimony before the legislative committee various witnesses, investigator for the state and others effectively denied your existence.

On Feb 25, 1999, Attorney John W DeCamp, who had represented Paul Bonnaci for ten years issued this challenge in a To Whom It May Concern Letter, accompanied by the transcript of the trial.

I believe the U.S. Attorney has no choice but to either CHARGE THE WITNESSES WITH PERJURY HAVING TESTIFIED UNDER OATH IN A FEDERAL COURT ON VERY MATERIAL MATTERS (from Murder to Bribery to Perjury to the vilest corruption involving young people) OR, THE U.S. ATTORNEY HAS AN OBLIGATION TO INVESTIGATE FURTHER INTO THE FRANKLIN SAGA AND REOPEN MATTERS. This

time there ARE PICTURES. This time RUSTY NELSON exists and testified completely contrary to Chief Wadman's (Omaha Chief of Police) testimony under oath to the legislature.

Let us repeat DeCamp: This time there ARE PICTURES!!! But where are the pictures... Judge Urbom has sealed the photos, the audio and videotapes. He has honored the request of Larry King from his jail cell in Colorado, that releasing the photos and tapes would cause harm to the Nebraska community. Who is he kidding.... we would have a mad rush by members of congress to resign. Congressmen Barney Fag would not beat this rap.

DeCamp concludes his letter saying: "If my witnesses in Court on February 5, 1999 are telling the truth... then Alisha Owen is also. If Alisha Owen is LYING as the jury said, then my witnesses are lying. It appears to me to put the U.S Attorney, Nebraska Attorney General and Judicial System on the horns of a dilemma and failure to act would to me at least appear to be a deliberate obstruction of justice at minimum." The pictures which were not are sealed by Judge Urbom .... Have been confiscated by the FBI.

To understand what is going on here you must realize two things. The so-called checks and balances of one branch of government acting as watchdog for the other two branches are no longer true. At both the state and the federal level the Executive, Legislative and Judicial Branch now constitute a gang. A gang sworn to defend each other on pain of death. Like the Mafia anyone who squeals is a marked man. Unlike the Mafia, who used to sink their defectors in cement shoes and drop them in the river, the ruling elite prefer blacklists. It often means, they will never work again in their chosen professions. More than a few whistleblowers have gone from six-figure jobs to being homeless and on the street.

What about the bill of rights, both state and federal, which grants an individual the right to "due process"? These rights have been replaced by the law of "judicial sovereignty" any judge may rule for his friends regardless of evidence presented. If the opposing attorney objects—at worst he will be disbarred and best him, might have to find a job at McDonalds to help support his family.

There are many people who claim: "Well at least America is better than other countries." Not so. The murder rate in America is 73 times higher than the murder rate of any other country in the Western World. Nine out of ten children murdered anywhere in the Industrial world are murder in the U.S. Children in Northern Ireland are far safer in school than those in Chicago."

RUSSELL "RUSTY" NELSON

Sign outside Larry King's house in D.C.

The house Larry King rented on Embassy Row.... where he held all of his "parties". This is where Rusty was stationed to photograph all the "Activities' at the parties. And the parties "after the parties.

Caradori Story Published, "The Ralston Recorder, Jan 10, 1985, shows Caradori to be an excellent investigator with worldwide connections. FBI Agent Says "Caradori work suspicious June 11, 1991"…...states The Omaha World Herald.

For private investigator Gary Caradori, the mean streets aren't in Lincoln. They're in Chandler's L.A. and Mickey Spillane's New York City—places where the hostile exterior only masks an even more violent interior.

The 35-year-old Caradori, born and raised in Ralston and a 1967 Ralston High School graduate, specializes in finding people….stolen kids, lost adults, in particular, teen-age prostitutes, and bringing them home. The consequences of his work could be fatal.

"They would kill you. Those young gals are worth a lot of money. That's their hardware. It's hard for people to understand that living here, "Caradori said. *"In some places in Los Angeles, Detroit or Florida, there are people out there that would cut your throat"*

When you start running around the streets of New York, in the Harlem area, in a lot of areas. I could name a hundred towns, don't think you're not thinking about those things. It's a lot different than going to a movie here in town

Leave Yourself and Out.

"You don't try to come on strong. A good investigator will blend in. The idea is no one will really know you're here. You just kind of slip in get done whatever you have to do and get out." Caradori said, "You go with whatever you're working with. You won't do anything people will want to remember."

Caradori said he's been roughed up a few times by both cops and cons, but unlike the TV operative, he's never had to shoot his way out of a jam.

"A couple of times I thought: "Maybe I'll have to use it (a gun) to get myself out of a situation. But I never have. That just comes from common sense and trying to leave yourself an out."

Good Investigative Techniques

Most detective work boils down to good investigative techniques. Although he couldn't share trade secrets or discuss specific cases, Caradori described how he and his partner, Mike Weatherl, go about their work.

We have a set of items we go through when we start out looking for somebody. Some of it pans out and some of it doesn't," he said "We do a complete psychological background on an individual before we even start, to get their makeup and pattern.

You have to put yourself in that individual's condition prior to leaving, trying to determine where they might go and what their thinking was. We have built a network of contacts all over the country. Those contacts are worth their weight in gold that really helps. You don't just walk in or fly in to some location and people just give you things. It comes with the rapport you've made with those individuals; it comes with your professionalism with certain individuals.

The bottom line is to have the ability to look in all directions and not have tunnel vision. Never assume anything and never take no for an answer. So you rely on your investigative knowledge and you really come to rely on yourself and you always try to leave a way out. Leave the door open so you can get the hell out."

Made ABC News

When it comes time to get the person out of town, particularly in the case of the young prostitutes, the key is to move fast and be very mobile, Caradori said. "In some cases, two or three vehicles and airplanes have been necessary to stay ahead of the game."

Caradori was successful making ABC news five months ago for finding two children, who disappeared 11 years ago. In another widely reported case, Caradori found a woman's father in East Germany 39 years after they were separated.

Home is a Sanctuary

The risk of being hurt is real, Caradori said.

"People sometimes they want to get back at you. Last year, I had a guy threaten to kill my kids. I guess that goes with the territory. However, that doesn't mean you don't take the necessary precautions to prevent that and you certainly don't want to look for it." Caradori said. "We try not to take those kinds of cases where we live. It's kind of a rule with us. You don't want to look over your shoulder every time you turn around." For that reason, only about 20 percent of Caradori's business is in Nebraska...primarily corporate security, while most of his missing person's work is out of state. That makes it possible for him to return home, away from the mean streets to relative safety and security of Nebraska. "People don't even lock their doors here, so there's a lot to teach them about security. Lincoln is a good community to live in. Who wants to hassle with the crime problems of Detroit and L.A.?

"It's always good to get home. This is like a sanctuary," the investigator concluded.

This was more than four years before he was hired by the Nebraska Legislator to investigate the Franklin Credit Union Franklin. He learned that Lincoln and Omaha had mean streets as well. He and his son would pay with their lives for trying to help the child prostitutes of Nebraska. He told his wife Sandy, just before his death, "I know what happened to Johnny Gosch!"

Above: Sandra Caradori
Below: Her son A.J. (eight years old)

The death of Gary Caradori and his son, A.J. sealed the fate of the Franklin Investigation. "There were a lot of people who wanted to see Gary dead" ....said Sen. Loren Schmit.

JOHN DECAMP...
RELUCTANT HERO

It is hard to say what John De Camp is most proud of—his 16 years as a Nebraska State Senator or his life since his downfall—trying to protect eighty sexually abused young people and awaken a sleeping nation to the corruption he uncovered.

John DeCamp is not your usual kind of hero... in his present life he appears unassuming, and yet out of desperation and the need to survive, he has written a book to awaken *the conscience of the nation.* "The Franklin Cover-up" now in its second revised and expanded printing is a labor of frustration and of necessity. It was friend and mentor Colonel William Colby, his one-time boss in Viet Nam later head of the CIA, who inspired this book.

It was undoubtedly DeCamps suggestion to state Senator Loren Schmitt that they hire Colby to determine who or what caused the death of Legislative investigator Gary Caradori and his eight year old son A. J.. DeCamp in the forward to the first edition of "The Franklin Cover-up" quotes Colby:

Colby said, "What you have to understand, John, is that sometimes there are forces and events too big, too powerful, with so much at stake for other people or institutions. That you cannot do anything about them, no matter how evil or wrong they are or how much evidence you have…that is simply one of the hard facts of life you must face. You have done your part. You have tried to expose the evil and wrongdoing. It has hurt you terribly. But it has not killed you up to this point. I am telling you, get out of this before it does. Sometimes things are just too big for us to deal with, and we must step aside and let history take its course. For you, John, this is one of those times."

Although this Colby statement would seem to be preaching John DeCamp, to forget it! Decamp sets the record straight in the revised edition of his book in the Chapter "In Memoriam Bill Colby."

"More than once, I was determined to put Franklin behind me, and write it off as a horrible experience that I could do nothing about. Often, I would ask myself, "Why should I have any responsibility to do something, when others in positions of power and government responsibility do nothing? I know that Senator Schmit…felt the same way. I told Bill one time "I have done all I can do and have been burned badly— financially and credibility-wise—and I am sure politically. I think it's time to just let it drop."

It was at those times that Bill Colby kept encouraging me and Senator Schmit, kept pushing us, almost forcing us to keep going, and to keep the press apprised. To quote his exact words: *"This case is so much bigger than you think. It goes to the very highest levels; we have to keeping pulling the strings."* His idea was not to investigate further— which he repeatedly warned me could be very dangerous—as to shine the sharp glare of publicity onto what had already been discovered to create the possibility of a real investigation.

It is a story of our government at both state and federal levels running amuck …child sexual abuse, Satanism and murder…is this what any Governor or Congressmen should be about? If they are not directly involved, they are willing to go to almost any length to cover it up.

DeCamp points the finger at Nebraska Governor Bob Kerrey, who became U.S. Senator. DeCamp reports in his book, The Franklin Cover Up that Kerrey was not only involved in the cover-up but may well have been involved in the crime. Kerrey in turn helped Iowa's Democratic Governor Tom Vilsack become elected. To return the favor, Kerrey sister Jessie Rasmussen, in charge of the Nebraska Department of Health and Human services from 97-99 was hired to run the Iowa Department of Human Services.

John De Camp served 16 years as a Senator in the Nebraska Unicameral, some of the time side by side with State Senator Bob Kerrey. At one time, De Camp considered him a friend, they were fellow Viet Nam veterans, but DeCamp began to find him less than honorable. There is an old saying: "If you are not part of the solution, then you are part of the problem." Bob Kerrey is not just a corrupt politician covering for his peers, he himself is directly involved according to Larry King's photographer. Rusty Nelson photographed him at the punch bowl full of white powder. Who knows what other recreational activities Kerrey participated in at King's house on embassy row in Washington D.C.. (See A Man Called Rusty) King maintained a stable of child prostitutes both boys and girls. While his business partner, Craig Spence reported to be with the CIA, supplied young men, some aged fourteen years old, for a discerning clientele in D.C. especially Congress, the White House and the Pentagon.

Because of the enormous growth of AIDS in children and reports of Satanism in Nebraska. Was Rasmussen's job in part to hold the line and not let the information become public? Her performance is under scrutiny in Iowa. The politicians behind Project Monarch aimed to dissolve the American family. What better way to do it than to control state by state the Department of Human Services, which is supposed to aid and protect children.

During August and September of 2000 one only needs to read the local Des Moines papers to see children dying or being badly injured because the

DHS didn't do its job. Rasmussen cries for more money while paying consulting fees of $5,000 a week to have her department evaluated.

September 17th, 2000, Des Moines Sunday Register reports nine children have died, all cases of abuse had been reported to DHS, prior to their deaths. Serious questions are being raised about the policies of DHS under its current director, Jesse Rasmussen. Brent Siegrist, Speaker of the Iowa House, called for further investigation of the conduct of DHS and Rasmussen in handling child abuse cases in Iowa. DHS director, Jesse Rasmussen has just asked the State Legislature for additional millions to properly protect children.

John DeCamp is a lawyer and an honest man—a patriotic man. Among those who despise lawyers, there is an old joke. Two men are walking in a graveyard when one spots a head stone. Here lies a lawyer and an honest man. Look said the other; they buried two men in the same grave. John DeCamp is an exception—he really cares for his God his country and its people.

DeCamp has taken up the causes of street kids, because he once was one. DeCamp has exposed the sexual abuse of children at Boy's Town because he once lived there. At thirteen his parents divorced. In his own words: "I split." He headed for Minneapolis where he was living on the streets. Police picked him up and a judge offered him two choices the Crosier Fathers or reform school. He took the priest and stayed with them over two years. Returning to Nebraska, he was still to young to be on his own and ended up in Boys Town.

He went to college and graduate from Law School before going to Viet Nam. Despite the fresh law degree, he requested a combat assignment. DeCamp spent 1969-1970 as a Combat Infantry Captain in the Mekong Delta. DeCamp was detailed to work directly under Ambassador William E. Colby, who was actually CIA Chief for S.E. Asia. Colby and DeCamp both Catholics, sharing similar views became friends. Colby was to be his mentor and friend over the years. Colby later became director of the CIA under President Nixon and later Ford.

Disillusioned with how the war was being fought DeCamp became a minor celebrity when in an open letter, from the battlefield "Let Us Win or Get Us Out" demand. The World Press picked up on it and it became the campaign slogan that allowed him to successfully campaign for the Nebraska Senate seat, from the rice paddies of Vietnam.

In 1975, as Saigon was collapsing and the North Vietnamese Communist were invading, Senator DeCamp again made military and political history. DeCamp boarded a plane, returned to Viet Nam and organized what would be called "Operation Baby Lift" humanitarian rescue mission in which 2834 half-American, half Vietnamese orphans were brought to this country.

For this work, Senator DeCamp was honored and decorated by the President at the White House and was named one of the Eight Most Outstanding Vietnam War Veterans by the Veterans support group. DeCamp always a veterans' advocate is one of two Nebraska Attorney licensed to practice before the U.S. Court of Veterans Appeals.

DeCamp had a stellar career in Nebraska. He was a delegate to the 1988 Republican Party convention. He had no idea that Larry King was there with an entourage of children to satisfy the desires of politicians and fellow delegates. A $100,000 party is given under the auspices of the Council of Minority Americans formed in May of 1988 with Alexander Haig, Jack Kemp, and Former Pres. Gerald Ford on its committee.

Back in Nebraska, Carol Stitt with the Foster Care Review Board is giving information to the Nebraska Attorney General Robert Spires relating to child sexual abuse. She had specific instructions from Nebraska Governor Orr, to pursue further investigations, which include not only foster care abuse but Boy's Town., the Girls Town.

What John De Camp did not realize was that the seeds of his own downfall were being sown around him. He had gone from a much touted (by the News Media of Nebraska) successful politician to a successful lobbyist but all this was about to change, and he would lose eighty percent of his business and must consider it lucky, that he did not lose his life in the process.

On Nov 4, 1988, the FBI and IRS raided the Franklin Credit Union of Omaha run by Larry King, who despite his $17,000 a year salary managed to throw frequent elaborate parties in Washington D.C. On December 25th, 1988 the State Foster Care Review Board turns over to the Executive Board of the Nebraska Legislator, a foot high pile of reports of sexual abuse of children. Two seemingly unrelated items were to unite and create the greatest explosion that ever-hit Nebraska.

THE INDICTMENT AND CONVICTION OF ALISHA OWEN FOR PERJURY

Is It Constitutional? Is it Legal? Is it Valid?

There are 3 main points of law that would indicate a justification to set aside the guilty verdict of perjury, in the recent court case of Alisha Owen. Perjury is legally defined as: "willful lying under oath".

The FIRST point of Law being Amendment V of the U.S .Constitution. The Operative phase being "nor shall be compelled in any criminal case to be a witness against himself." Alisha was under the compulsion of a subpoena and Neb. State Law 1977 LB 38 156, to testify as to her knowledge of child abuse in connection with the Franklin Credit Union Case. 2. Alisha was not advised of her rights prior to testimony before the Grand Jury.

The second point of Law being: Nebraska State Law 1977, LB38 156 28711 "When any physician, medical institution, nurse, school employee, social worker, or other person has reasonable cause to believe that a child has been subjected to abuse or neglect or observes such child being subjected to conditions or circumstances which reasonably would result in abuse or neglect. He or she shall report such an incident or cause a report to be made to the proper law enforcement agency.

Under this statute, based on what Alisha saw and experienced herself and of what she had seen other children experience, Alisha had reasonable cause to believe that she herself, and other children were being subjected to child abuse.

Nebraska State Law 28 716 declares that any person making such a report or participating in an investigation shall be immune from civil, or criminal liability for making maliciously false statements. Alisha should have been granted immunity for her testimony.

28-717 Violations: Penalty. Any person who willfully fails to make any report required by the provisions of sections 28-710 to 28-717…shall be guilty of a class III misdemeanor. Alisha could have been liable under this law for failure to tell what she knew about child abuse in the Franklin Case.

The third point of Law being: The Douglas County Grand Jury was charged to specifically make a determination whether there was enough evidence to support an indictment of the individuals named as perpetrators in the allegations from the 'victim witness' reports of child abuse in connection with the Franklin child abuse investigation. The Grand Jury did not have legal jurisdiction to indict the witnesses to this case. The powers granted to grand juries are very specific and limited for good reason.

The grand jury in any case failed to offer any evidence of perjury by Alisha. The Grand Jury speculated that there may have been some business arrangement between Alisha Owen, Mike Casey and Gary Caradori (Investigator hired by the Franklin Committee). This alleged motive has no basis in fact or evidence. The grant jury is charged with the duty of finding evidence to indict for the crime.

THE EVIDENCE IS:

1. Alisha has never contracted with any firm or person for the purpose of "selling her story."
2. She has never granted ANY interviews to ANY reporters or ANY magazine, television or newspaper.

3. It is not proven that Alisha had any relationship but one of casual acquaintance with Mike Casey. (Sometime local freelance writer)
4. Paul Bonacci made the same types of allegations against the same people in 1986. This was 3 years prior to the formation of the Franklin Committee. Paul made these allegations to the Omaha Public School, Omaha Police Department and Nebraska Psychiatric Institute. These are some of the institutions named in his civil suit for deprivation of civil rights and negligence, because of their alleged lack of attention to his allegations. This supports Alisha's testimony and also shows that her testimony was not initiated because of some corroborative effort between Alisha and Mike Casey, the legislative committee, and Gary Caridori.

It appears evident that it was a violation of Alisha's Fifth Amendment Rights to be charged with perjury as the result of her compelled testimony before the Grand Jury. It is unheard of in the United States to bring an indictment of perjury against a victim witness of a Grand Jury, **and much more bring that indictment on the basis of a compelled testimony to that Grand Jury.**

Secondly, the Douglas County Grand Jury was charged to specifically make a determination whether there was enough evidence to support indictment of the individuals named as perpetrators in the allegations from the victim witnesses" reports of child abuse in connection with the **Franklin Child abuse investigation.** Never in the history of Nebraska has a Grand Jury attempted, or much more, succeeded in bringing an indictment against someone who did not fall under the scope of their charge of duty.

Thirdly, we believe that she should have been granted immunity under LB 28-716. We believe that a person in her situation is just what this law was created for. **The public needs to know that never in the history of Nebraska has such a travesty of justice occurred.** Perhaps that is because in Nebraska the courts have followed the rule of state and federal constitutional law.

This travesty of justice certainly gives credence to the thought that perhaps the Douglas County Grand Jury was manned as an instrument to punish and silence the victims of these terrible crimes and to protect prominent and powerful alleged perpetrators, as well as send a message to any other victims. This message has been heard very loud and clear.

John DeCamp is a man who has faced the ultimate frustration. The laws of this country and his birth State of Nebraska have failed the very people they are designed to serve. The actions of the courts, of the Governors, Legislators, U.S. Senators, Representative, FBI, police and sheriffs departments have made a mockery of his years of service to his country, in the military and to the State of Nebraska in 16 years' service in the Legislature.

The people he sought to serve were cowered and manipulated to imprison the very children who were being harmed while the very guilty sexual perverts and deviants were being celebrated almost as heroes for the ability to beat down and jail their accusers. In the words of William Colby "there are forces and events too big, too powerful with so much at stake for other people or institutions, that you cannot do anything about them, no matter how evil or wrong they are and no matter how dedicated or sincere you are or how much evidence you have."

If there is a Nebraska Hall of Fame, an honor roll of heros, then John DeCamp deserves that special high place among them. In more than 12 years he has done battle with the corrupt system of Nebraska. He has often been knocked down but like Rocky Balboa, he never failed to get up and continue to fight.

William Colby

The following materials are excerpts from:
"Secret Agenda Operation PaperClip Linda Hunt

"Blank Check: Pentagon's Black Budget" p-132-33 Tom Weiner

William Colby entered John DeCamps life, while he was in Viet Nam serving as a Captain in Military Intelligence. Colby was chief of CIA's far eastern division from 1962-67. Since the 1950s Colby had been involved in CIA clandestine operations.

Quoting from Tom Weiner's book: "He took time out only to run the Phoenix program, a civilian led counter-insurgency operation that had led to the death of more than 20,000 Vietnamese." In reality this was a joint military/CIA operation that made the Mafia Murder Inc. look like child's play. I have personally talked to ex-soldiers, marksmen, who had a civilian CIA man, stand behind him with a cocked pistol saying: "See that old man in the village below. Kill him or I will blow your brains out!" This was Project Phoenix in action. Anyone who was remotely suspected as a leader in the small villages in Viet Nam was marked for death by execution from afar. According to Wiener the number in which the CIA acted as judge, jury and executioner was at least 20,000.

No war before Viet Nam has produced the number of post-traumatic stressed syndromes, as has the Viet Nam war. The number of those killed in Viet Nam exceeded 50,000. The number of Viet Nam vets, who have since committed suicide exceed to the number killed in action. A company clerk in Vietnam, who handled the personnel files, reported, the CIA scoured records looking for psychos, which were put into a special division. The clerk remembers the CIA co-opting the printing presses used to make up multiple copies of new directives etc. When he returned, he found in the trash discards with satanic symbols on them. He was forced to accompany a group of soldiers once, but he remembers nothing of it except leaving and coming back. But he does know that the psycho units murdered and pillaged, did not hesitate to bash in the head of children before raping the mothers and then killing them.

These were part of the CIA operations that William Colby commanded during part of that war. They were part also of Captain John DeCamp's job. How then was this a counter-insurgency movement, which suggests

Vietnamese killing Vietnamese? They might indeed have had a part in it but it was the CIA that acted as judge and jury, and then supplied the executioner. There is no record of how many men were killed rather than be forced to kill from ambush, civilian.

Here is Tom Weiner's description of Colby "Colby was a graduate.

of Princeton, Princetonian in his demeanor and speech: proper, almost patrician, in bearing; mild manner but capable of being cold blooded…

Colby's family background was military and devoutly Roman Catholic; both facts are clue to his apostasy. He would follow any legitimate order. "

It should be noted here that like all employees, he was subjected to a mild form of mind control propaganda, which suggested that even dirty deadly deeds were possible in the service of country for the protection of national security. It was the National Security Act of 1947, that allowed the CIA to begin using any or all of the American population as a kind of laboratory animal preserve for trying out various means of mind control, both individual and in groups.

The CIA and another secret covert operation behind the government have infected whole towns with airborne virus designed to test the ability of infrastructure to sustain itself. Author Leonard Horowitz in his "Aids and Ebola" book produces documentary evidence that individuals and organization—including Universities under government contract produced the AIDS virus and set about disseminating it to promiscuous homosexual before including it in a hepatitis B vaccine and inoculated half of Africa.

In April 1971, Richard Helms, Director of the CIA gave a speech to the Society of Newspaper Editors. In which he declared "take it on faith that we too are honorable men." Four years later it fell to then Director Colby to admit that Helms had lied to Congress. From this point Colby was no longer well respected in the Intelligence community. He had committed the unpardonable sin, he told Congress the truth.

WHY JOHNNY CAN'T COME HOME!

**WILLIAM COLBY... FORMER DIRECTOR OF THE
CIA SHOWN IN "CONSPIRACY OF SILENCE"
A BRITISH DOCUMENTARY...BANNED IN AMERICA**

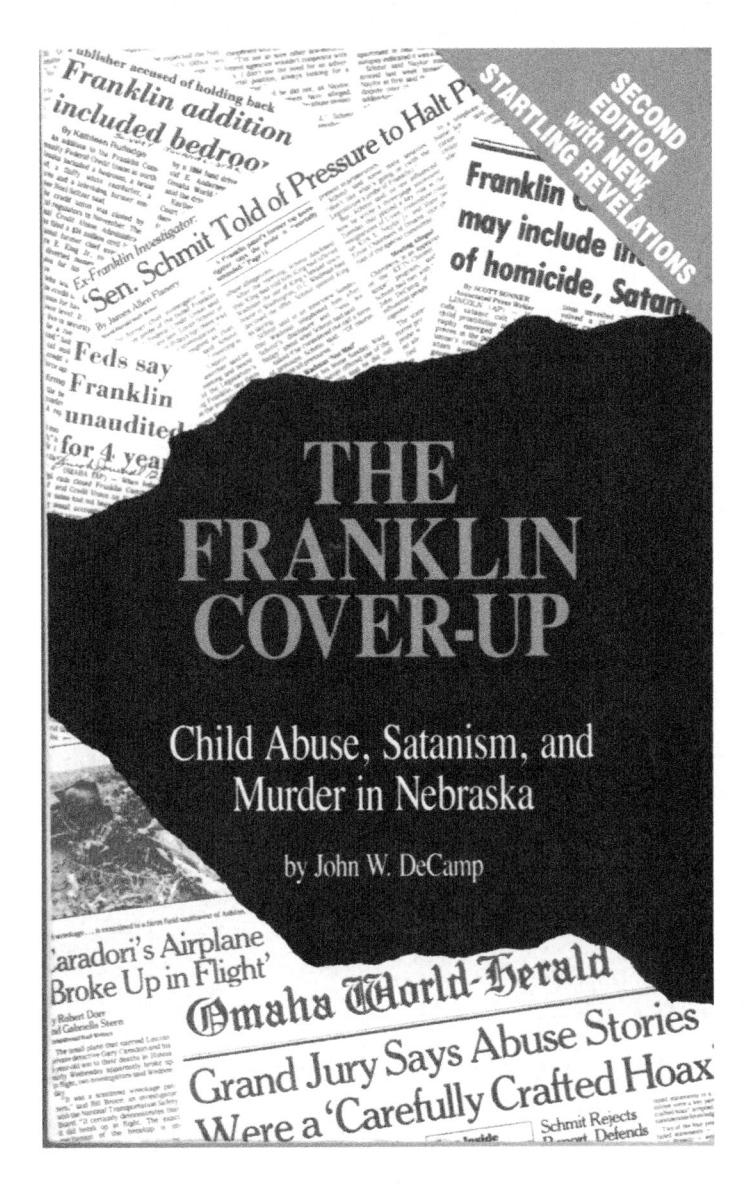

THE FRANKLIN COVER UP IS AVAILABLE AT: AWT, INC.
P.O. BOX 85461
LINCOLN, NE 68501

EMAIL: decamplegal@inebraska.com
$9.95 plus postage/handling $3.25

WHY JOHNNY CAN'T COME HOME!

Above: John DeCamp at his office in Lincoln, NE Below:
DeCamp with Paul Bonacci, outside the White House...
See Conspiracy of Silence

TED L. GUNDERSON, FBI SPECIAL AGENT IN CHARGE LOS ANGELES, RET.

TED GUNDERSON – MAN WITH A MISSION

The Real FBI Story

Ted L. Gunderson retired from the FBI in 1979 after 28 years. He was head of the Los Angeles Bureau of the FBI at the time, covering not only L.A but also a large section of California. Ted looked forward to forming a lucrative Private Investigative Practice and bouncing his grandchildren on his knees. Instead, 21 years later, some regard him as a kook and crazy conspiracy theorist. Gunderson chose to put his time and energy into investigating the unthinkable that in America women and children were victims of Satanic and pedophilic abuse. The pursuit of the truth has cost him a great deal!

For those of you who are old enough to remember Efrem Zimbalist Jr. in The FBI Story, which aired in the late 60s early 70s, you have a perfect picture of FBI Man Ted Gunderson. His job was to preserve and protect the public not to protect high ranking political pedophiles.

When Gunderson retired in 1979, he formed Ted L. Gunderson and Associates, of Santa Monica, California, an international security consulting and investigation firm. World-renowned trial lawyer F. Lee Bailey often hired Gunderson's firm. Bailey describes him as "a person whose investigative skills are unsurpassed by anyone I know or have known."

In 1979, just after his retirement U.S. Attorney General Griffin Bell appointed him special consultant to the Pan America Olympic Games, San Juan, and Puerto Rico. He was a consultant on international terrorism and security matters. In 1981-82, he was appointed by California Governor Jerry Brown and later became a consultant on terrorism and security for the Los Angeles Olympic Committee in 1984.

His service record was exemplary. Yet he has been removed from the Retired FBI Association, primarily because he does his job too well. In his first 9 years, he was in counterintelligence/espionage. But before his retirement, he was the senior agent in charge of Nashville, Dallas and finally in Los Angeles.

Gunderson is an author, lecturer and radio broadcaster. E.P. Dutton published his: "How to Locate Anyone Anywhere Without Leaving Home." He has lectured and published numerous reports and articles on Satanism and missing children. His investigation includes the Oklahoma Bombing and the CIA Drug smuggling.

A retired FBI Man investigating the CIA is not exactly healthy. Gunderson was forced to go underground and eventually lost his business while trying to avoid a series of murder attempts. Gunderson has no difficulty understanding how such death threats could have been lodged against Noreen Gosch. Gunderson has come to realize that the government eliminates its foes...by discrediting or death. Here are his words:

"For the last 20 years, there have been numerous stationery and moving surveillances of me. When I see stationery surveillance, I strap on my gun and confront the individual or individuals. On two occasions, I chased the subjects out of the neighborhood. One ran a red light to get away from me. The individuals involved are probably contracted employees for the CIA, members, I suspect, of the "shadow government". They discontinued stationery surveillance in 1993. Since then, they have

periodically entered my automobile, usually at night, and turned on the directional signal to let me know they have been in my car and are watching me.

On several occasions, they entered my condominium in Las Vegas, at night while I was sleeping and took files from my cabinet. From May 3 to May 10, 2000, while I was in Philadelphia, my condominium was burglarized. There was no forced entry. The suspected CIA burglars took four of my storage boxes of documents, which contained sensitive material and research. I have since been able to replace these. They also stole my FBI memorabilia, cherished items commemorating the days when I worked with my fellow agents on clean operations.

I have been photographed and videotaped on numerous occasions from automobiles and on one occasion on the golf course and on another occasion, at a picnic in a public park. I suspect the individuals taking these pictures are CIA contract employees. I have also received numerous threatening and hang up phone calls. Their favorite phone calls involve the sound of a phonograph needle at the end of a record. I have also received numerous phone calls of individuals chanting on the line. I have recorded these calls. My mail has also been opened and I filed a formal complaint with the postal inspectors.

In May 1993, while driving from Omaha, Nebraska to Lincoln, Nebraska, at 75 miles an hour, my right front wheel came off. I was in Nebraska is working on the Franklin case. I called the Nebraska Highway Patrol. The Patrolman, Officer Lamb, told me the lug nuts on the right front wheel had been loosened, which caused the accident. Fortunately, I was able to control the car. The Repairman later told me that some of the lug nuts on the left front wheel were also loosened, but apparently the intruder was interrupted while loosening the lug nuts, as the others were intact.

ATTEMPTS TO FRAME TED L. GUNDERSON FOR A CRIMINAL VIOLATION

Between March and August 1983, the FBI and DEA attempted to frame Ted Gunderson (this writer) through a girl named Pam Fawsett, an FBI informant. In August 1983, Fawsett called me and said she wanted to meet with me. She told me of her assignment by the FBI, a plot that involved a series of recorded telephone conversations between her and me. She furnished a hand-written note by an agent, which listed the questions she was to ask in one of the phone calls. The agent carelessly forgets to retrieve the note.

During the 6 months she was working with the FBI in an attempt to frame me, she was paid $2000 and had access to the FBI Modesto, California office. She even had her own coffee cup. She then furnished a series of three signed statements, and for documentation, the hand-written note the agent failed to retrieve. When I asked Pam Fawsett, why she came over to my side, she told me, "Ted, I woke up the other morning and realized you were the only honest son of a bitch I have talked to in 6 months".

The last time I talked to Pam, she said she was going into hiding because she was on a "hit" list. Pam was heavily involved in drugs and had numerous contacts in the drug community. Up to that time, I had worked several cases involving drug activity; among those was the Dr. Jeffrey R. MacDonald case. This case involved a major drug cover-up involving the transporting of drugs from Southeast Asia in military planes in plastic bags in the body cavities of dead G.I.'s coming into the United States (Time magazine, January 1, 1973). It is very possible that this planned "hit" is due to her involvement in this case.

WIRETAP ON GUNDERSON

In April 1985, I learned there was an illegal telephone tap on my office line at 1100 Glendon Avenue, Suite 1200, Los Angeles, CA. I filed a lawsuit and subsequently received an out of court settlement from GTE. I was placed in a position of taking the settlement rather than pursuing the lawsuit because I could not afford an attorney and could not locate one who would take the case on a contingency basis. I learned that the tap was administered by a telephone answer-

ing service known as Answer All Answering Service, on W. Pico Boulevard, in Los Angeles. I visited the site and noted approximately 150 wires coming into the building that appeared to have been abruptly cut. The occupants apparently left in a hurry with their equipment.

Prior to filing the lawsuit with the phone company, I was tipped by a confidential source inside the phone company and was able to obtain photographs of automobiles parked in the area and people coming and going from that location. These photographs are in safekeeping.

TED GUNDERSON, CIA FILE

In July of 1999, a confidential source advised me, this writer, that my CIA file at Langley, Virginia is the thickest he has ever seen. Despite attempts by the "Shadow Government" to wipe out my documentation through burglaries, my file on CIA-FBI corruption is also the thickest one I have ever seen, except for the copies securely hidden in several places (recall Rusty Nelson), which are about the same size of the original, give or take a stolen box here and there."

Gunderson has continued to fight for the lost souls in America, who fall between the cracks, mostly because the public is asleep or busy listening to the propagandist, who runs most of the major media. In his late 70s, Gunderson is flying, faxing, phoning and fighting in every way to restore law and order to this country, to restore a Constitutional form of government.

July 6, 2000, Ted Gunderson was on the phone at 5 a.m., to save the life of Rusty Nelson marked for extermination. Rusty was imprisoned because he had taken photographs at parties by Larry King, implicating some of the nation's leading politicians. After more than 10 years on the run Rusty Nelson was jailed for taking pornographic pictures. Paroled from the state of Oregon, in the custody of Nebraska Attorney John DeCamp. Judge Urbom ordered all files and photos sealed, claiming that it would ruin many of the outstanding citizens of the state of Nebraska. Why would a Federal Judge consider people who had sex with children outstanding citizens?

Rusty took the pictures, Rusty had the negatives, so suddenly it became imperative that he be put back into prison and if possible, die quickly. Gunderson has mounted and Internet campaign with hundreds of copies of a 50-page report fired off to Bill Clinton, Janet Reno Al Gore—anyone and everyone in any authority in this country.

Noreen Gosch drove to Omaha Nebraska to personally hand deliver the report to the prison where Rusty was being held. The abusive treatment included withholding epilepsy drugs.

Gunderson wrote the foreword to the book "The Mystery of the Careful Crafted Hoax". The book was published by the Nebraska Leadership Conference to refute the Omaha World Herald campaign branding the Franklin Investigation as a hoax. Gunderson explains, how he became involved in investigations cases that the FBI would not touch…or as he came to realize later that the FBI deliberately covered up even to resorting to murder (see FBI Friend or Foe).

Gunderson states "After I retired in March 1979 as Senior Special Agent in charge of the FBI in Los Angeles, California, I was contacted by friends of Doctor Jeffrey R. McDonald, the former green beret, who had been convicted of murdering his wife and two children at Fort Bragg, North Carolina in February of 1970. McDonald, as well as a group of close personal friends, claimed that he was innocent of the crime.

After hundreds of hours of investigation, he interviewed Helena Stoeckley, who had become a suspect in the murders. In 1978, Stoeckley had contacted the FBI to make a full confession. The FBI refused to talk to her. She had told others that she was part of a "satanic cult" that had only meant to frighten McDonald because he was identifying soldiers who OD'd on drugs to hospital officials. The cult oversaw moving the heroine from Fort Bragg to the eastern market. It was being smuggled in the body cavities of dead soldiers.

Gunderson states: "In October of 1989, my associate and I convinced Stoeckley that it would be in her best interest to confess. She then gave us a signed statement in which she admitted her satanic cult had murdered McDonald's family. Stoeckley's admission was ignored. The Dept of Justice attorneys, and the FBI, stuck to their theory that McDonald committed the crimes. Despite the evidence of innocence, Jeffrey McDonald is still serving two life sentences. All efforts to secure another trial have failed.

At the time, Gunderson says, he had heard about satanic cults but didn't truly believe in their existence. But during the past 21 years, he has had contact with hundreds of adult survivors of satanic cults. These include former law enforcement officers, and politicians along with ordinary people. "I have talked with psychiatrist, psychologist and sociologist. I have developed confidential sources and informants who have had direct contact with cult members. *Unfortunately, 44 of them have been killed during investigations.* I have received and gathered hard evidence from journalists, who have written stories about the numerous "satanic murders" in America (Gunderson was always a field agent, Ken Lanning, who claims to be an analyst for the FBI at Quantico claims there is not one incident of satanic murders that he knows about).

Gunderson goes on to explain I have helped gather information for books such as "The Ultimate Evil" by Maury Terry's and "Cults that Kill" by Larry Kahaner. I have been a guest on numerous radio and television shows. Today, I am regarded as an expert around satanic cult crime."

Even though 20/20 secured boxes of police file documents on Satanism and child kidnapping from Gunderson, which they have now misplaced.

They also regarded him as "a conspiracy nut". Why would they bother to gather these documents if they regarded him as such a "nut"?

Without hesitation Gunderson declares: "I can state without hesitation, that there is, indeed, a national cult network—including satanic, witchcraft, pedophile and occult groups—which is operating at full throttle within our society today. The activities of these groups (It is one group which operates on many levels) include the kidnapping and molestation of children, as well as the torture and murder of human beings. Their favorite victims are children and newborn babies, the younger the better.

The cult lives, indeed thrives on drug sales, pornography and prostitution. The cult network is largely responsible for the recent rash of "snuff" films, which are sold at high prices to people who crave this sick, degenerate material. Children kidnapped and literally "owned" by the cult are sold on the open market to the highest bidder. These children are taken right off the streets of our cities and traded through a national pedophile network."

If you check the Chapter on Satanism, you will see two sides of the government involvement in the deepest level of Satanism. Aquino became a Satanist high priest with under Anton LeVay, who created the Church of Satan in California. Aquino rose to the rank of Lieutenant to Lieutenant. Col. military. Despite the fact he was accused at the Presidio Military base of molesting children.

Aquino later founded Temple of Set in the military. Satanism through his efforts is now a recognized religion in the military. He continued to receive the best military training ranging from the Command and Staff College at Fort Leavenworth, (School for Generals) to the War College in Washington D.C. National Security Agency documents indicated he was engaged in mind war experiment "creating for the government the perfect "Manchurian Candidates." Ken Lanning...supposedly an expert in Behavioral Science at Quantico, he and others in this department create profiles of cannibals, serial killers, Satanists and pedophiles. However, Lanning continues to assure everyone who logs into **www.fbi.org** that there is no satanic crime in America. This totally contradicts thousands of police reports.

Gunderson continues: The cult guards its secrets and controls its people primarily using fear. They have an intricate system of reward and punishment. They also deal in disinformation, intimidation, blackmail and murder. My investigations have revealed that the satanic cult network has even set up preschools across the country, which they use as a source for kiddy-pornography and child prostitution. They have successfully infiltrated the public school system as well. (In the Chapter "A Man Called Rusty" Russell Nelson claims to have been beside Larry King on a Lear Jet, flying into Washington D.C., when King called Ronald Reagan about re-opening the pre-school. He claims he recognized Reagan's voice, and the pre-school was re-opened by the time they landed in Washington) Several tabloids and the Franklin Cover-up book have shown pictures of Maureen Reagan draped over Larry King. The picture by its very nature suggests a close relationship. King sang the National Anthem at the 1988 Republican Party Convention.

Throughout this country Gunderson has met with the media and shown them mountains of police reports, newspaper clippings that clearly indicate there is an epidemic of satanic human sacrifice and cannibalism. Rusty Nelson can confirm this with photographs; Paul Bonnaci was witness to it and participated in human sacrifice and snuff films.

Due to his relentless investigation of Satanic crime, sexual abuse of children and drugs. "Two confidential and reliable sources advised Ted Gunderson (this writer) in July, 1982, that there were two contracts on my life, one by the Israeli Mafia (on an unrelated matter) and the other by "the satanic cult" out of Florida and Houston, Texas.

My landlady advised me that on the first Thursday in July of 1982, at 1:30 a.m., when she was parking her car, she noticed two men sitting in an automobile across the street from my front door. One of the men got out of the car, walked over to her and asked if she knew where Ted Gunderson lived. I had previously told her, if anyone asks about me to tell them she didn't know me. She told the man she didn't know Ted Gunderson. She went into her apartment and watched from her window until 1:45 a.m. until she saw them leave. By divine intervention, I did not go home that night but was visiting a friend.

I successfully eliminated the Israeli 'hit' almost immediately through one of my confidential contacts. It took me a year and a half to eliminate the satanic cult 'hit.' Because I had to go undercover, I was not able to work openly during this year and a half and lost my private investigation business.

A third attempt on my life, occurred on May 19, 1987. By divine intervention, I stayed at my daughter's home and did not return that evening to my business partner's home, where I was living. My business partner was out of the country; his wife and 12-year-old son were home. The next morning, when I met my partner's wife at work, she told me that at 11:00 p.m. that past evening, she heard an intruder come in the front door, on the first floor. She was on the third floor and locked herself in the bedroom. She went to the telephone extension located in the bedroom, but the phone was dead. She laid awake in bed terrified from 11:00

p.m. till 2:00 a.m., when the intruder left.

The next day, I contacted an informant, who advised me that Bill Mentzer, known in the satanic cult/sex/drug network as Charles Manson, II, was the individual who was waiting for me to come home the previous night."

Gunderson has indicated that over four hundred individuals, who are knowledgeable about the CIA's involvement in drugs and other criminal activities have been marked for death.

Although Ted Gunderson is now nearly 80, he continues to travel… to investigate. One day his in Las Vegas, then Canada, Washington State, New York and Connecticut. Often, he is running on a shoestring financially. His investigative business was forced to shut down, after he had to go into hiding to avoid yet another attempt to kill him.

In 1996, Gunderson threw his hat in ring, as a Presidential Candidate in the Democratic Party. Gunderson got himself on the primary ballot in New Hampshire. He was scheduled to take part in the debates. He had videotape, which he felt went a long way toward explaining why he was getting involved. On a Friday, a TV station told him it would cost five thousand dollars to put the program on and had agreed to air it. On Monday, they had decided that someone on the sales staff had misspoken, and the price was $25,000. Not only was this beyond the budget, but also shortly before flying east to take part in the debate, he was notified he had been dropped.

No one who knows Ted would doubt that he is.... a man with a mission. He has watched in horror as the FBI, where he served for 28 years, turned into a Gestapo, who harass witnesses and victims of satanic sexual abuse. He has viewed Ken Lanning's findings, on the FBI Web site, as a disservice to the America public. When Gunderson served in the 50sthrough the 70's, when protecting the public, was the FBI's job!

Gunderson is like John DeCamp, a reluctant hero, who fights on today long past the age of retirement. Those who know him feel that if an honest President by some miracle could be elected, Ted L. Gunderson could make an ideal and honest head of the FBI.

Before dying of AIDS, Thorstad watched his organization grow from one in 1978 that had $600 in the bank and a handful of subscribers to a multimillion-dollar organization.

FBI statement on Johnny Gosch: "WE HAVE NO CRIME.!"
NOREEN replies: "I have no son, he was kidnapped ……
Kidnapping is a Federal Crime.!"

FBI FRIEND OR FOE?

September 5, 1982, Police Chief Orval Cooney kept telling me that the FBI would not be entering the case. I called the local FBI office and requested an agent to come to my home. They sent Special Agents Ed Mall and David Oxler. When they arrived, they sat down at the table and told me they would not be entering the case because, in their words "WE HAVE NO CRIME." I responded, "I have no son, he was kid- napped, you have all the information from the witness's, kidnapping is a Federal Crime." The agents informed me the Police Chief, Orval Cooney had briefed them telling them there was no need for them to enter the case… That he could handle the situation. I could not believe what was happening. It seemed the world had gone completely nuts. A little boy was kidnapped off the street and the FBI would not enter the case. The FBI also told me that night that I had not proved Johnny's life was in danger. So, they would not enter the case. At that point I had heard enough and told them to get out of my home. They told me I could not speak to them that way because they were special agents. I just said "You do not look special to me so GET OUT OF MY HOUSE! At that point they left. We had no police or FBI assistance when Johnny was kidnapped.

We learned later that a phone call was made to the West Des Moines police... call was answered by the Captain. The phone call was to tell the WDMPD to take no action/ stand down on the Johnny Gosch Case. We later learned that the phone call was made from the Omaha FBI office. Why would the FBI tell the police to stand down and then later inform the parents that the FBI would not be entering the case? What were they hiding? Who were they protecting?

I grew up watching the FBI Story with Efrem Zimbalist Jr. and really believed that they entered kidnap cases and set up a command post in the homes of the families. NOT TRUE…. THEY DON'T!

…. **Noreen N. Gosch**

I used to be disturbed by the fact that the media, police and FBI were not doing the job of finding my son or the people who took him. But it seemed that they were determined to place as many obstacles in front of me as they could…. I felt like a one-armed fireman jumping from fire to fire.

My life was worse, when I didn't know why…THEY were trying to stifle the investigation and any hopes of my seeing my son alive again. They did not investigate my son's case .. DELIBERATLY! I believe my son and I were pawns in a much bigger game than I could even imagine.

Every time a clue or lead surfaced indicating Johnny might be alive…. the FBI…. The same FBI, who said "We Have No Crime", would gallop in and suck up all information, never to be seen again. I always referred to them like a huge "vacuum cleaner" …. Information and dirt go one way…

In 1985, I received a letter from a woman in Sioux City, Iowa, she sent me a dollar bill she received in change at the grocery store. The dollar bill contained a handwritten message from Johnny. It said," I am alive…Johnny Gosch". The handwriting looked like samples I had of Johnny's. I immediately contacted a hand-writing expert to verify the sig- nature…. He said it was Johnny's handwriting and the approximate time frame the signature had been applied. It meant my son was alive.

I did not tell the authorities until I had the opportunity to contact Iowa Senators Charles Grassley and Tom Harkin asking for their help in this matter. They put me in touch with someone from the U.S. Treasury Office in Washington, D.C. It was at that time I learned the "travel route" of this dollar bill. I learned that a dollar bill generally only travels in a short radius of the area it is released, and it has a very short life. We think of a dollar bill as turning up on either coast etc., they do but the local area is more often the case.

I called back to Senators Grassley and Harken, telling them I wanted to do a "press conference" from the Nation's capital to show the dollar bill and appeal to the kidnappers to return my son. Both Senators cooperated and did their part in setting up a date, time and place in the Capitol for the press conference. I took care of the rest. I sent packets of material to all the people I had worked with in the media to that point. I gave them the location, date and time of the press conference.

When I arrived in Washington D.C., I was treated most graciously by both Senators and the men from the Treasury Dept. We discussed the plan for the press conference and the continued investigation of the "dol- lar bill".

While we were riding the "inter-building tram" from Grassley's office to the Capitol, Senator Grassley leaned over and said "Now please do not be disappointed if you only have a few reporters show up…. The Washington Press is very independent." I smiled and said, "thank you". When we walked up to the Capitol, into the room for the press confer- ence, the room was filled with press nearly a hundred from newspapers, television (both local and network) and radio. Senator Grassley looked at Senator Harkin and said, "My God how did she do this, I can get this many people to come to one of my press conferences."

The FBI by now had heard of the existence of the dollar bill, they no doubt saw the press conference. When I arrived home, the FBI paid a visit to my home and demanded "the dollar bill." I had made plenty of copies of it, verified it was my son's signature by experts and conferred with the U.S. Treasury Dept., so at that point, I turned over the dollar bill to the agents. The dollar bill has never been seen again…. It went up into the huge FBI Vacuum cleaner. At a later time the FBI denied there ever was a dollar bill with the message "I am alive…. Johnny Gosch" received by them. They lied!

Kidnapped children are being kept alive and transported around the country… evidence such as the dollar bill in our case supported the fact Johnny was still alive. The case of the girl in Florida, whose picture was found in a convenience store parking lot, showing her tied and gagged in the back of a van. She is originally from Arizona and yet three years later, photos of her are found in Florida. I have spoken a few times to her mother and the photo was validated as "current". Did the FBI investigate this? Did they do any investigation on the dollar bill? I did my own investigation. I have learned the hard way that if you want something to be done…. You must do it yourself.

It has been more than 18 years since my son was kidnapped. I have relied upon my private investigators, who have been able to supply me with evidence not only of what happened to Johnny but that he is still alive.

According to former Mayor of West Des Moines, George Mills; "Orval Cooney, West Des Moines Police Chief was a friend of Omaha Chief of Police Robert Wadman. "In a recent conversation with George Mills, he quickly stated he had only met Wadman one time, but he was "really Orval's friend".

Many influential men according to Senator Loren Schmit and the Nebraska Franklin Investigation was a major figure in pedophile activity in the Omaha area as well as a major figure in the cover up. Shortly after the legislature had formed the Franklin Investigative Committee, Schmit received a threatening phone call from Wadman stating "I've got something on you."

When evidence mounted in the investigation that led Loren Schmit to believe it was beyond the boundaries of the legislature, he sought out friend

FBI FRIEND OR FOE?

and legal representative John DeCamp to accompany him to the FBI offices. The Regional Head of the FBI, Nick Ohara, informed DeCamp and Schmit that Wadman was his close friend and a friend to the FBI. When the scandal ran Wadman out of town, he apparently had the assis- tance of the FBI in securing the job of Chief of Police of Aurora, Il. This was suspiciously near the site where Chief Investigator for the Nebraska Legislature, Gary Caradori's plane crashed, killing him and his eight-year- old son A.J.

A phone call from Caradori to Senator Loren Schmit, the night before the crash, stating; "I have the evidence to put them away," this might have jeopardized Caradori's life. Schmit and others involved later agreed the telephone lines must have been tapped. The question is .... Who has the capacity to tap the telephone lines to the Nebraska Legisla- ture?

DeCamp states; "mystery surrounded not only the crash of the airplane, but Caradori's whole trip." The Lakefront Hotel in Chicago where Caradori stayed, the management of the hotel claimed they had no record of him. However, both his wife and business associate had made phone calls to him at the hotel.

Ted Gunderson, FBI Retired, in a report made public on the Internet, June 28, 2000, stated that the investigation of the crash was conducted on a military base.... This is unheard of in the investigation of a civilian plane crash.

Ten years ago, Paul Bonacci, a prisoner in the Lincoln Nebraska Federal Prison confessed to his participation in the kidnapping of my son. Bonacci's attorney, John DeCamp had the confession transcribed and it was hand carried to the FBI office in Omaha Nebraska, in 1989. That confession contained information about the kidnapping of my son Johnny.

The FBI did not act upon this information. Does the FBI have any obliga tion to notify parents when new evidence surfaces? The answer is "NO, the FBI operates much like a vacuum cleaner.... All information and de- bris go one way." In this instance, the FBI had a vested interest too.

...Ignore and disregard any information concerning Johnny Gosch, which connected to the Franklin Scandal.

I did not learn of Bonacci until March 1991, although Johnny's father, John Gosch had not only received the information from DeCamp. But had been to the prison with a woman impersonating me to interview Bonacci. He made the decision to keep this from me. I found out following massive press coverage. Both the FBI and the West Des Moines Police announced they "were not interested in talking to Bonacci "Detective Gary Scott of the West Des Moines Police also stated in a TV interview "We do not want to try and reinvent the wheel." Which was a stupid remark given the circumstances.

The West Des Moines Police were shown viewing Bonacci's videotaped confession, shrugging their shoulders and looking bewildered during the interview. When I watched it .... I kept wondering what kind of "wheels" they were trying to not reinvent.... And what did wheels have to do with it anyway"? It was such a dumb statement.

Battling the FBI in Nebraska

Over a ten-year period, DeCamp repeatedly filed a Civil Rights Law Suit on behalf of Paul Bonacci was indeed telling the truth, concern- ing his abuse by Larry King but also **the kidnapping of Johnny Gosch.** It had been rejected year after year until February 1999, when Bonacci was allowed to go before Judge Urbom, in Federal Court. Following the hear- ing, Judge Urbom awarded Bonacci one million dollars in punitive dam- ages to be paid by Larry King. The ruling by Judge Urbom was the catalyst of new information to be used in Johnny's case.

Following this hearing, the FBI made no comment whatsoever. The West Des Moines Police stated, "we still do not consider Bonacci

credible, despite the Federal Court Ruling!" What on earth does it take for Bonacci to be considered credible in Des Moines, when the Federal Court has ruled?

Governor Vilsack, when contacted for his assistance said; "This is not my concern…. Take your problem to the Dept. of Public Safety!" Presi- dent Harry S. Truman stated, "The Buck stops here." Obviously not with Governor Vilsack. In Nebraska, the last four Governors, including Vilsack's friend Bob Kerrey, ignored even their own legislative investigation, which uncovered massive sexual abuse of children.

The Governor should have referred it to the Department of Crimi- nal Investigation …The DCI, as this was new damning evidence in kid- napping of my son. The DCI is the proper investigating branch of law enforcement. It raises a question about Vilsack's knowledge of State gov- ernment. It was obvious from the response I received, the Governor is not that concerned about what happens to children in this state or in solving the kidnappings of Johnny or Eugene Martin.

When Johnny was first kidnapped, the DCI was involved. One DCI Detective, Chuck Wood was sent to my home on several occasions. He and a detective from the West Des Moines Police always worked as a team. During interviews as they would ask me questions and I answered…Wood would look at me and always say, "If what you are saying is true…. And I doubt that it is!" That became his refrain each time we met his message was clear …. He was not only belittling me but also trying to intimidate and discourage me.

There were numerous times I had to be in meetings with Detective Wood, I had finally instructed my attorney to tell Wood, that he would have to submit his questions in writing. I would only answer them in writing, if he was going to continue his intimidating behavior. The very last time I saw Wood, was at a "summit meeting with authorities, my private detective and me". I brought my knitting along… As we discussed the case, I kept on knitting, it finally unnerved Police Chief Cooney, he yelled at me : "**WHY THE HELL ARE YOU KNITTING, WHY WOULD BRING KNITTING TO A MEETING LIKE THIS?**" I replied, "Knitting keeps me calm, and it will stop me from acting on the temptation to smack the hell out of you…for your

OUTRAGEOUS behavior towards me and my son's kidnapping." Cooney was taken back that I would respond in that manner, however, I had decided I would take no more of the rude remarks from these men.

It doesn't matter if remarks come from local law enforcement or the FBI, the impact is still the same. Why should I be surprised! The FBI is still not investigating the case. What has changed in eighteen years? NOTHING! I have talked to countless parents of missing and murdered children over eighteen years. The report is always the same.... **THE FBI DID NOT HELP US AT ALL.**

When you finish reading this chapter, there will be no question in your mind, if you can accept the truth of what is being said....

In Nebraska, the FBI raided of the office of Gary Caradori investi- gator for the Nebraska Legislature, who uncovered information on the kidnapping of Johnny Gosch and the sexual misuse of young children. The FBI confiscated Caradori's files the day after his death.... those records have never been released.

Johnny Gosch was kidnapped! Eugene Martin was kidnapped! Jacob Wetterling was kidnapped! Is it possible that the FBI has had the job of covering the tracks of any kidnappers working in conjunction with the CIA?

Paul Bonnaci comments that Emilio, who oversaw the kidnapping of Johnny Gosch, bragged "The FBI lets me do whatever I want with children."

Arrogance and apathy prevail in our country to the highest level. People see a Johnny Gosch case here and there but as long as it doesn't affect "me or mine", then people can turn away, as though it never hap- penned. Arrogance on the part of law enforcement officials.... Apathy on the part of the public and media. Sometimes an informant can become an agent provocateur who ends up participating in, perhaps instigating and even leading the activity he was paid to report upon.

The FBI seems to have played a major role in the Nebraska Cover Up as early as 1982 – 83. An investigation had uncovered what was termed "male prostitution ring was identified in Omaha." An FBI press release in the Omaha World Herald in October 1983, stated "this thing is so big and involves so many prominent people around this state." It was sug- gested that was the motive for covering up the ring then, as it is today.

Two days after the death of the chief investigator of the Nebraska Legislature, Gary Caradori …before Caradori's body had been delivered home, the FBI presented a subpoena to Caradori's wife, Sandy for all his investigative notes, documents, receipts and files.

Once again, the evidence is sucked up into the FBI Vacuum cleaner, never to be seen again.

The FBI then proceeded to launch several investigations of Franklin Committee Chairman Senator Loren Schmit. Several spurious lawsuits were filed against Senator Schmit over the period of a year, to break him financially. At least one of the lawsuits was almost certainly instigated by an FBI agent.

WHY JOHNNY CAN'T COME HOME!

Dear Mr. Gosch,
I'm very interested in knowing if this is his signature. I would appreciate hearing what you find out. I pray this is not a sick joke.
Jeanette M.
14th St
Sioux City, Iowa
51103

Johnny and other kidnapped kids, traveled a circuit which brought them back to Sioux City, IA on a regular basis.

14th St.
Sioux City Iowa
51103

[Postmark: SIOUX CITY, IA — PM — 13 JUN 1985]

John Gosch
1004 45th St.
West Des Moines, Iowa
50265

FBI FRIEND OR FOE?

ST. PAUL PIONEER PRESS AND DISPATai
- Tl-UmAY, .U. Y 11, 1985 P'tl-/

Associated Presa
Noreen Gosch display doAar bill at press conference
wtth the words "I am aivei Johnny Gosch."

$400,000 offered for return of boy

NAMBLA

The North America Man Boy Love Association was formed in 1978. According to the minutes of the meeting they had six hundred dollars in the bank and about 225 member subscribers to their publication. Ten years later, when the Franklin Credit Union in Omaha was raided, it was discovered that this Credit Union had five million in NAMBLA money.

They have vehemently denied charges that they had anything to do with the creation of a whole new subclass of pornography. They absolutely denied that they vigorously recruited run away and throw away child not to mention kidnapped children and even young infants being in kiddie porn.

Paul Bonacci, a young man who detailed his part in the kidnapping of Johnny Gosch so thoroughly, that Noreen Gosch totally believes him. In February 1999, a Federal Court Judge in Lincoln, Nebraska ruled that Bonacci had been repeatedly sexually abused. If this court ruling makes Bonacci creditable then he should also be believed when he says he went to Washington D.C, to have sex with U.S. Representative Barney Frank. He traveled to New York to become a "boytoy" for Peter Thorstad, head of NAMBLA.

Bonacci has MPD/DID and one of those personalities is based on Thorstad. He personally heard Thorstad speaking of Dr Judi-Ann Densen

Gerber, a psychiatrist who was called "Public Enemy No. 1," by NAMBLA. She exposed NAMBLA, who promote their civil right to have sex with children. Thorstad said: "I'm going to have to get rid of that bitch." It has been established that Paul possesses a photographic memory, which allows him to recall every person he has been with, every location he has seen and describe it in detail.

Under the control of Larry King, Bonacci made snuff films and had sex with the corpses, made child/child and child/adult porno films…was routinely sent around the country to have sex with over 1000 men. How then was NAMBLA not related to what was going on? How then did NAMBLA increase its bank account from six hundred dollars to five million in the Franklin Credit Union in ten years?

Under Thorstad's leadership NAMBLA was the first American member of the International Lesbian and Gay Association granted consultative status to the United Nations Economic and Social Council. According to the American Family Association on July 30, 1994, the United States and 21 other nations voted to approve this status.

NAMBLA has grown since it first reported membership of two hundred to a worldwide organization with members in Europe and Asia. Robert Rhoades, NAMBLA's former membership secretary, is a government employee with the U.S. Veterans Administration, Roy B. Radow worked as the school psychologist at the P.S. 75 school in Queens, and Peter Melzer has held a teaching position at New York City's prestigious Bronx High School of Science. It is certain that Catholic priests have actively participated in recruiting boys for NAMBLA's organization.

NAMBLA defends sex between men and young boys. They favor abolishing all age-of-consent laws designed to protect minors. In 1993, the Constitution and Position Papers claim that they engage in no activities that violate the law. But in the next paragraph they proclaim: "We support the rights of youth, as well as adults to choose the partners with whom they wish to share and enjoy their bodies. We encourage young people to rebel against the anti-sexual prohibitions imposed on them by authorities: parents, school officials, so called 'moral' crusaders, the church, the law, the news media and the state." They further declare: "We oppose age of consent laws.

On December 29, 1982, on a nationally televised show, Thorstad was asked by the Host of the ABC talk program, The Last Word, if a boy as young as nine would give consent to have sex with a man. "Of course,", Thorstad replied: "They do it all the time.!"

This was confirmed by anyone reading the NAMBLA Bulletin, where one man described receiving oral sex from his six-year-old brother. And a writer from Nebraska stated his first lover turned out to be a boy of seven and a half.

American Family Association Journal states "Realizing the incredible public relations disaster pedophiles represent to their cause, homosexual leaders have consistently tried to keep NAMBLA "out of sight".

The "Overhauling of Straight America" which the journal describes as "the landmark playbook for homosexual strategy, they quote an old Arab proverb: "First let the camel get his nose inside the tent and only later his unsightly derriere…the masses must not be repulsed by premature exposure to homosexual behavior itself."

Today Chicago and other cities believe that any child in the third grade is old enough to know how homosexuals have sex. Years ago, most kids were too busy playing baseball and roller-skating. Why do children this young need to be educated in pursuing "alternate lifestyles"?

NAMBLA INVESTIGATION

From "The Survivor Activist" publication, summer 1998. Survivor Connection web site http://www.angelfire.com/ri/survivorconnection. Angel fire network has a whole series of website dealing with the sexual abuse of children. For example, ri is for Rhode Island, 52 Lyndon Rd., Cranston, RI 02905-1121 (401) 941-2548.

This is a statement made by Larry Echols.

"From July 3, 1997, to October 27, 1997, I was a paid informant working under FBI Special Agent Richard K. Lack of the Monterey, C.A., FBI Field Office (408/375-3123) under the code name "Pedbuster" During that time, I personally handed Agent Lack over 200 original letters from members of the North American Man/Boy Love Association (NAMBLA) which had been given to me by a NAMBLA member-turncoat. The authors of those letters detailed their sexual lust for and in some cases their actual rapes of young boys...and approximately 30% of those letters contained the writers" real names, addresses, phone and fax numbers, e-mail addresses, and other personal information.

In late July of 1997, I introduced Agent Lack to a gay, prominent member of NAMBLA, who is not a pedophile or pederast and Lack hired him as a paid undercover informant to work for the FBI. From July until late October, I was the principal conduit for providing NAMBLA informant's intelligence and evidence of criminal sexual activity involving children to Lack, including Internet posts, e-mails, and other Internet communications between the mole and NAMBLA members and BoyChat participants as well as some photographs of self-identified child rapists and their victims, some of them boys as young as eight.

Remarkably, this arrangement was necessary because the Monterey (CA) FBI office had no Internet connection, and the San Jose (CA) FBI office...the one responsible for Silicon Valley...had but one computer with access to the Internet.

Repeatedly the NAMBLA mole suggested to the FBI that he be wired for his frequent in-person meetings with sexually active NAMBLA members and other pederasts. But much to Agent Lack's chagrin, this never happened because FBI Headquarters in Washington refused to approve it.

On October 23, 1997, at the FBI's Monterey office I met with FBI Assistant Director George Martinez, FBI Internet Child Sex Predator Task Force (i.e., "Innocent Images" in Baltimore, Maryland) Supervisor Linda

Hooper (301/572-5400), San Francisco FBI Administrator Lillian Zillias, and Agent Lack. At that meeting, I brought examples of extremely egregious Internet child pornography featuring totally naked and sexuallyaroused boys as young as eight which I had recently downloaded from the Internet and handed to Martinez, Hooper, Zillias, and Lack, and asked them if this was sufficient evidence for them to begin investigations.

I had thought that Agent Lack would get angry with me for downloading and bringing this material; however, his ire was directed instead at Martinez and Hooper when they pointed out to him that...even though such pornography was illegal...they would not authorize his or any other FBI Agent to investigate such pornography because U.S. Attorney General Janet Reno had instructed U.S. Attorneys around the United States not to prosecute such cases.

Four days later, Agent Lack called me into the Monterey office and told me that Martinez and Hooper had ordered him to terminate me. However, he said that the NAMBLA mole would continue to work with the FBI. But in late December, the mole was totally disrespected by a FBI polygraph examiner to whom Lack was required to send him...a bigot who accused this courageous man of "f_little boys" totally contrary to the mole's past, including his criminal history—and at that the mole resigned from working with the FBI.

On November 17, 1997, I went to the U.S. Customs Service and from then until January 8, 1998, I was a paid informant under U.S. Customs Special Agent Robin Sterzer (408/535-5149) of San Jose, CA, with the code name "Alex Cole". During those seven weeks I provided both she and an unpaid informant, a California Department of Justice Special Agent Robert DeMiguel (415/351-3374) of San Francisco with their own sets of the aforementioned NAMBLA letters, as well as hundreds of downloaded pages of evidence of Internet activity by child sex predators and child pornographers which included copies of posts from BoyChat, emails, IRC communications, and even detailed photographs of child sex predators and some of their victims.

On December 19, 1997, I asked Special Agent Sterzer to reimburse me for over $1,000 in out-of-pocket expenses which I had incurred in my work for U.S. Customs, but she delayed doing so until Jan 8, 1997, at which time she told me that Customs would not reimburse me "Until we can give you a polygraph conducted by one of our examiners; but we don't have any in this part of the country and we don't know when we will have."

I refused to go along with this duplicity and also due to the continuing failure of the California Department of Justice to even reimburse my expenses, I ended my undercover work for law enforcement.

What will it take to get Janet Reno and the Justice Department to conduct a thorough investigation of the conduct of NAMBLA members? Surely the evidence indicated here proves that NAMBLA members are perverted criminals.

NORTH AMERICAN MAN/BOY LOVE ASSOCIATION

The North American Man/Boy Love Association (NAMBLA) is an organization founded in response to the extreme oppression of men and boys involved in consensual sexual and emotional relationships with each other. Its membership is open to all individuals sympathetic to man/boy love in particular and sexual freedom in general. NAMBLA is strongly opposed to age-of-consent laws and other restrictions which deny adults and youth the full enjoyment of their bodies and control over their lives. NAMBLA's goal is to end the long-standing oppression of men and boys involved in any mutually consensual relationship by:

1) building a support network for such men and boys;
2) educating the public on the benevolent nature of man/boy love;
3) cooperating with the lesbian, gay, and other movements for sexual liberation;
4) supporting the liberation of persons of all ages from sexual prejudice and oppression.

If you are interested in more information about NAMBLA, our regional meetings, national conferences, political actions, and publications, please send $1 to:

NAMBLA
P.O. Box 174
Midtown Station
New York, NY 10018

june 1983 nambla BULLETIN vol. 4 n. 5
VOICE OF THE NORTH AMERICAN MAN/BOY LOVE ASSOCIATION
$2

We have received reports that the FBI has visited members of NAMBLA, asking about John Gosch (see elsewhere in this issue).

If accosted or visited by the FBI, do not think you are dealing with reasonable people interested in determining the truth. You are dealing with the American equivalent (in methods and ethics) of the Soviet KGB. Since the emphasis is on the justification of thus-far squandered taxpayers' money, agents' salaries, etc., rather than on the finding of the truth, beware!

Be firm! Protect your right to privacy by cutting such encounters short. DO NOT SPEAK, EXCEPT FOR A REFUSAL TO SPEAK. REMEMBER, REFUSING TO TALK TO THE FBI IS NOT A CRIME, IT'S YOUR CONSTITUTIONAL RIGHT.

Read guidelines and detailed instructions in another part of this issue.

JOHN GOSCH - PHONE HOME!

NAMBLA has received an inquiry regarding the whereabouts of a missing love youth, John Gosch, whose disappearance has generated considerable media attention. John is a 13-year-old youth of West Des Moines, who disappeared on September 5, 1982, while delivering newspapers.

NAMBLA firmly believes that youths should be allowed to determine whom they shall live with. At the same time, the request for our assistance has come in a unique form: a polite phone conversation between Brian McNaught (Boston mayor Kevin White's liaison to the gay and lesbian community) and NAMBLA spokesperson Brian Quinby.

The idea that NAMBLA would be well informed on runaways is both wrong and being used by the FBI against us. However, if anyone does know any runaways, suggest to him that he call the National Runaway Youth Hot Line (1-800-231-6946) to relieve anxiety at home and resolve the question about the conditions under which leaving occurred. The Hot Line is confidential and young people who use it can do so without being pressured into divulging any more information than they choose to.

WHY JOHNNY CAN'T COME HOME!

december 1982 — nambla BULLETIN — VOLUME 3, No. 10
VOICE OF THE NORTH AMERICAN MAN/BOY LOVE ASSOCIATION

NAMBLA HERE TO STAY!

NAMBLA HOLDS PRESS CONFERENCES • ATTRACTS WORLDWIDE ATTENTION

NAMBLA's first-ever news conferences, held within an hour of each other in New York and Boston, propelled our four-year-old organization into the newspapers and on to the airwaves across America. By revealing the source of the picture alleged to be that of missing Etan Patz, NAMBLA quashed reports that members David Groat and Brett Portmann, whose Wareham, MA house was raided on December 3rd, were in any way connected with the disappearance of Patz. The existence of the picture was confirmed by Nassau County Police the next day, clearing NAMBLA of any involvement in the kidnapping. The conferences served also to refute the sensationalized press coverage that declared NAMBLA to be a pornography and sex ring that accepts major credit cards and delivers hapless lads via Learjet.

The Boston news conference began at 9:15 on Tuesday, December 28th. Held at the Glad Day Bookshop, the thirty-minute conference attracted

continued on page 2

Photo the FBI and the local police allegedly found in a cottage in Wareham, Mass., where members David Groat, Brett Portmann and Harold Baker III were arrested. Conveniently construed as a photo of Etan Patz, a 6-year-old boy missing from SoHo since 1979, it was passed along and used in the uninformative, gutter-snipe style of the sensationalist press to defame NAMBLA, "a bizarre sex club," with quasi-allegations and innuendos of having kidnapped Etan Patz. The effort to destroy the legitimacy of the Organization failed...

...Whose, thanks to the efforts of NAMBLA, the source of the photo and the identity of the model were revealed in press conferences held simultaneously in Boston and New York.
Published in the Boyhood Calendar dated 1968, it is the photo of a model who now must be in his late twenties. The FBI has declined any comment to the press, except for an occasional "it was thought, at the time... ." NAMBLA maintains the FBI knew all along of the falsehood of the accusations it was leaking to the press.

NAMBLA

Division of Criminal Investigation

Iowa Sex Offender Registration

Not all of these registrants will appear on this web site's searchable database.

The searchable database only contains information regarding persons who have been assessed as "at-risk" to reoffend, and who were convicted of an offense requiring registration after July 1, 1995, and who were previously notified that electronic access would be part of their public notification. A registrant who has not been assessed as "at-risk" and not been the subject of public notification will not appear in this file.

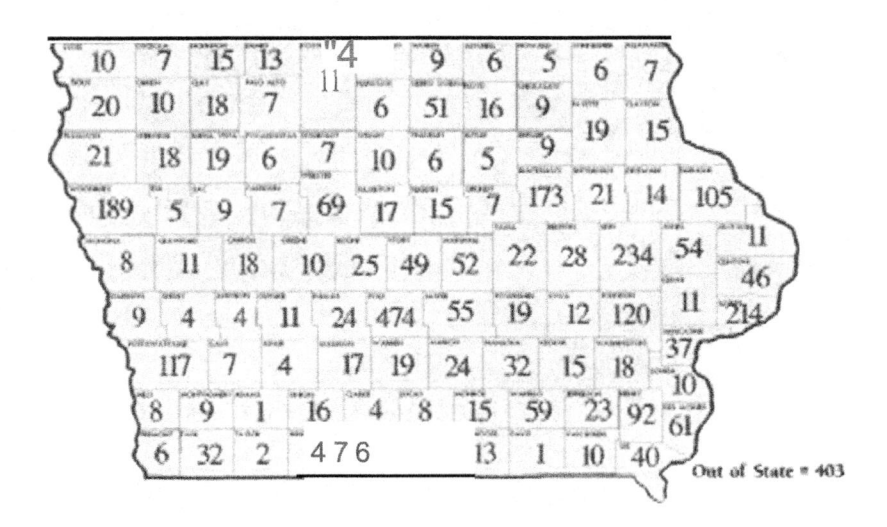

Number of Registrants by County

http://www.state.ia.us/government/dps/dci/isor/sorstats.htm

Iowa Sex Offender Registry Statistics

Adair	4	Adams	1	Allamakee	7	Appanoose	13	Audubon	4	Benton	
Black Hawk	173	Boone	25	Bremer	9	Buchanan	21	Buena Vista	19	Butler	
Calhoun	7	Carroll	18	Cass	7	Cedar	11	Cerro Gordo	51	Cherokee	
Chickasaw	9	Clarke	4	Clay	18	Clayton	15	Clinton	46	Crawford	
Dallas	24	Davis	1	Decatur	7	Delaware	14	Des Moines	61	Dickinson	
Dubuque	105	Emmet	13	Fayette	19	Floyd	16	Franklin	6	Fremont	
Greene	10	Grundy	7	Guthrie	11	Hamilton	17	Hancock	6	Hardin	
Harrison	9	Henry	92	Howard	5	Humboldt	7	Ida	5	Iowa	
Jackson	11	Jasper	55	Jefferson	23	Johnson	120	Jones	54	Keokuk	
Kossuth	11	Lee	40	Linn	234	Louisa	10	Lucas	8	Lyon	
Madison	17	Mahaska	32	Marion	24	Marshall	52	Mills	8	Mitchell	
Monona	8	Monroe	15	Montgomery	9	Muscatine	37	O'Brien	10	Osceola	
Page	32	Palo Alto	7	Plymouth	21	Pocahontas	6	Polk	474	Pottawattam	
Poweshiek	19	Ringgold	4	Sac	9	Scott	214	Shelby	4	Sioux	
Story	48	Tama	22	Taylor	2	Union	16	Van Buren	10	Wapello	
Warren	19	Washington	18	Wayne	6	Webster	69	Winnebago	4	Winneshiek	
Woodbury	189	Worth	9	Wright	10						

Iowa Sex Offender Registry Home Page
Iowa Division of Criminal Investigation | Iowa Department of Public Safety Home Page
State of Iowa Home Page

http://www.state.ia.us/government/dps/dci/isor/sorstats.htm

SATANISM IN AMERICA
A Reality.... Not a Myth

CURRENT RITUAL ABUSE

A recent study by Bennett Brown, a University of Chicago Psychiatrist, involved 37 adult ritual abuse survivors. These individuals did not know each other and were interviewed from differing locations around the U.S. The results of this study revealed 10 common factors of ritual abuse experience. They are as follows:

> 97% talked about the use of drugs in the cult 100% were sexually molested.
> 100% were tortured.
> 100% witnessed animal mutilations & killings.
> 72% talked about coffins, graves & being buried alive with dead bodies.
> 100% had death threats.
> 83% witnessed sacrifices of animals, children and adults 78% of women had stories of marriage ceremonies.
> 60% of the women had stories of sacrifice of their own children and were impregnated for this purpose (breeders)
> 81% were involved in cannibalism and consumption of human body parts.
> .... Nebraska Leadership Conference

We have heard it all before. I don't believe you. This can't happen in America. You are just trying to scare us. People shy away from those trying to get the message out, as if carrying a warning about Satanism was akin to being a smallpox carrier.

Two men have surfaced in the debate over Satanism, Lt. Colonel Michael Aquino (Satanist and mind control specialist in the military) and Ken Lanning, a supposed FBI specialist who monitors groups. Lanning's statement that Christians have done more harm than Satanism ever did has led many to call him a Satanist. Lanning has used the power of his position with the FBI to "claim that there is no satanic crime wave" in total contradiction to police reports by the thousands. An entire issue of "The Journal of Psychohistory" documents tens of thousands of cases being brought to the attention of psychiatrists and psychologists.

The editor, Dr. deMause states: It was not, however, until word began to get around the psychotherapy community that I was editing an issue of my journal on "Cult Abuse of Children" that I began to realize the full extent of cult activity in America today. Phone calls from all over the country poured into my editorial office from psychotherapists, who told me that they would like to read the cult abuse issue because they had treated cult abuse victims. When I then asked them if they wished to contribute somehow to the issue, they often said they couldn't…they were afraid to talk in print about their clients, even anonymously, because the cults had threatened them or their families with violence. Phone threats, dead cats on doorsteps, burning crosses on lawns and other convincing communications made them understandably reluctant to write anything about cults."

DeMause continues that one psychiatrist wrote him, after he learned the psychiatrist had given a paper on treating cult abuse victims, but he declined the invitation to publish his paper, stating:

"As you may know, there is some risk attached to treating satanic ritual abuse victims. A recent study by Dr. Nancy Perry indicates that as many as 10% of therapists treating such patients have been threatened or attacked by the groups to which their patients formerly belonged.

DeMause went on: In fact, even that therapist who had agreed to write about their clients for the cult issue often had second thoughts. Most promised articles but then didn't send them in. After I heard one psychiatrist give…a detailed account of his patient being sexually abused by a cult, I requested he write an article, which I published in this issue as it was written, attributing the increase in cult reports to "the contagious nature of group hysteria" …but without a single word about his own cultabused patient!"

Dr deMause goes on to say that authors of false memory books also turned out to be pedophile advocates. Paul and Shirley Eberle's book "The Abuse of Innocence: The McMartin Preschool Trial" taken seriously by reviewers and widely quoted in magazine articles as authorities, were producers and publishers of kiddie porn.

Sgt. Toby Tyler, a San Bernardino deputy sheriff, who is a recognized expert on child pornography stated: "I have seen articles they have published such as "I Was a Sexpot at Five "and "Little Lolitas" included illustrations of children involved in sodomy and oral copulation and featured pornographic photos of the Eberles."

Yet when Ted Gunderson, recently retired head of the FBI in California and a team led by an archeologist uncovered the tunnels at the McMartin Day Care, Gunderson could not get the L.A. Times or other major media to run the story. The tunnels contained satanic objects and were as the children described them.

Dr. deMause also comments on FBI's Ken Lanning, who says he has "been unable to find one murder of anyone by two or more people following typical satanic ritualistic prescriptions." Lanning ignores all kinds of convictions for cult abuse that are in police and court records, while others who have done ritual abuse investigation work for the FBI are ignored by the press. "

Dr deMause concludes: The more I dug into the literature; the "curiouser and curiouser" seemed the claims that investigation of cults are only witch hunts.

There is a group called the Cult Crime Impact Network, which estimates that as many as 50,000 human sacrifices a year are being performed by a nationwide covert network of satanic cults."

From Kenneth V. Lanning, M.S. Supervisory Special Agent National Center for the Analysis of Violent Crime, FBI Academy, Quantico, Virginia comes a series of pronouncements. A selection from his outline will give you an idea of what he is trying to debunk.

He saves the "Big Conspiracy theory for last "which implies that Satanist are responsible for such things as Adolph Hitler, World War II, abortion, pornography, Watergate, Irangate, and infiltration of the Department of Justice, the Pentagon and the White House" (All these connections surfaced in the Nebraska Franklin Investigation)

Add to that "Organized, Traditional, or Multigenerational satanic groups involved in organized conspiracies, such as taking over day care centers, infiltrating police departments, and trafficking in human sacrifice victims. (Proven in Nebraska)

About music: Lyrics, symbolism, and influence of rock and roll, Heavy Metal and Black Metal music. Teenage suicide by adolescent's dabbling in the occult. Lee Orr, Kansas City Homicide detective and satanic cult investigator said, "Omaha youth were carpooling to Kansas City to buy Death Metal. Which features the sacrifice of mother and baby real or simulated?

Although Lanning does his best to explain away each and ever step of the "Big Conspiracy Theory." The exception is leaving out the major drug trafficking connections that bind the DIA/CIA to the Satanist drug traffickers. He has given a perfect outline of what is going on. A Chicago University survey of Satanic activity around the country revealed that 100% of the cult survivors were using drugs.

Lanning writes: What is Ritualistic Crime?

Lanning smoothly explains. "Ritual can refer to a prescribed religious ceremony, but in its broader meaning refers to any customarily repeated act or series of acts. The need to repeat these acts can be cultural, sexual, or psychological as well as spiritual. Cultural rituals could include such things as what a family eats on Thanksgiving Day.

What Lanning fails to mention is the thousands of reported cultural ceremonies involving satanic murders with the child's hand involved?

...held firmly in the grip of an adult to kill a playmate, or a child snatched off the streets. At least hundreds of convictions are in the courthouses of America. Tens of thousands of complaints have been filed from every corner of America. No amount of false memory manufactured covers these stories.

Charles Highams two books "Trading with the Enemy "and "America Swastika "shows how the Nazi worked in America before, during and after WW II. One factory even manufactured ball bearings for German fighter planes while telling the U.S. government it lacked the proper metals. He wrote of how Nazi war criminals found a place for themselves in America after Germany was literally destroyed.

"The Plot Against the Peace" published in 1946, revealed how the Nazi began training schools in 1943 for agents whose job it would be to carry on the Reich at the end of the war along with Teutonic Satanism. They were given new names and new passports, often of dead eastern Europeans and told to wait out the end of the war and apply for political asylum, fleeing communism. Switzerland was fully cooperative in this venture and the monies for the new Reich were held safe in "neutral" Swiss banks.

Col. Michael Aquino has long been claimed to oversee a Mindwar project for the U, S Military. He is the illegitimate son of a Nazi SS officer. As a young lieutenant, he joined the Church of Satan founded by Anton La Vey, a former circus barker, who found a new stichk. He was the sensation of the Men's magazines of the 1950s, conducting his satanic masses with the likes of Jayne Mansfield and with such followers as Sammy Davis Jr. Rising to the rank of High Priest did not seem to hinder Aquino's military career, even charges of molesting children did not stop his rise. What better place to molest them than in the military. They are the largest provider of day care in the world. Day Care centers at West Point, New York and Fort Leavenworth, Kansas have carefully been dealt with, so another fall guy took the rap for higher ups.

Ken Lanning, the so-called specialist in cult crimes claimed there are no Satanists. Although Aquino was on trial at the Presidio in California for molesting children as a High Priest of LaVey's Church of Satan. Aquino broke away and founded in the military the Temple of Set. Satanism now has a place on an America soldiers dog tags just like Catholic, Protestant, Jew, Moslem and Witch—yes Witch.

Lanning would have you believe that no such groups exist or if they do they are of little significance. Yet police throughout America are reporting more and more cases of satanic connections to murders and disappearances of both children and adults.

According to Johnny Gosch and at least three others. It was Aquino, who picked him up and paid for him in Sioux City weeks after he was kidnapped. Referred to as the "Col.," …Reports have connected him to Johnny Gosch, Eugene Martin, Jacob Wetterling and other Midwestern boys. All kidnapped to participate in a government program designed to create the perfect vessel for sabotage for blackmail and for murder. To accomplish this. …They had to be subjected to satanic programming which created MPD or DID (Multiple Personality Disorder or Dissociate Identity Disorder) which provided more than just Doctor Jeykle and Mr. Hyde but a series of personalities suited to a variety of assignments.

Directly from Lt. Colonel Michael Angelo Aquino's own website comes the information that he was in Military Intelligence. During the time of Johnny's kidnapping, he was with the Defense Intelligence Agency and attended the Foreign Service Institute at the Department of State. From 1981 through 84, he was in Washington D.C. If Cathy O'Brien can be believed, he regularly attended White House functions and hobnobbed with George Bush and Cheney. His last course attended was the Joint Intelligence Operations Course at Fort Leavenworth, Kansas in 1990. He had graduated from U.S. Army Command & General Staff College in 1979 on the Commandant's List, like the Dean's list in college it meant he was in the top ten per cent of his class.

Paul Bonnaci states, he met Aquino. Rusty Nelson narrates for the federal court record his picking up bearer bonds from Larry King in a Suite at the Ritz in Minneapolis, allegedly Iran-Contra money. John Gosch identifies him as the man who picked him up and paid for him two weeks after he was kidnapped.

The record is established that he was in military service during the time of the kidnapping. He was then a Major writing from "Psyops to Mindwar" describing mind control techniques and their use in the military.

At the conclusion of the report of the Nebraska Legislature and the Franklin Investigation they did not shrink from reporting on Satanism, unfortunately absolutely nothing came of it.

Many Nebraskans remember the horror of the occurrences in Rulo, but there is a temptation to think of the murderous cult behavior in Rulo as an aberration. Or to think of Satanism, witchcraft, and other cult activity as being things that happen elsewhere than Nebraska. (On July 17, 1991, John M. Zielinski on WHO Talk Radio Jan Michaelson show challenged the Iowa Legislature: "To walk down the hill to the Des Moines River, up past the Botanical Gardens and have a look under the bridge over university. 'Missing Children our Dead' 'Satan Rules' an off-duty police intelligence officer showed Zielinski this site in daylight saying, "After midnight, we do not come here. When the Satanist meet... they have guards with AK-47." (This officer also talked about local shoot outs that were in police reports but never made the Des Moines Register.)

The report introduces Priscilla Coates, from New York, a representative of Citizen's Freedom Foundation, a support group of former cult members.

"She describes cults as destructive groups, that are a problem on an international basis. She testified extensively about cults, and other destructive groups, (including Jonestown), in which children were constantly abused for purposes of cult discipline. She testified, that she had information of cults encouraging people to commit numerous crimes ranging from prostitution to theft to selling drugs. She described the cult at Rulo, Nebraska as being somewhat typical, in terms of isolation, group paranoia, excessive discipline and demands for obedience, etc.

She discussed how destructive groups prepare customized versions of the Bible, so that they can use biblical authority to influence people. She testified that many of them have no life experiences to which they can return, and she discussed the difficulty in rehabilitating children who had been subjected to cult abuse. She stated that information regarding Rulo, in terms of forcing cult members to have sexual relations with their children and with each other, was not uncommon, and that bestiality (making people have sex with animals) was also not uncommon,

The members of the Committee are fully aware of the fact that people do not want to hear about cult activity and are fully aware of the fact that to discuss witchcraft and Satanism is to risk being the subject of ridicule and even hostility.

We understand this.

Nevertheless, because Satanism and witchcraft, and other forms of cult abuse demonstratively do exist, it is our duty to report our findings and discoveries, in the hope that perhaps the public may be made aware of such dangers as may exist.

The report states: "Because under the First Amendment… Congress may make no law respecting an establishment of religion, or prohibiting the free exercise thereof, or abridging the freedom thereof, there is a satanic church which functions as a legitimate organization.

After declaring Satanism as a Constitutional protected religion, the report continues: Their practices include 1) sexual child abuse: 2)

prostitution; 3) incest; 4) orgies; 5) physical abuse; 6) homicides; 7) brainwashing towards suicide.

What in the above paragraph can be considered protected under the First Amendment? Quantico based, FBI Man Ken Lanning claims there is no satanic crime!

Kathleen Sorenson, Foster Mother

Attorney John DeCamp, like Ted Gunderson and Noreen Gosch stands ever ready to present the stories of the men, women and children who were abused and murdered to cover up the satanic activity that is rampant in Nebraska, Iowa, Minnesota, etc. From "The Fatima Crusader this account of Kathleen Sorenson, who lived and died trying to do right by the foster children she took into her home.

Sorenson appeared on the Geraldo Rivera's national televised special on Satanism. What follows is a transcription of an interview she gave on Christian TV in 1989, shortly before her death. It was based on her experience with over 30 children who spent months or years in her home. "We got involved and learned about this subject because we were.

foster parents and worked with several children. And several years back, several of the children began, after a period and building up trust, to talk about some very bizarre events that had happened in their past and they were frightening and very confusing.

I really didn't know what to think. We went to the police, and we went to social services and there was really nothing anyone could do. (Or would do). These children we worked with are now adopted, in safe homes, and probably would never have talked had they not felt able to trust the people they were living with....

There are certain things that are in common in the children's' stories when we talk about devil worship...There are things that come up in every single story, such as candles. They all talk about sex. Sex is without a doubt a part of every area of this, all sorts of perverted sex. This is what you will hear, about the sex, about the incest, and it is so hard to believe. But once, we get that, we have learned that we can go on and ask and find out...and it will involve pornography. Part of the reason is that they use it to threaten the children. "We have pictures we will show the police if you talk." It makes the children feel that they are in great danger, and they are all very frightened of the law. They talk about the garish makeup that the people in the group wear, they talk about the singing that they didn't understand. Obviously, that is chanting, and that has come up in every one of these stories, and none of them call it chanting. There will be dancing. Most often that will involve sexual acts. There will always be a leader and they will be very frightened of the leader.

The children, from a very young age, and I am talking about children who came out of birth homes, the family they were born to, worshipped the devil.

The children I have talked to have all had to murder before the age of two. That is something beyond anything I could comprehend. But in some way, whether with the help of an adult's hand over theirs, by having them practice, by getting them excited to be part of the adult scene, they do murder.

They are told they will never get out, no one will ever believe them, that there is no freedom that the law will get you. They are hopeless before they get someone willing to listen. They are threatened with death. Every time a child is killed in their group, they are told, if you tell, this will happen to you.... They believe that these people know everything they are doing, everyone they're talking to. One teenager told me that she had been told, that if she ever got married, that they would fool her, it would be one of them. They set them up to fail in every area.

It is very prevalent in the Midwest... Iowa, Nebraska, and Missouri. Some people speculated that these states are headquarters....

As you listen to us talk about these things, there will be a natural part of you, which will deny much of what you hear. Believe me, we did too. I would like to share this with you, partly in the children's words, so that you can hear the things that they said that nobody could make up, that no child could know. That's what eventually convinced me, along with the deep emotion.

The grieving, screeching damage and hurt that they cry out as they talk. They are today (1989) between the ages of 5 and 17. We are talking about children forming consciences at that time, learning right from wrong. These children do not know. They come out and do not know what is right. They are confused, and most often they have been in multiple placements, they will go to a home, they will steal, they will lie, they will hurt animals. One little guy would sharpen pencils and try to stab people. I don't mean poke, I mean stab. People don't like that in their homes. Many are sent to psychiatric hospitals, where they are labeled psychotics, schizophrenics, and who would want them...

I will begin with the first stories that we heard, which will seem horrible to you, but are very mild to me, because we have progressed and heard far worse things. The first story is about two little boys, who were 7 and 9 when they talked about sexual abuse at one point and were very grieved. We talked about good and bad touching, and we thought we really had gotten to the bottom of it. Then one afternoon the little one began to cry, and when we couldn't get the answer from him, the older brother said, "He is probably crying because he was in the room, when they killed his friend".

That was the first one we knew about. They talked about that victim being brought into a room, hands and arms tied, mouth tapped, and how there had been x's marked on his body, on his vital organs. That was bad enough. Within a very few weeks, we learned that it was not the adults who had killed that child. It was this oldest boy, who was talking.

The next person that we talked was a little boy, who was very borderline mentally. He had language problems; it was very hard for him to explain himself. And when he began to come out of it, everyone was startled by the way he talked. We were sure; we knew he had not been around these other children and heard anything.

"The part which made me believe this child's story, he talked about different babies being killed, but this one being stabbed, curled up in a fetal position. He was 9-years old when he was telling the story. His eyes became glazed as he said: 'They cooked that baby on the grill' And I thought, he has really flipped out. And he said "Oh, gross, it smelled like rotten chicken, or rotten deer.'

He then went on to tell us how they would cut out the heart, or cut off the sex organs, and save them in the refrigerator. A very typical thing that these kids talk about. They worship the sex organs. They kept it for another ceremony. I asked him where the bodies went. Eventually they talked about throwing babies in the fire.

And I asked them: You mean they were dead when they threw them in the fire?

And the littlest on said: "NO NO…Them was alive and then threw them." By this time, we were really freaked out. How can you help these kids? Where do you find a therapist who can deal with this?

The next child I will share about, and I am going sort of by categories here with the types of killings. This little girl is 11 today, she was 9 when she first talked. It was a very painful thing when she first started to share the sex things. The sex things are so harmful to children…She began to draw pictures of cats, and the cats all had tails that were on the other side of the page, or their leg was someplace else. She said she had to kill a pregnant cat. She had to kill the cat…. with a knife.

It progressed, the next time she had to kill a baby, the same way…. The baby was alive, and he was screaming. That child heard that, to this day, she has nightmares and flashbacks. They cut the baby open, and they ate him. They do this, so there are no bodies left. They burn what is left and grind up the bones. And she talked about that, pouring gasoline on the bodies and burning them in the back yard.

We know there are mortuaries involved, to cremate the bodies… The most horrible story about fire is extremely disturbing. She was a little girl when it happened and a teenager when she was telling me. She was describing a barn where they used to go to have their meetings. They used to gather outside the barn, and there would be chanting. Then as they went inside the barn they would split into different groups. She was never with any of her family. They all went to different places. I asked her where she had to go and she said, "I was always in the burning room."

They would take in children, probably preschoolers, and they would hang them from the rafters in this barn. There would be as many as five or ten hung in a row. This group was fully clothed, which was unusual, because frequently they were naked. The children, like this girl, were all given candles.

You can picture the ceremony as she described it. The candles were lit. Then the adults would go forward and would pour liquid from a cup on each of the children's clothing, which was obviously gasoline or kerosene. Then they would give a signal and the others would have to go forward and set the children on fire. When they were done, they would cut them down. The first child that this girl had to kill was a cousin, a little cousin.

What does that do to you? But you couldn't object... because the children who objected were killed. Frequently, she said, people would come in families, not knowing that their child would be sacrificed. She described the screams when they realized that their child had been killed... A child, about two years ago, just fell to the ground at Christmas.

time: everyone thinks that Christmas is such a wonderful time. She confessed that she hated Christmas; she couldn't wait until everything was put away, because all she could hear was babies crying. Christmas is the time when the most babies die. She covered her ears and cried for 2 hours. She screamed.... Stop it... stop it... stop it! Talk to God and make Him stop it! All she could hear is the screams and the babies crying...

Christmas for the children has been one of the worst times. I have had three children tell me about a very similar ceremony. I will kind of merge and tell you how it went. They were taken to a church (three different children, three different churches). It is a very festive occasion. They are taken to the front of the church. A small child is now brought in. Two of them talked about babies and they put them on a platform. The adults are all celebrating, dancing and singing. The children are getting into the spirit of it. What they are doing is forming a circle around the child. The child represents the Child Jesus, and they begin mocking, spitting, and calling names. They encourage the children to begin doing it and you can imagine how it gets out of control. At some point they hand all the children's knives and then they are all hacking, and slashing until the baby is dead. And then they all celebrate because the Child Jesus is dead.

DeCamp comments. Kathleen Sorenson was aware that it was dangerous to tell the public what she did. She appealed to friends, "Pray for me." She was killed in a head-on car crash in October 1989. Ted Gunderson evaluated the accident and believed Sorenson was killed by a satanic contract suicide. The other driver didn't die, but well could have. In satanic lore, a person who loses his life in such a contract murder/ suicide will be reincarnated with more power granted by Satan. Both the young woman driver and her husband had prior arrest records for cruelty to animals, a common marker for Satanism.

Not long after Sorenson's death, a teenager in a youth care facility told a worker, "You better watch out or we will get you like we got that lady from Blair." The youth went on to describe a ceremony of drawing lots for the privilege.

DeCamp concluded: "A few years ago if anyone had recounted something like her testimony, I would have recommended that they be hauled off to the loony farm. Today, I have no doubt that much—maybe all of it is true. I have been confronted with documentation of a world, I did not know about or believe existed."

Ted Gunderson has estimated that human sacrifice practicing Satanist group in U.S., Canada and Mexico number between three and three and one half million.

LETTER FROM A MURDERER

By David (Son of Sam) Berkowitz
From his private correspondence
Secured by Ted Gunderson

…You asked about Satanists. I'm not talking of thrill seekers, who hang onto and join every anti-establishment group that comes along. I'm not talking about those who remain on the fringe of such groups. My letter is about the elite and dedicated hardcore members of the Occult groups. You see, these people cannot be taken lightly. Please try to understand their philosophy of life and society. They have no fear of manmade laws nor the laws of God. To them, murder comes easy. Being antiGod, they love nothing better than a good kill.

These people will stop at nothing to fulfill their desires. They have the complete ability to elude the police and to cover their tracks complexly.

Many members of these hidden and secret groups are participating of their own free wills. Others aren't. Yet, they are there to obey every command and complete every task without question…lost souls, half-mad zombies they are.

There is a very important key that cannot be overlooked…it ALL ends in tragedy! So many people, who have followed the Left-Handed Path (black magic) have met either sudden death via accident, suicide or murder. Or they have suffered financial loss, the ruination of their reputation, or they just ended up totally insane. It is the same story!

John and Michael (fellow members of his coven, and fellow murderers) are dead. My life is ruined, too. And I also came close to death several months ago.

Personally, I think it is best if you leave all this alone, you or whoever started this investigation. Just drop it! It's for your own good…Look; there are a fearless lot. They HATE God! I'm not talking about common criminals. You know who I am talking about.

There are people who will follow a "Chosen Lamb" throughout the ends of the earth. If they feel that this person is the "next one" …well, they have money. They have brains and hate.

They will even kill in a church. Do you think I'm joking? Do you think I'm just bending your ear? I'm serious about all this. There is no reason why I shouldn't be. Sir, Satanists (genuine ones) are peculiar people. They aren't ignorant peasants or semi-illiterate natives. Rather, their ranks are filled with responsible citizens. They are normal on the outside, at least.

They are not a careless group who are apt to make mistakes. But They are secretive and bonded together by a common need and a desire to cause havoc on society. It was Aleister Crowley who said. "I want blasphemy, murder, rape, revolution, anything bad." Surely you will agree that death literally followed Crowley's footsteps.

Do you still doubt me? You know damn well that these Satanists cover their tracks pretty good. You are aware of their intelligence (businessmen, doctors, military personnel, professors, etc) Cults, as you know flourish around college campuses. They flourish around military bases, too. Drugs flow all over these places (universities and bases). Young service men and young college students are involved in sexual relations. So, mix the two of them up. Put them near each other and what do you have? You've got a wild, dedicated and nasty bunch of zealous, anti-establishment devil worshippers. And what a deadly mixture it is...

Above: Michael Aquino & wife Lilith Below: Lt. Col. Michael Aquino

WHY JOHNNY CAN'T COME HOME!

PROJECT MKULTRA, THE CIA'S PROGRAM OF RESEARCH IN BEHAVIORAL MODIFICATION

JOINT HEARING
BEFORE THE
SELECT COMMITTEE ON INTELLIGENCE
AND THE
SUBCOMMITTEE ON HEALTH AND SCIENTIFIC RESEARCH
OF THE
COMMITTEE ON HUMAN RESOURCES UNITED STATES SENATE

NINETY-FIFTH CONGRESS

FIRST SESSION

AUGUST 3, 1977

Printed for the use of the Select Committee on Intelligence
and Committee on Human Resources

U.S. GOVERNMENT PRINTING OFFICE
96-408 O   WASHINGTON : 1977

For sale by the Superintendent of Documents, U.S. Government Printing Office
Washington, D.C., 20402
Stock No. 052-070-04357-1

AND YE SHALL KNOW THE TRUTH AND THE TRUTH SHALL MAKE YOU FREE

John, VIII: 32

(Inscribed on the marble wall of the main lobby at CIA headquarter, Langley, Virginia)

George White who started with the OSS and continued in the CIA, dying of cirrhosis of the liver, wrote: "I toiled wholeheartedly in the vineyards because it was fun, fun, fun. Where else could a redblooded American boy lie, kill, cheat, steal, rape and pillage with the sanction and bidding of the All-Highest."

MIND CONTROL, MONARCH & MK ULTRA

If you asked the average thinking citizen: Do you believe the government? Do you believe the government lies? Remember the Warren Commission. Kennedy was the victim of a lone assassin –Lee Harvey Oswald. The finger of evidence points to the CIA as a major player in the Kennedy's assassinations, with the total co-operation of J. Edgar Hoover and the FBI, and the Media.

The President, shaking his finger: "I did not have sex with that woman! Over the past twenty years at least two books have been written with the word: Whistleblowers in the title. Who are these whistle blowers? They are individuals in government, industry, congress, CIA, FBI, military who see something that is at the least morally wrong, against the law or at the worst horrifyingly evil.

The United States government has conducted human experiments on a level with the worst human experiment conducted by the Nazi before and during WW II. Those same doctors and scientists were brought to this country by the hundreds to continue their mind control and drug experiments. Ex-CIA authors such as Phil Agee has implicated the CIA and other covert government operations to the genocide of at least 9 million people as the Covert Community sought to exercise its control outside the United States.

CIA man Terry Reed wrote in his book "Compromised" the Bush/Clinton Connection going back to a time when Clinton was governor. It involved using the Mena, Arkansas National Guard Base to fly in planes loaded with drugs and fly them out carrying arms for the Contras, drug dealers, and drug revolutionaries. Other whistleblowers writing about the people the CIA has put in power evil men who have caused the death of at 30 million people. If the Moslems call America "The Great Satan" it is because of the CIA manipulation and murders around the world. They have toppled hundreds of democratically elected leaders and replaced them with the military or a repressive dictator.

Yes, many of those Nazi doctors guilty of the worst atrocities were cleared of criminal charges brought to this country and allowed to go on with their experiments. None was more deadly; none more harmful to the young people of this country than the MK Ultra program and its many branches.

Mark Philips told the listeners of KCXL a Kansas City area radio station. "There are now hundreds of books in print that describe the involvement of the CIA in drugs and mind control. To follow this story, you only need to go to the largest library and start looking. Or you may find hundreds of sites on the Internet about drugs, about slavery, about mind control, about Satanism and all lead back to the government or someone connected to the government. "Under the terms of Operation Paperclip there was cutthroat competition among the Armed services to see who could secure the best Nazi scientists and engineers. "For its part, the US Navy was equally eager to snare its measure of war criminals. One of the first men picked up by the navy was a Nazi scientist named Theodore Benzinger. Benzinger was an expert on battlefield wounds, expertise he gained through explosive experiments conducted on human subjects during the waning stages of World War II. Benzinger ended up with a lucrative government contract working as a researcher at Bethesda Naval Hospital in Maryland. Quoted from "Whiteout: The CIA, Drugs and The Press by Cockburn and St. Clair

Mark Philips worked for NASA as an independent contractor supply monitoring equipment for behavior modification in what he assumed were animal experiments. Astronaut Gordon Cooper reveals that at least 54 of those experimental animals were children. He refers to them as NASA children and they were subjected to drug and centrifuge experiments which were supposed to give them "out of body" experience and improve the ability to communicate telepathically with "aliens" Gordon doesn't explain what aliens!

As with all whistle blowers, there have been major efforts to discredit Philips. Philips told Interviewer Richard Boyden: "MK Ultra is not an experimental program but an active program, which has been underway for at least two decades. It is a trauma-based program. This program was a direct result of our importation of Nazi/fascist scientist under "Operation Paper Clip. President Truman attempted to put a stop to this in 1949 but was unsuccessful."

Mark Philips speaks firsthand because he rescued a Monarch Mind Slave called Cathy O'Brien. The book they authored together "Transformation of America" is almost beyond belief—except that Paul Bonnaci and other children went through much the same thing. More than 80 children were identified in the Omaha/Lincoln area. They in turn talked about hundreds of others in major cities across America, especially in Washington D.C. The investigation of the Nebraska Legislature turned up evidence of a mind control project run at Offutt Air Force Base near Omaha.

Johnny Gosch when he visited his mother Noreen in the middle of the night told the same story. He asked his mother to do something about the congressmen, the generals, the governors, and the DIA, CIA and FBI men, who had participated in his torture and the torture of thousands of other children. Johnny was able to talk only because he escaped along with a group of other young men from their handlers—using the very training they have been given to escape their captors. Both Johnny and Paul have been trained to drastically change their appearance, dying hair and skin to pass as an Indian or becoming a blond.

Mark Phillips calls this a "U.S. Defense Intelligence Agency project for radically modifying human behaviors through MIND CONTROL Mind Control was begun by are importation of the Nazi/fascist scientists into this country—supposedly for the research involving propulsion and rockets. Actually, of the 900 initially brought over in 44 in only 200 were involved rocketry, the other 700 were psychiatrist and doctors who had participated in experiments to control the human mind."

Mind control literally began in earnest under Adolph Hitler in the late 1930s. He assigned Heinrich Himmler, Gestapo Chief, the task of researching multi-generational incest families in Northern Europe. Hitlers early background in the Satanic and Occult provided the impetus for this examination of occult trained individuals who could be totally obedient to a strong leader, even unto death.

Philips continues: "These families were the basis of all mind control research because Adoph Hitler believed, like many of our so-called leadership in this country believed, that nuclear war and nuclear proliferation was not the viable answer. There would not be anything left, no spoils for the victor. So, Hitler thought it best to be able to control the minds of his subjects. They began by developing what Hitler and Heinrich Himmler called "The Chosen Ones" (See also "Plot Against the Peace" 1946 which details this operation which trained 8,000 agents designed to carry on the Reich after Germany lost the war)

These chosen ones were the children of the multi-generation incest abusing, psychological and physically abusing families (see Satan Ch). They had developed a peculiar psychiatric malady, dysfunctional identity disorder DID. Many years ago, it was referred to as multiple personality disorder, which is a misnomer since they barely had any personality at all. The personality was fragment literally from abuse that began at birth. The father substitutes his penis for the mother's nipple, and it goes downhill from there. (In a statement to the Nebraska Legislature Dr. Judi-Anne Densen Gerber told of a baby 8 months old being diagnosed with gonorrhea of the throat.}

The DID individuals develop some strange traits, for example, they develop visual acuity 44 times that of you or I Adolph Hitler envisioned using these so-called chosen ones. He would put them in positions of extraordinary control and power like heads of state. He would use them in "special forces" and upon certain cues, codes, keys and triggers, these people would act antigenically, and just an automatic response to whatever their program consisted of. The program was quite sophisticated even in the 1930s when it was in an experimental mode and after Project Paper Clip took over this scientist brought all the information with them. And we placed them in our institution of higher learning (Kinsey Sex Research had Nazi data). In military complexes and with corporations with a fair number of them going into NASA.

These scientists were developing according to several congressional hearings project that were abused human rights and abused the field of psychiatry. The 95 Presidential Hearings revealed the MK Ultra name, and I am sure it has evolved into another unnamed program by now. Under the MK Ultra Umbrella there were many MK Ultra sub projects. Many of these involved tracking the same kind of multi-generational satanic/incest involved families in the United States and Canada, some of them even descendants of the original groups that Hitler had studied.

Some of these children would end up being programmed for robotic human beings that were used in special forces that were used in drug mule operations, money laundering, were used in the field of computers. There have been people surfacing in "legitimate" psychiatric facilities who were able to prove some of their background. They had been used for the sheer pleasure of some and to help fund the "Pentagon's Black Budget Operation". I am sure many of your listeners regard the drug problem as one that is separate from the government, when in fact the United States Government is the world's largest drug dealer."

In this radio program, Philips roundly condemns the psychiatric community for its failure to stand up and be counted. When Phillips rescued Presidential Mind Slave Cathy O'Brien (yes, Presidential) he sought help from psychiatrists to help deprogram her. Whether they were simply frightened by the consequence or already knew too much is the question.

The Monarch Project was a code name assigned to a new brainwashing formula, which was originally called "Bluebird." It was an outgrowth of Nazi experiment utilized by intelligence personnel in the U.S. Army during the 1950s. Unlike the Chinese who used something ancient like water torture, the U.S military resorted to drugs to gain control of the human mind.

In total violation of the Geneva Convention and the Nuremberg Laws they transported Chinese and North Korean prisoners to Japan. There they were subjected to LSD and a whole plethora of drugs designed not merely to elicit information but to turn them in to mind control slaves. In the next 50 years nearly 150 drugs would be tried on everyone from inmates in prison to fellow co-workers at corporations to students in universities.

Most of the American people can recite many of these drugs without prompting. Cocaine, heroin, amphetamines, marijuana, date rape drugs, etc. For all we know Viagra might have been developed out of these experiments. There were drugs that would render the subjects incapable of judging right from wrong, drugs that would turn them on sexually and prey on whatever weakness they showed.

Thus experiments, which began with the "enemies of America", were gradually administered to the people of America. In a brilliant move, the ruling elite decided to sell them they very drugs that would enslave them. The CIA bought at one time enough LSD to have drugged one quarter of the US population. FBI man Gunderson claims one drug proved to be capable of causing a heart attack within a half hour of being administered and was untraceable. Is this what happened to CIA Director William Colby?

While the military worked on prisoners of war, the CIA and FBI were experimenting with Candy Jones, a model turned modeling instructor, whom they turned into a secret (even from herself) undercover agent. British Secret Agent Intrepid, Sir William Stephenson told her she a "zombie" Agent. He stated to her that he had been able to use such agents during WWII, if captured their surface personality knew nothing.

Philips & O'Brien talk of the refined "zombie" drug, which made Cathy totally unaware of her past and indeed who she was in the present. If she were told she was Marilyn Monroe, she would from that point introduce herself as such until another command gave her another identity. Cathy was a Presidential model zombie and had far more scientific know how and care applied to her training than that Paul B, or Johnny

G. had. Although one of Paul's alters is totally fluent in German. There is no record of his ever leaving the country, although he can describe Hotels in Cologne, Germany.

For the next 15 years, the new-formed CIA took control from the

U.S. Army Ultra secret Monarch project, now code name MKI and MKII. Project Monarch was declared stopped by then President Gerald Ford. The CIA did stop experimentation but all records, equipment developed and under development were secretly handed over to the U.S. Defense Intelligence Agency. The DIA then secretly and illegally re-assigned the Monarch Project experiments right back to its original founders.... The

U.S. Army. Now it was cloaked under TOP SECRET U.S. Army Psychological Warfare Division.

The DIA used the excuse that it was for safekeeping. The discoveries detailed how to seize total control, undetected of a human mind for any "patriotic" purpose. The formula was so simple that even a person of average intellect and no moral foundation could successfully enslave almost anyone for any purpose. See the movie "Telefon" starring Charles Bronson for the best dramatic portrayal of how it worked. Although the film points a finger at the Russians, the adviser was said to have been from the U.S. governments mind control program.

Again, the words of Mark Philips: "The DIA is a politically governed/operated U.S. government intelligence gathering agency whose responsibilities, progress, and assignments are "monitored" by the intelligence committees of both the House and Senate. This equates to politicians having access to ultra secret, ultra dangerous information.... which? they could and HAVE USED against innocent US. citizens for their perverse pleasure and profits...undetected.

The original purpose of Monarch was to be used to "deprogram" captured espionage agents and to determine just what they had learned, second to make them "forget" what they had learned so they could be traded to their country in exchange for our agents.

The next step was to program the captured agent with a "cue" from one of our in-place agents to retrieve secrets from them.

The Russians out did us by devoting billions of dollars to research and development of a new method...a complex formula of precisely timed and orchestrated physical and psychological tortures that were administered to "young recruits" (in the U.S. it became government authorized kidnapping and child breeding), children over a long period of time. These normally above average intellect children were chosen due to their intelligence and genetics for being "conditioned" as the new generation of "super spies".

The U.S. aggressively began pursuing more exacting methods of super spy development. Michael Aquino, who had joined Anton LaVey's Church of Satan in California, broke off and formed the Temple of Set in the military, quickly winning both military approval and promotion. (Every indication suggests Bonacci, Johnny Gosch and others is that Aquino spearheaded the acquisition of new young Aryan type recruits.)

They were programmed to perform a variety of superhuman tasks with an incredible success rate. Meanwhile, Jimmy Carter signed another Presidential Executive Order, which supposedly halted the remaining Mind Control experimentations. This was the second false "death blow" to Monarch Project aka MKI, MKII, and MKIII. It was business as usual at the DIOA and the U.S. Army Psychological Warfare "

Mark Phillips states: "At this point in time, this writer was no longer associated directly with the intelligence community and therefore has no espionage statistics other than hearsay (which I will not repeat) except for the following.

The New Revised Monarch Project was now under the direction of a U.S. Army Major (now Colonel) Michael Angelo Aquino…who would put a new dark twist into the Monarch Project…Satanism. Colonel Aquino says he himself was sexually abused as a child and is a sociopath…. with a lot of political friends. Ronald Reagan, a proponent of mind control since he was governor of California, insisted Aquino attends White House parties in his satanic regalia. According to Cathy O'Brien he resented this and considered Satanism only a means to an end, but he reluctantly complied with Reagans wishes."

What follows in the next ten pages of the report is a list of the kind of mind control programs, Alpha, Beta, Delta, Theta. Children are buried alive with spiders or snakes. Cattle prods or high voltage law enforcement type stun guns are used to command instant obedience. If they are ordered to have sex, or to kill the obedience must be made a reflex. See Bonnaci Documents

The Theta program, which involved mind reading and out of body experiments ultimately evolved into electronic possession. Using the proper electronic high frequency broadcaster, they can make a room full of people suddenly decided they all need to use the bathroom at once. Individual with implants and the right stimulation can go from nice guy to crazed killer in a matter of minutes.

The first victims were captured spies, from friendly and hostile nations. "The second groups were bright aggressive young men who applied to Officers Candidate School. After a battery of tests, these eager young men were allegedly told, they couldn't go to OCS, but they could "volunteer" for a career in Intelligence where they would be given TOP SECRET training, James Bond "007" stuff. This true, but very misleading, information created powerful patriotic images in their minds. They envisioned being "special" espionage agents in just months instead of the years of OSC training."

The final recruits were a little younger than the college types, more like two or three years old. Some were given by fathers, who got caught sending kiddie porn through the U.S. Mails, others got caught having sex with underage boys or girls. CIA agents offered them money, business favors, and protection from prosecution.

Some fathers were educated at government expense on how to precondition their little girl with tortures of the mind and body and with sex... which would give this child a "gift of insanity" an MPD/DID super child. Some fathers became manufacturers to Uncle Sam producing dozens of children for the New Monarch project. Organized crime bosses dealing in child/adult porn, opened Day Care Centers to create a virtual "kiddie smorgasbord" When some of the occult conspirators got too sloppy as in the Franklin Legislative Investigation, the McMartin Day Care Center it could be taken care of.

West Point, N.Y., Fort Leavenworth, Kansas, Presidio, California— all military day care centers—all had incidents of child sexual abuse...all covered up.

Mark Phillips concludes: "Mind Control techniques/formulas unlike nuclear weapons systems can be reproduce without exotic and expensive component systems...in the privacy one's own home by anyone of average intelligence and absolutely no conscience. "Mind Control, "states Phillips" is just as lethal as nuclear war."

He predicts the Mind Control, he also termed "white slavery" will be the largest "cottage industry of the 21 Century. The U.S. now has nuclear regulatory agencies which oversee everything from nuclear weapons to nuclear power plants. But Mind Control thanks to corrupt U.S. Government officials...is out of control.

Before 1980, when Aquino took over Monarch, there were reported only 200 cases of MPD/DID, one of the rarest diagnosed psychiatric disorders. Today there are 24,000—which could mean from a quarter to half a million undiagnosed DIDs waiting around to explode with rage as a serial killer, child abuser, or mass murderer.

He concludes while, we're waiting for the answers, another child is being raped, mostly by the very person biologically designed to protect them…their father. Anyone who reads a newspaper or listens to the local news will be struck by the amount of child abuse and murder. Recent headlines are filled with mothers and fathers, or stepfathers, or boyfriend/girlfriend who kill their own children, or stepchildren.

Psychiatry: The Ultimate Betrayal

Bruce Wiseman, U.S. National President of the Citizens Commission on Human Rights and former chairman of the Department of History at the John F. Kennedy University. Wiseman in writing his book "Psychiatry: The Ultimate Betrayal" indites the entire psychiatric community in this country for its cooperation with the CIA drug experiments. Government records show the CIA ordered LSD by the ton from a midwestern drug manufacturer It was handed out to doctors and psychiatrist like a "candy" cure all for mental illness, when in fact it did far more harm than good.

This drug was not only dispersed to military bases but to many psychiatrists and doctors throughout the University communities who tested it on student "volunteers" One psychiatrist, Dr Ewen Cameron, former president of the America Psychiatric Association, used LSD in combination with electric shock to "depattern" the minds of paying patients. Wiseman state." It is ironic that Camerion, who was a member of the Nuremberg tribunal hearings of Nazi war atrocities, would later work for the CIA and violate the Nuremberg Code for medical ethics by sponsoring experiment on unwitting and unwilling subjects."

Wiseman's experiments were conducted in Canada with the financial backing of the CIA. Those patients are the only ones to successful sue the CIA and win—perhaps because they were Canadian and could not be blocked by invoking the National Security Act. These experiment and the subsequent lawsuit were dramatized in a made for TV mini-series shown in the U.S.

An Iowa City newspaper" ICON" exposed the University of Iowa Hospitals to participate in such experiments. Later, information revealed that University Hospital also participated in radiation experiments in which mothers and newborn babies were given radiation pills as vitamin supplements. The government needed to test the effects of radiation on human beings.

Psychiatrist Louis Jolyon West created the greatest misstep in LSD experiments when he overdosed on an elephant. The animal immediately fell over in a stupor. All attempts to revive the animal failed. Most of the animal experiments at universities were conducted on two-legged animals. Some students were paid a dollar for each time they took part in experiments.

Tens of thousands of soldiers from the 50s through the 80s, were used without their knowledge. They were sometimes told they were taking part in flu medicine development. These experiments on soldiers went far beyond LSD, hypnosis combined with drug cocktails were designed to create "a Manchurian Candidate".

Wiseman stated by the late 1950s, psychiatrists who administered LSD were all the rage. Cary Grant was among those who promoted the use of the drug and soon psychiatrists who used LSD in therapy were inundated with clients. Yet in the years to come the use of LSD will come to be known for its bad trips and its ruined minds. LSD was first discovered in Switzerland and was first probably used by the Nazi's who exercised control of Switzerland during WWII

Where was mind control going?

The CIA for over 50 years has been developing mind control technology, a technology designed to alter the basic mindset of a people. Its purpose is to devise operation techniques to disturb the memory, to discredit people through aberrant behavior, to alter sex patterns, to elicit information and to create emotional dependence.

Its goal is to program individuals to carry out any mission of espionage or assassination even against their will even against such fundamental laws of nature as self-preservation.

The newspapers have been full of stories of mind control victims who have gone on to commit crimes. Sirhan, Sirhan with the assassination of Robert Kennedy. John Hinckley in the attempted assassination of President Ronald Reagan. In each instance these people have appeared dazed and out of it afterwards. Lee Harvey Oswald did have a memory and information he could have called upon. Therefore, had to be killed. The other men remembered nothing. It was safe then to put them away in a jail or a mental institution.

It is interesting that Walter Bowart was born in Omaha, Nebraska; the center for the only real investigation of mind control conducted by other than a do-nothing Congress. The reason for the "Franklin Credit Union" investigation was the missing forty million dollars. It led to CIA/Satanism and FBI/NAMBLA connections, which in the end brought forward the Paul Bonacci's and the Johnny Gosch. Both later talked about mind control, Monarch and MKUltra. (see Bonaci Documents)

Walter Bowart in his book "Operation Mind Control" states in his author's note that the book is an exercise in Citizens' Intelligence and that the majority who contributed to it were private citizens working on their own efforts. Like the author, they too were shocked and outraged at the many citizens of this country, who have been victimized by their own government.

Published in 1978, this was well before the information surfaced about the black men who were allowed to die of syphilis in order to study its long-term effects, or those mothers and babies who were given radiation pills in order to study radiations effect on the human body.

Bowart describes the circumstances surrounding the four-year enlistment of David, described as a young Air Force Sergeant. "Ever since I got out of the service, I haven't been able to give a day-to-day account of what happened to me during those four years. The scary thing is that I still have a horrible fear of talking. I tend to speed up my speech when I'm being pressed on something: I get very tense when anyone asks me about my service duties. ...Something has happened to my mind."

David joined the service in 1969. David had not been part of the 60s revolution he had not smoke pot or used LSD. David had hoped to be a doctor and, therefore, sought something in the Air Force related to this field. He was put instead in supply but told it was a cover for an Intelligence Operation; he was to be a part of it. But weeks passed and he was still making supply entries on a computer.

Next, he woke up in a hospital and was told he had tried to commit suicide. He has no memory of this. Interrogation and drugs followed, then suddenly he is granted, and two weeks leave home. After his leave he is shipped to Guam. Instead of remaining at the main base, he is shipped to a small facility eight miles away. Here things were different. He was suddenly paired up with a woman, Pat, who throughout his stay would be wife and companion. They planned a meeting when they got out.

Yet afterward David could not remember her last name and had misplaced her address. Moreover, when he applied for jobs that asked what he had done the past four years, he would break out in a sweat and flee the office.

David spent years under psychiatric care. He was finally asked to decide, did he wanted to spend the next 18 months unraveling the mind block, and so he could remember what he did in the Air Force. Or did he want to concentrate on functioning normally in his life today. He chose today and decided to forget his past. How many military personal walks around America with blank spots in the memory?

A "flashback" caused by a remembered incident the causes of "a rage" that under the write circumstance can lead to death. And in less trying circumstances to lose of job or marriage. America's future rests with coming to a true understanding of what happened in our past. A lone gunman did not kill Kennedy! Did Franklin D. Roosevelt know about the bombing of Pearl Harbor in advance? Do you have a blank spot in your memory bank where you cannot remember what happened for days, months or years as David has?

Do not be afraid to ask questions. I talked to a young lady, a recent high school graduate working in a department story. When she had heard part of the story of what went on in Nebraska, she said: "My parents told me that if we criticize this government, they will come and arrest us!" Are we liking the little old lady who fears to look under the bed for the burglar and instead covers here head and hopes he will go away?

Where are "The Manchurian Candidates?

Richard Condon author of the fictional "The Manchurian Candidate" wrote a Forward to "Operation Mind-Control" Condon writes: "As demonstrated inescapably by Walter Bowart in his book: Our Father who art in the American secret police has endowed hundreds of scientists at American universities to unravel methods of fracturing American minds… In this book, Walter Bowart has proven each step of this official, terminal, government anarchy, even though that appears to be a contradiction in terms. To alter and control human minds is the ultimate anarchy. What is offered by official apologists as a tribute to the needs of daring-do by romantic spies are acts of hatred and sadism against all people in an insane and degraded determination to extirpate conscience from society." No better explanation can be made of what has gone on in Nebraska and to some extent Iowa. When the investigation of the Nebraska legislature began revealing almost every person in positions of power were and are more interested in maintaining their position than respecting either the laws of man or God. In Nebraska sadistic pedophiles have been taken under the wing of protection of both the Republican and Democratic parties. Nebraska Governor, after Governor simply says: "It's not my responsibility". Although governors, legislators and all elected officials take an oath of office. "I will uphold the Constitution of the United States and the Constitution of the State of Nebraska.... Iowa, etc."

What happened to Johnny Gosch. We know from both Johnny and Paul Bonacci that immediately after he was kidnapped, he was repeatedly raped and molested while being photographed for pornography purposes. He was kept locked in a boarded-up basement room. This was only the beginning of his journey for survival. Bonacci reported, Johnny was later taken by Col. Michael Aquino to Colorado, to begin his life of terror. Noreen Gosch has said of her son. He is no longer the same Johnny...not the boy who wanted to be an architect.

David entered the service because he faced being drafted but Johnny was not drafted.... He did not choose to serve his country at the age of 12. Those who saw him, as another kind of guinea pig gave him no other choice. Johnny came to his mother seeking justice, for himself. He wanted to live as a free man. "The Lost/Missing Children" posters are mounted on the walls of every Wal Mart in the country.

Ray Bilger writing in an article from **www.davidicke.com**

"I lived with Gail for a very stormy year and a half. She died in January of 1996, MDP (DID) and involvement in MK Ultra; pictures with Ronald Reagan, pictures at the Hefner Mansion, or was that her twin? And much more, I sit on quiet evening, maybe sipping a little Chardonnay... I speculate on what more I could have done ...to help "put Humpty together again." She committed suicide.

Jim Gentry on the same site replied: "My best wishes to all in this ongoing tragedy, even to the MK Ultra Handlers, those master behaviorists, with all the codes, keys and triggers. Guys, I wish you would all get religion: realize that your pet robots are real people, and defect: come over to our side. We need your skills to help heal what you have wrought over these many years."

A Doctors Boast

"I can hypnotize a man—without his knowledge or consent—into committing treason against the United States," boasted Dr. George Eastabrook in the early 1940s. This was the beginning of what would later be called Mind Control. Eastbrook conducted experiments on U.S soldiers to prove his point. One of the experiments involved placing a normal, stable private in a deep trance. He was told the officer was an enemy soldier who was going to kill him. When brought out of the trance he leaped for the officer's throat. The cardinal sin in the military is to attack a superior officer.

In 1958, Dr Louis Gottschalk, the CIA's "independent contractor" had prepared a think tank report which suggested that the intelligence agencies might control people through addiction. It was recommended that GIs newly discharged from hospitals would make subjects worth studying since their need for pain medication made them easy to control. So, our government began a series of experiments using a variety of drugs to control the people.

In a report from the U.S. Senate, August 3, 1977, entitled: "Project MKUltra, The CIA's program of research in behavioral modification. Behavioral modification sounds so pristine, so medical, it amounted to experiments to modify individuals, especially children, so they could be "Manchurian Candidate" assassins, human computers with photographic memories, drug couriers, and prostitutes. What they discovered thanks to the Nazi scientists is that one individual could be all of the above without their main personality knowing anything about it.

Here is an Excerpt

"3. The Surreptitious Administration of LSD to Unwitting NonVolunteer Human Subjects by the CIA After the Death of Dr. Olson." (Understand that today the use of all kinds of drugs is the number one problem in America)

Much violent crime in this country is due to the need of the drug addicted, to get more money to buy drugs. Drugs also destroy the reasoning power and the brain, hence robberies of gas station, quick food places often result in killing of the clerks for what is often a few dollars to a few hundred dollars.

The government report continues: "The death of Dr Olson could be viewed, as some argued at the time, as a tragic accident, one of the risks inherent in the testing of a new substances. It might be argued that LSD was thought to be benign (Note: human experiments of a new drug were being conducted without the knowledge of the subject that he or she was being drugged). After the death of Dr. Olson the dangers of the surreptitious administration of LSD were clear. Yet the CIA continued or initiated a project involving the surreptitious administration of LSD to non-volunteer human subjects. This program exposed numerous individuals in the United States to the risk of death or serious injury without their informed consent, without medical supervision, and without necessary follow-up to determine any long-term effects."

A letter to Richard Helm, then Director of the CIA, in 1954 suggested:

"We intend to investigate the development of a chemical material, which causes a reversible non-toxic aberrant mental state, the specific nature of which can be reasonably well predicted for everyone. This material could potentially aid in the discrediting individuals, eliciting information, and implanting suggestions and other forms of mental control."

This report made it quite clear that although the CIA and other covert governmental agencies used and continued to use a variety of drugs to discredit individuals. In Bowart's book there is an incident described of how an agent slipped a drug into the drinking glass on the podium. The speaker made a complete fool of himself because he was so disoriented. Any reader who gets the idea that this was done only to "foreign" individuals better think again. Anyone who attempts to expose bad conduct an even murderous practices would becoming a potential target for chemical warfare Following the bad behavior, due to being drugged, an article would be written about the speaker, by a CIA asset, further discrediting him or her.

One of the most cited books on mind control is John Marks "The Search for the Manchurian Candidate." A declassified memorandum, from the Deputy Director for Science and Technology to Deputy Director of Central Intelligence, comments on John Marks FOIA (Freedom of Information Act) request. Notes the difficulty in finding records.

"Dr Gottlieb retrieved and destroyed all the MKULTRA documents he was able to locate, it is not surprising that the earlier search for MKULTRA document was unsuccessful. The purpose of establishing the MKULTRA mechanism was to limit knowledge of the sensitive work being performed to those with an absolute" need to know basis." If those precepts had been followed, the recently found B & F files should have contained only financial and administrative documents." Instead of these there were documents which could give the outside reader, the outside reporter, the feeling that they had uncovered experiments worthy of Dr. Frankenstein. It allowed Joseph Mingle similar experiments by the same Nazi doctors who had worked for him…perhaps even by Mingle himself, under Cold War Secrecy Acts and under the umbrella of National Security.

What U.S government documents reveal is that not only were mind controlling type drugs developed and used on people without their knowledge, but they also developed Shellfish toxin for the purpose of poisoning the enemy were developed and retained in the face of a Presidential Directive that they be destroyed. Marks obtained 20,000 documents relating to mind control under the FIOA.

In the 1970s, CIA Director Richard Helm ordered all files relating to the CIA Mind Control experiments destroyed. A few years later a small number of them surfaced and were review by the Senate. One surviving document bears an uncanny resemblance to the circumstances surrounding the assassination of Robert Kennedy. The document dated 1954, describes efforts to find a way to induce an individual **"to perform an act, involuntarily, of attempted assassination against a prominent politician or if necessary, against an official"** It suggested that the subject be "surreptitiously drugged through the medium of an alcoholic cocktail at a social party." Sirhan last memory was of pouring coffee for a pretty girl wearing a polka dot dress. When Sirhan was taken from the assassination scene, patrolmen shined a flashlight in his eyes and stated that Sirhan's eye didn't react. The officials of the LA Police department lost Sirhans blood test, and the policemen could not recall his earlier statements. About Sirhans eyes.

Witness Sandra Serrann claimed she saw Sirhan with a "Latin" man and a girl in a polka-dot dress just prior to the shooting. Los Angeles Police Department polygraph operator Sgt Enrique Hernandez harassed/intimidated/ridiculed her attempting to get her to change her story. Hernandez apparently had ties to the CIA.

Congressional records show that the CIA continued to perform experiments on a psychiatric patient and later lobotomized him. The list of atrocities performed on captive patients is only matched by the chemical warfare experiments performed on whole small communities.

Everything from chemical warfare to mosquitoes infected with yellow fever. The experiments were successful, many people died.

Perhaps one of the greatest mistakes made by any President made was Harry Truman when September of 1946, he signed permission for "Operation Paper Clip." Truman expressly excluded anyone found "to have been a member of the Nazi party and more than a nominal participant in its activities, or an active supporter of Nazism or militarism" The first set of scientists were rejected by the State Department as "ardent Nazis."

Director of the War Department's Joint Intelligence Objective Agency, Bosquet Wev wrote a scathing memo warning the State Department "the best interests of the United States have been subjugated to the efforts expended in 'beating a dead Nazi horse." We learn from a host of books that the Nazi party only restructured beginning in 1943's. "The Plot Against the Peace" outlines how the Nazi's realizing they were losing the war began to plan for the peacetime continuance of the Nazi party not in Germany but in the World at large.

Nazi's trained at several centers, were given new identities and new backgrounds, especially speaking German eastern European countries and told to await the end of the war. Then apply for asylum in various free world countries. The excuse being they were fleeing communism.

At the same time, Allen Dulles, then CIA director was meeting with General Reinhard Gehlen, a Nazi general who had run the spy network inside what became the Soviet Union. Dulles promised Gehlen that his spy network was safe inside the CIA. Dulles had the scientists' dossiers re-written to eliminate incriminating evidence that tied them in to the most severe atrocities against both Jewish and Gentle prisoners.

Allen Dulles' efforts opened a whole host of projects stemming from Nazi Research. Unfortunately for America… MK Ultra/Artichoke, Bluebird and other projects were brought forth under the umbrella of protected the CIA afforded them.

Truman virtually opened a Pandora box of ills for this country and the world; because he did not realize that power hungry members of the military establishment would lust after the information on mind control experiments. Although Warner Van Braun and others experimenting with military rockets, planes, and weapons were brought into this country, they numbered only about 200. An additional 700 psychiatrist and other scientists who had been working on mind control were brought in and ordered to begin experiments all over again with the American military and finally an unwilling and unknowing American public.

In 1985, Linda Hunt writing in the Bulletin of the Atomic Scientists examined 130 reports on Project Paperclip subjects. Everyone "had been changed to eliminate the security threat classification." This may have sparked the interest which eventually led her to complete in 1991 "Secret Agenda: Operation Paperclip" a damning indictment of Allen Dulles and those who conspired not only to alter the dossiers of scientists who fit the description of Nazi War Criminals, but promoted them in position of power in the academic community and war industries.

The Occult in Mindwar

"Satan Wants You" declares author Arthur Lyons. His books link the in the occult to the psychedelic revolution. With the likes of Timothy Leary touting LSD as a religious experience, Lyon claims it only led to interest in the occult. Today with the knowledge Leary worked for the CIA, the connection becomes clearer.

From Christopher Simpson book "The Splendid Blond Beast" "Friedrich Nietzsche called the aristocratic predators who write society's laws "the splendid blond beast" precisely because they so often behave as though they are beyond the reach of elementary morality. We can imagine them returning from an orgy of murder, arson, rape and torture, jubilant and at peace with themselves as though they had committed a fraternity prank."

Anyone who examines the way CIA Agents were recruited and indoctrinated would recognize that it was very similar to the way the SS trained their soldiers. For the service to the fatherland (for the matter of national security) nothing was beyond the scope of an agent (like James Bond) was licensed to kill, not just the guilty. The CIA judged and executed, but the innocent who might have exposed "a plot" and therefore had to be eliminated.

Philip Agee, CIA, who became disgusted with the murderous ways of the CIA was accused of treason for "revealing their secrets". He escaped several attempts to kill him. President Ronald Reagan declared him a traitor and removed his citizenship. Today Agee is a man without a country. Agee has no passport, and no country will give him citizenship because of the pressure from the U.S. government. Agee's life may be an extreme example but many "whistleblowers" both in government and in industry have found themselves ostracized in their profession and often vilified by the news media.

What most people have not realized is that the DIA/CIA and other covert "government" have infiltrated into all walks of life. Today there are five branches of Government, Executive, Legislative, Judicial, Media and Clergy. And examination of newspaper, magazines and books will reveal that members of the clergy and journalist are CIA assets, the work for and guard against a public being informed.

"If people truly want to combat this phenomenon, it must be brought out into the public; it must be brought out into the light of day, and it must be done so very publicly so as to protect the people coming forth. It cannot be combated just on a national level, because it is international in nature. Governments work in collusion with other governments throughout the world; people who want power work in collusion with others; they use each other to gain social, economic and political power."

Dr. Green (A programming alter)
Quoted from: Thanks For The Memories…. By Brice Taylor

Brice Taylor is one among many of the Presidential Mind Control Slaves, who have courageously come forward to tell their story in books, videos, Television and talk radio. The following is a quote from her book, in which she describes in detail the creation of a Mind Controlled Slave.

THANKS FOR THE MEMORIES BY BRICE TAYLOR

"MANUFACTURING THE MIND CONTROLLED SLAVE"

I would like to define some terms that you will hear when learning about people with "multiple personalities." Dissociation is a key term that refers to the ability of the mind to "cut off" a part of itself from conscious awareness. An everyday example of this ability, which we all have in varying degrees, is the experience of driving down the freeway and missing the exit you take every day because you are thinking about something else. You "come to" an exit or two late and realize you missed your exit, even noticing that you "saw" the exit sign, but it didn't "register" within you to take it!

Part of your mind was dissociated, or separated from, the real world around you while you focused on internal thoughts. Another example is reading every word on a page in a book, and then realizing you had not comprehended a single word, because you were thinking of something else. All of us have these experiences.

This ability of the mind to detach from itself is a brilliant coping mechanism that the mind uses in situations of extreme threat to protect itself from the full awareness of a traumatic situation. You may recall reading about Vietnam veterans, who had amnesia for their war experiences, but would have difficulty coping with life. They would fee detached or estranged from others; they would have difficulty feeling any kind of feelings, except for outbursts of anger; they would have difficulty concentrating, would feel anxious and on edge without knowing why, and would have an exaggerated startle response (over-responsive to stimuli). These are all characteristics of the diagnosis "Post Traumatic Stress Disorder" or PTSD. In addition, these veterans would have sudden memories of the horrors of war. These memories would be "triggered" by something that reminded their unconscious mind of the war experience) for example, the sound of a car backfiring, reminding them of gunfire). In these sudden memories, they felt as if they were re-living the experience, smelling, tasting, felling, hearing and seeing in vivid detail everything they went through during an actual battle. These memories, complete with all the sensory memories, are called flashbacks. During those flashbacks, the veteran would be out of touch with the reality around them; they would no longer know it was 1985 and they were in America; they would think it was 1968, and they were in the jungle, reliving a battle. They were totally dissociated from reality and were reliving a past reality that was now only in their minds. Later, in processing these experiences, the soldiers would report that during the actual battle, they would feel very detached, even numb, from what was happening, even though they may have been wounded themselves. At times, they reported feeling as though they were standing outside of themselves, observing themselves going through the trauma of the battle, but not feeling anything. They were dissociated from their reality. But their brain was recording all the experience, exactly as it occurred, and those "mind and body" memories were being re-experienced during a flashback.

When someone is exposed to a "psychologically distressing event that is outside the range of usual human experience... is usually experienced with intense fear, terror and helplessness, (DSM III) then dissociation usually occurs as a way for the mind to process the event without overwhelming the person. Parts of the experience (either knowledge of what happened; the feelings associated with the event; the sensory experiences of the event, or the behaviors expressed during the event) become separated from one's conscious awareness. The more frequent the trauma, the more dissociation occurs. This phenomenon is why children who have been severely sexually abused and tortured, are amnesic for those events. In a landmark university study by Linda Williams hundreds of children were brought into a hospital emergency room who received medical confirmation of sexual abuse, were contacted at intervals throughout a 20-year period. Only one-third of these children, when reaching adulthood, retained conscious memories of sexual abuse— all others had repressed, or dissociated, those awful memories. Such is the power of the mind to block out painful experiences.

During times of torture and extreme pain, the mind is in an altered state, as it dissociates itself from reality. But there are other ways to alter the mind state, for example, by sensory deprivation, or meditation, whereby one focuses internally, with sensory stimulation from the outside minimized or eliminated. You may recall in the 1980's that "float tanks" were popular. In a float tank, you are floating on very heavily salted water; you are enclosed in a totally darkened metal tank, and you float for an hour without any sensory stimulation. Many people felt claustrophobic and couldn't take it. But if you could stand it, you would eventually report having a euphoric experience. If you had been hooked up to a brainwave machine (EEG), your brain would no longer be producing beta waves (the brain state associated with usual waking activity). Instead, you would be in a theta state, the state associated with deep relaxation, as when you are just about ready to fall asleep (the twilight state).

In this state, the pain produces lots of endorphins, the body's natural "feel good" chemicals that give you a profound sense of well-being. It is important to note that this twilight state is associated with the ability to rapidly absorb and learn information. Without the "filtering" mechanism of the conscious waking mind, information seen or heard "pours" into the subconscious mind.

Biofeedback expert Thomas Budzynski of the University of Colorado Medical Center reports "We take advantage of the fact that the twilight state, between waking and sleep, has these properties of uncritical acceptance of verbal material, or almost any material it can process; it is in such "altered" states of consciousness that a lot of work gets done very quickly." (For much more information about brain research and technology associated with producing altered states, read the fascinating book Mega Brain, by Michael Hutchison) Other methods used to alter brainwave states include, but are not limited to, rapid flashing lights, drugs, phased sound waves, negative ions (electromagnetic energy fields), electroshock, alterations in gravity in the cerebellum (spinning), microwave emitters, and lasers.

It is vitally important to understand dissociation, because in learning about how someone's mind can be controlled by someone else, you must understand how it is possible to program the human mind as you would a computer. "Programming" is recent term in history of mind control (and is of course associated with computer technology). Perhaps you'd recognize it better as "brainwashing."

In the POW camps, captors would refer to "freezing," a term used to destroy the person's identity. Using food and sleep deprivation, isolation, torture, chronic assault on a person's values, and instilling total dependence on the captors for survival, a person's whole sense of self would be destroyed. They would be totally helpless, broken, with no will of their own left. They would then be ready for the "brainwashing," or "refreezing" whereby a new value system and a new identity would be put in through reward and punishment, conditioning or "programming" that person to believe or do only what the captors wanted them to believe or do. (For more information on brainwashing, including USA and Canadian government experimentation, read: Brain Control by Elliot Vallenstein; Deep Self by John C. Lilly; Inside the Black Room by Jack Vernon; In Search of the Manchurian Candidate by John Marks; Journey into Madness by Gordon Thomas; I Swear by Apollo (author unknown; published by Canadian publisher).

Just as it is possible to break down a person to create someone you can control (by getting them to do anything you want them to do), so it is possible to program a part of a person's mind (a dissociated part that is split off, by trauma or other means, from connection with reality). You can "teach" that part of the mind to do what you want it to do without the part of the mind that is conscious and aware knowing what's going on. Hence, people with multiple personalities report that they "lose time," whereby they don't remember where they have been or what they have been doing.

TECHNIQUES ON "CREATING" NEW CHILDREN

"Daub fingertip size glob of Vaseline or K-Y jelly on pressure points – wrists, inner elbows, behind knees, under ears. Take ends of 2 wires (black and red are easiest, negative/positive easier identified) with mental attachments (round, copper, holes in center) and tape with surgical tape on top of Vaseline. Calibration – watch for muscular reactions, eye glazing, sweating, involuntary loss of bladder control, bowel control. Want to give enough of a current w/o being too much. Want my child to remain alert. Words, cords given. Assignments given. "Yes, one finger, No, raise two; Confused – raised right hand." Clarify instructions. If still confusion, time to stop, take a break. Do not allow any contact between patient and others until the cycle is completed. Do not, under any circumstances, offer juices, snacks, etc. which could be construed as a "reward" until the cycle is completed. Check carotid pulse for significant elevation in blood pressure. ? Do not wish to have a heart attack. Heart attacks can occur in children. (Children are outfitted with diapers before the sessions begin, are also taken to the bathroom beforehand. Keeps down unnecessary interruptions). Always keep voice on same level. Not hurried, not raised or lowered. Same pace always. Droning, hypnotic effect. Helps to stabilize heart rate.

When instructions are given to child, and received, then are only then give reward of name for identification purposes. Code phrases – "well done," "very good," or "you did really good." Avoid hugs, touch, and any other forms of physical contact. Eye contact is necessary, stabilizing. Allow alter-state to form place of safety within, encourage alter to describe internal surroundings. (All is taped, voice-activated, recorded later in the computer records for others to refer to). "

In March of 1995, before a Presidential Hearing in the United States the horrific radiation and mind control experiments, performed on unwitting subjects, was ONCE AGAIN brought to the U.S. Government's attention. At the conclusion of the hearing the Committee recommended further exploration of the mind control experimentation, however NOTHING FURTHER WAS DONE.

So, in 1997, a group of fifteen survivors and professionals, organized by ACHES-MC (Advocacy Committee for Human Experimentstion Survivors—MIND CONTROL) came together and testified in regard to their own experiences of mind control atrocities. This was recorded on video by Wayne Morris (CKLN Radio out of Canada) and sent with a letter to President Clinton requesting further investigation. To this very day nothing has been done and the pleas for investigation into these matters has been completely ignored… one has to wonder why?

WHY JOHNNY CAN'T COME HOME!

The United States declared the 1990's as "The Decade of the Brain" In 2000 and beyond, let us join together to do whatever it takes to insure the express right and freedom of our brains and insure the freedom of our minds. Putting fear aside, let us join in **TRUTH AND LOVE**

As we face the year 2000, are we going to allow this most precious human asset, OUR MINDS, to be abused, used and harnessed by ANYONE?

It's bad enough to think that any individual would interfere with these basic freedoms, but to know that the perpetrators are some of the most influential people in the world is unconscionable. Many are our World Political Leaders, Corporate Business Heads, Sports and Entertainment figures, World Banking Leaders, plus a group of publicly nameless puppet masters who work strategically from the top, and are pulling the strings

...... Brice Taylor

Thanks For the Memories

To order: Thanks For The Memories
Brice Taylor Trust
P.O. Box 655
Landrum, SC 29356

MIND CONTROL, MONARCH & MK ULTRA

The single most important book to detail how Nazi experiments became Project Monark/MKUltra

SECTION THREE

INTRODUCTION TO 2024

We are beginning a new year of 2024! This year marks 24 years since my first book was written. In this second edition of my book, I have kept the initial story of Johnny's kidnapping and what followed for several years. Including all the details we knew at that time. With this update I will elaborate on some of the things which happened and are still relevant to the case now.

Most of the activity which was changing daily did take place in the first number of years. I have kept detailed records of the situation for the sake of clarity as I will go forward on the case.

Going through something so traumatic is never ending when it continues for decades. My mission was to try and find my son, Johnny. But also, to bring awareness to people in our country about what was happening to children.

One thing I learned firsthand was about the different types of pedophiles. We have the garden variety who live in our communities. They may use and abuse a child but rarely kill or kidnap. They bribe children to remain silent and to live with that secret. This is a bad situation. However, when one thinks about the larger scale of this crime. The pedophiles who take children for their business, sell them and make profits off our children. It is the unthinkable that is taking place.

My private detectives were able to find evidence through the years of this taking place locally. I began speaking out about this information twenty-five years before this crime was given the name Human trafficking.

Did people want to hear it? No, they did not. The subject was to horrible to consider. I can remember when my detectives brought this information to me and explained it all. I sat there and kept saying "This can't be…this is America, and we don't do that to our children". But it was all true. For me it was difficult to get my mind around this horrific news. However, with time and reading the information over and over. I realized this was all true and more than likely this is what happened to Johnny.

When we lose a loved one and particularly a child to a violent crime. The survivors feel actual pain in the region of their heart. It is said to last up to five years with some variance among people. When I was a speaker for one of the groups in Des Moines… my audience were people who all lost their children to a crime someone committed. It was asked during the meeting by one of the people "how long has the pain in your heart lasted"! Several people volunteered for the information. Then one person asked me how long mine lasted and I told the crowd it was four years, a six months and ten days. I knew exactly how long that physical pain was with me. Then one day I woke up and the pain was gone. I never knew this existed and that people took notice of the length of time it lasted with different individuals.

Another thing I have wanted to accomplish is the solving of the kidnapping cases of Johnny, Eugene Martin and Marc Allen. To bring peace to the families who have suffered enough. It is my hope that this second edition of my book will continue to help people who have lost their children and inspire those who can spread awareness.

INTRODUCTION TO 2024

AND NOW FOR "THE REST OF THE STORY"

Many years ago, Paul Harvey a radio personality would give the highlights in the news reports. Then after a pause he would say.

And "now for the rest of the story". I always liked that phrase.

During the past 40+ years since Johnny was kidnapped many incidents have taken place. I am going to begin with the Police Chief in 1982, Orval Cooney. The day Johnny was kidnapped as you know from reading the chapter on the kidnapping. We filled out a missing person's report and the officer left. We did not see another member of the police dept. until three p.m. However, we had a visit from 23 people who had been out searching wooded areas any place that was secluded. The police chief arrived in a squad car; he was under the influence of alcohol at the time. He climbed up on the picnic table and used a bull horn yelling to the crowd... "everyone go home this kid is nothing more than a G.... D.... runaway. All the volunteers were shocked and immediately came to tell us what took place. I got a very dark feeling from the police chief and did not trust him from the beginning.

It was difficult to believe what they were saying... Who does that??? That action set the tone for the investigation. He would not initiate any action to find Johnny. He turned away other police departments and Sheriff's officers who came and volunteered to help. Again, who does that? This attitude by the police chief continued for months.

No FBI came, we were in this tragedy by ourselves. I finally called the FBI office and asked for agents to come to our home. When they arrived, they informed us that this was only a courtesy call, and they had no intention of entering the case. They told me it was our responsibility to prove Johnny's life was in danger. This was just a slick way to toss parents aside and not to take on the cases. I told them to leave.

We learned later that a call was made from the Omaha FBI office which is the headquarters for five states. The police dept. was told to stand down and take no action on the Gosch kidnapping. Why? The reason came out later. Instructions were being issued to all that nothing be investigated if it came near the Franklin Credit Union Scandal… which in later years was exposed. We had no way of knowing that this had taken place. This set the stage for a big cover up which has lasted four decades and counting.

A week after my book was published in the fall of 2000. I was contacted by Mayor George Mills in Des Moines. He told me that Orval Cooney who had been police chief and fired was a regular at the sex parties held in Omaha, Nebraska and he joined other friends there. The sex parties were hosted by a man named Larry King/ Franklin Credit Union and a pedophile named Alan Baer. They had many children who were being used as prostitutes… Kings men and Baer's boys. I asked the mayor why he was giving me this information. He said, "you deserve to know what really happened". I was grateful to the mayor and now it made sense why Cooney treated Johnny's case so badly. He was protecting himself and his friends who were attending the sex parties. My original feeling about him was correct. I did not trust him from Day 1 of Johnny's kidnapping.

THE SECOND KIDNAPPING

I have shared what took place with Sam Soda regarding his predicting the second kidnapping of Eugene Martin. Witnesses have identified Sam as the man who brought photos of Johnny and said, "this is the Sam Soda was the common denominator in both kidnappings.

THE BURNING CAR

Two years ago, in the summer of 2022, I received a phone call at four a.m. The woman on the phone said, "You don't know me, but we were up by your house the night before Johnny was kidnapped". She went on to say that she and her husband stole cars and would drive them to Chicago to sell. But that night they did not see any vehicles on our street. So, they went a few blocks away to an apartment building. They selected a car and her husband jumped in the car, drove it away and she followed him. They took the car to the next country and stopped to look at what they had just stolen. In the car on the seat was a stack of kiddie porn photos of boys. And on the top of the pile was a school photo of Johnny.

They became afraid and set fire to the car. It was left burning as they drove away. The next morning, they heard on the news that Johnny had been kidnapped and people were searching for him. They saw his photo on Tv and realized it was the same as the school photo found in the car.

The woman continued to tell me that they found another car to steal and headed for Chicago again in a few days. But that when they got there the man who they sold their stolen cars to had been murdered and placed in the trunk of his own car. I patiently listened to this whole story and told her I appreciated the information. Then I asked, "where is your husband now"? She took a long breath and then said "Oh, I shot him dead in the living room. He tried to strangle me, and I grabbed the gun and killed him.". She said her husband was afraid she would talk about the car theft and get them in trouble. She then suggested that I check with the WDMPD for verification of her story. I did call to check on it and BINGO she was telling the truth.

The point of this story was that the car they took may well have been an extra car driven by someone involved in the kidnapping when we learned Johnny's school photo was in the car. That was the kid they were going to kidnap the following day.

Over the years there have been many strange stories I have listened to and some have information which we can use. Which in turn helps us put one more puzzle piece into this huge mystery. I appreciated the woman coming forward and her story was accurate.

MY FAMILY

Some have wondered and asked why I do not discuss or answer questions regarding my family. The reason being we are dealing with some very high-profile people in these trafficking cases. The people who handle, kidnap, spot the kids for abduction. The safety of all concerned is primary. Years ago, one of my children wanted to help at a booth for Johnny... where we handed out literature about pedophiles and what to watch for in their communities. A woman came up to the table and spit on one of my kids. From that day forward no contact with my other children was allowed. And many years later, I received a letter from the person who did this to my child. She explained that since that time… someone killed one of her grandchildren… so she now knew the pain of losing a child in the family. I was shocked by the letter, but she took the time to write it and to apologize.

THE GANNON CANON

Who is/was the Gannon Canon? He was a reporter going by the name of Jeff Gannon. He was at many press conferences at the White House. Someone watching TV News saw him and thought he looked like Johnny. Andy called me to give me the name. Somehow, this all got splashed all over the country in news shows. I finally called Jeff Gannon and asked him if he would take a DNA test and settle this mystery. At first, he said "sure he would do it". But then later changed his mind and wanted us to appear on Dr. Phil… Or Maury Povich. Have the DNA sample done and then announce it on TV as they do in some other shows. I said "no". Then he came back wanting thousands of dollars for his DNA (it must have been special) My answer was "no way am I sending you a huge amount of money". So, I sent two men there to visit him. The truth be known … Jeff Gannon was way too old to have been Johnny at the age he would have been, and he was much shorter in height than Johnny. So that cleared it up for me. I didn't need a DNA report. What he wanted was some money and his fifteen minutes of fame attaching himself to a huge kidnapping case.

THE MANY INTERVIEWS AND MOVIES

Through the years there have been many interviews by TV and other mediums of communication. For the most part they have all been positive. Occasionally you meet someone who isn't very friendly in that role. But they did a good job reporting the story and the need for information that could lead to a conclusion. The most recent interview in print was on the CNN website. It was done by Thomas Lake, who did a very thorough job of investigating, interviewing, and countless trips to various locations to gather information for his article. He did a fantastic job of reporting Johnny's story. I believe that he and the article were successful in raising awareness about the problem of Human Trafficking in our country and the world. The thing I always tried to remember was that it is business, and it is not personal. They have a job to do and must report "NEWS".

And if things go according to plan there may be another documentary movie that will be made. Things are in the planning stages so we will wait and see for that possibility. Each time there is a show or an article… it is amazing how much information does become available.

THE LAWS

Soon after Johnny was kidnapped, I realized that we needed new legislation concerning kidnapping. How long a person is missing before police enter the case. We kept hearing that it is 72 hours. When in fact there was absolutely no law on the Iowa books to indicate such a thing. They wouldn't wait 72 hours to investigate a bank robbery or a car theft. So, I sat down at my kitchen table and wrote things that were needed in a new law. I met with newly elected Gov. Terry Branstad. He listened and went to work on it. They put my suggestions into the new bill. Unfortunately, it didn't pass the first session it did, and it was signed by Gov. Branstad in July of 1984. Little did we know that the next victim would be in August 1984, and it would be Eugene Martin. When I proposed a new law, it was because I wanted something good, lasting in Johnny's name so his kidnapping did not happen for naught. The first family to be able to use that law was the Martin family. Our Johnny Gosch law was so successful that other states all around Iowa began to use it as well. When Marc Allen was kidnapped in March 1986 this law was not used. Police told his mother not to talk to anyone, keep quiet, no TV interviews and for heaven's sake do not call Noreen Gosch … she is a troublemaker. Sadly, no one really knew Mark was missing. Then twenty-five years later, I received a call from the Natl. Center for Missing Children… they said, "did you know you have a third child kidnapped in Des Moines." I told them I did not know, and they said they would send overnight Marc's file to me. As soon as I received it…I called Jan Mikkelson with WHO radio and asked if I could be on his show. I showed the file to Jan couldn't believe it either. The fact that boy was missing all these years and the police kept quiet. More than likely, they did not use the Johnny Gosch Law either. Jan talked about Marc's case and the story went all over Iowa. One would think that the police would want all the help they could get if they had 3 kidnappings unsolved in the community.

Sadly, Marc's mother, Nancy passed away in January 2024. She never was able to find out what happened or who took her son. This was so hard on their family. And for the police to suppress the news of Marc's case for 25 years was criminal. Marc's kidnapping wat the third boy taken. The police also told Nancy that if the residents of Des Moines knew there was another kidnapping it would cause panic in the city. Nancy was told to "let it go!" I think this was outrageous behavior. This directive by the police increased the pain and suffering of Marc's family.

HOW DID YOU MAKE IT THROUGH THIS TRAGEDY?

This is a question I am asked almost daily. What did you do to survive this tragedy and go on without becoming bitter. First, I knew Johnny would want me to keep on keeping on. And that his life hung in the balance of every decision I would be making for the next four decades as it has turned out.

I did things to stay healthy body, mind and spiritual. I exercised every day and taught Yoga classes for 55 years. I had many students in Des Moines and in the area. I ate in a healthy manner… so important. I drank a lot of water. Staying hydrated is a huge factor in everyone's health. When it came

INTRODUCTION TO 2024

to the spiritual …I have a very strong faith, discipline in myself and a positive thought pattern.

But just like anyone else there can be issues big or little which affect our lives. However, whatever it was "already happened". So "how we happen to it makes us or breaks us". I learned that a very long time ago. And to concentrate on the "solution rather than the problem". No one ever said any of this is easy. It isn't and probably the most difficult thing I have ever done. But I had to do something to keep the momentum up all these years on this case.

The spiritual part of us is a driving force from within. A person's faith and belief system are very important. It gives us the feeling that someone has our back and that it is going to be okay… and I am okay!

A book I recommend is "Rays of Dawn" by Dr. Thuran Fleet. It is a book that has been in print for many years. It is still available on Amazon.com and it is worth the read. I still have my original one which was given to me 50 years ago. I received mine years before Johnny was kidnapped. It explains the emotions we all have and/or go through. What they cause within us. Your blood pressure, blood sugar, heart rate changes more acid in your stomach etc. when one is very angry. So, if you become very angry several times a day this is what happens several times per day. I prefer to be calm. Now that doesn't mean one is stuffing their problems or issues. It just means you take a different approach.

I remember one evening something very upsetting took place, and I was angry. I read the chapter on "forgiveness" four times before I could get up from the chair and feel calm, the anger was gone. Everyone has something to bear it seems and being able to rise above some of it gives a person a better night's sleep and daytime life. Try it, you will like it!!!!

I still remember when the film crew came from the Charles Kuralt TV show came to spend several days filming us. The producer was a woman. She kept throwing very curt remarks toward me. On the last day before they flew back home, she came over to me and said, "You are the real deal aren't you"? I asked her what she was referring to. And she said, "you are known as the ICE WOMAN in the network media because no one can push you into a fit of anger or bring you to the point where you would fall apart". I was sent here to break you down! I just looked at her and finally said "With a young boy's life hanging by a thread that is what you wanted to do to me". Shame on you and whoever directed you to do that. Then she added "I am going back and will have to tell them that I failed to BREAK YOU"! Shock doesn't even describe what it felt like to hear such a diabolical plan to destroy someone who already was in so much pain after losing a child.

At an appearance one time… after my book came out. A lady said to me "your book sure isn't a Harry Potter". Well, it had been one of those days …we all have them occasionally. I stood there and began laughing… in fact I couldn't stop. She was giving me a little insult and couldn't understand my laughter. I think it is called "comic release" and occasionally people just need a good laugh. I finally composed myself and said, "well this book was designed for awareness to protect children so that they can enjoy reading a Harry Potter book". She just stared at me for a few minutes. Then she got the big idea of what I had said.

Sharing a few of these things gives the reader a glimpse of what it is like to be in this situation. Most all people have been kind but occasionally you run into a "clinker" who upsets the system. I am reminded daily concerning the loss of my son. The years which were robbed from him and our family. When that comes to mind… I shift my thoughts to a happy memory about him. It is a proven way to change a "brain wave pattern or thought pattern". It works!

DNA … TO GIVE OR NOT TO GIVE

In Crime solving, we have come a long way from the days right after Johnny was kidnapped. Using the DNA from people can help the
law enforcement solve crimes, identify unclaimed bodies and many other helpful ways.

INTRODUCTION TO 2024

Once DNA arrived on the scene there were many DNA shops that were open for business. Send us your DNA via technology and we will give you your history clear back to the cave man. And many of my friends did do it. It seemed important to them to know their history back to the beginning. I did not criticize nor make any comments. Some of these places were doing good work. I don't know how many there are now or if they are all reputable or not. And people pay a lot of money for this service. I am going to share several incidents that I have dealt with concerning this subject. Many people have questioned me about why I have not submitted my DNA on Johnny's case. Which by law one does not have to do so. Below are the reasons and the issues that came up.

There are several very good reasons that I will list below.

1. My attorney advised me not to give my DNA to the police. That is due to the corruption and the information we had about an individual in the police force who was involved in Johnny's kidnapping... it was not wise.

2. Several years ago, I got a phone call from a relative. She said " Noreen, I am so sorry about Johnny. When is his funeral to be held. I saw everything on Ancestry.com"? Well, that was news to me I had not been notified of anyone's death. I investigated Ancestry.com and found that Johnny was listed as dead, and someone even went so far as to reserve a cemetery plot for him in the cemetery which is only a mile from my home in West Des Moines. I contacted the police with all the information. They said they would investigate it. A couple days later they called me and discovered who did all of this but that they decided not to do anything legally about it. Nothing new there! Then several days later a woman in Davenport, Iowa listed Johnny as dead on Ancestry.com. Once again, I supplied information to the police. After looking into it they told me they would do nothing. I did ask them to try and get all this removed from Ancestry.com. They said they would try.

Hours and days went into this mess and Ancestry.com refused to remove these two fraudulent claims from their records and that it would remain visible to the public. Nothing was done. Who lists someone as dead and then goes so far as to make arrangements for a cemetery plot???

3. Then a few months later a body was found in Colorado. The Medical Examiner there called me herself and said " What is going on... I am getting extreme pressure from the West Des Moines Police to tag this body as your son, Johnny. Why are they doing this without any DNA or dental records supplied.?" I referred her to my private detective to validate what had happened and how the police labeled him a runaway when he was not, and the FBI refused to enter the case.

The Medical Examiner then called me a second time after talking with my detective and getting the information about how this case was handled from Day one.

She did tell me that a few days after we first spoke on the phone...Johnny's father supplied his DNA. But it was not satisfactory (her words not mine). I have no idea why it was not satisfactory but that is what she told me. I sent the dental records; they were sufficient, and the body was NOT JOHNNY!

After these above-mentioned issues ... why in the world would anyone think that I would voluntarily give the police my DNA or anything else????? I read all the possibilities of dumpster diving for my DNA etc. etc. However, this is the decision I have made with good reason. I would not trust Ancestry .com to do anything after the fiasco of the fraud and they would not even remove it after being asked repeatedly by the police. This was deliberate by both parties to do harm. Or that is the story I was told. And I am not so sure about that either. Did the police try to get it removed or just mention that they did so. I have no way of knowing.

This is a situation that most people will never find themselves in during their lifetime. A violent crime committed, and your child taken. It unleashes problems you would never dream existed. The above is just a couple of examples of what has taken place concerning the use of DNA currently. If or when it would be important then I would give it careful consideration.

INTRODUCTION TO 2024

WHO … WHAT … WHERE

Shortly after my first book was written and published, I was contacted by the Mayor of West Des Moines. He said he wanted to talk with me. I met with him, and he shared with me a frightening amount of information. Some years earlier the Police Chief, Orval Cooney was relieved of his job. This is all explained in an earlier chapter in this book. The Mayor began by telling me that Orval Cooney had been a "regular "going to the sex parties being given by pedophiles in Omaha, Nebraska. He had a couple friends who joined him from Omaha as well. The parties were all part of the Franklin Credit Union sex scandal by pedophiles were using young boys and girls as prostitutes for their own financial gain.

I was a bit shocked about the parties Orval Cooney was attending however, I did know he attended "movie night" at Barry's Lounge in Des Moines. That is where they were showing kiddie porn movies to those who wanted to be there. I am not sure if was by invitation. But this is what was taking place for several years. Eventually Barry's lounge caught fire and burned to the ground. The information about Movie night at Barry's was given to me years beforehand by someone who had worked there and thought it might be helpful in Johnny's investigation.

This information and more eventually was out in the open about the Franklin sex scandal. Information we learned pointed directly to the kidnappings in Des Moines, Iowa. It sometimes takes years before information of real substance appears in a case. I thanked Mayor Mills for his honesty and giving me the information to work with on the case. It answered a lot of questions.

From the very beginning of Johnny's case, I did not trust the police chief, Orval Cooney. There was something about him that just wasn't right. The decisions he made to label Johnny as a runaway when he was not. He makes disparaging remarks about me and our family to the public. Name calling and basically throwing every obstacle possible in our path as my private investigators joined the search for Johnny and the truth.

I felt it necessary to pursue this information legally. I talked to an attorney about a civil lawsuit against Orval Cooney. Plans for that were halted when he died suddenly.

THE LAST MAN STANDING

Sometime after my book was published for the first time, we began getting information on the actual kidnappers. Paul Bonacci had been very helpful with everything he could remember and information he would still receive from people he knew as fellow victims. It seems that some of the people involved in the actual kidnapping had died. It had been many years since the kidnapping, so some people do pass away.

We had worked for a long time to find the man who drove the van the morning of the kidnapping. My detectives went house to house after the kidnapping. They talked to all the residents asking if they had seen or heard anything unusual before the kidnapping or that day. They got to one house and a man opened the door. My investigators told him they were there to ask a few questions about the kidnapping of Johnny Gosch. The man thought they were with the police dept. He said "Thank God you came. I have been calling and calling the police station to ask someone to come to my home. I saw the kidnappers that morning. My detectives explained they were working for me.

The man living there began by saying he was up early and in the kitchen to get a drink of water. He heard an engine running outside. His house was right on the corner. He looked out without turning on any lights. He saw this dark colored van sitting there with the motor running. Soon a car pulled up and a couple people got out and pulled something long wrapped in what looked like a blanket. They quickly loaded it into the van. And the vehicles turned right on 42nd street. Heading North. He then told the detectives "Later that morning, I heard the news about the paperboy being taken about the same time, a couple blocks away. When they showed the make of the car on TV that day. It was the same as the one I saw outside my window by the van.

INTRODUCTION TO 2024

My detectives came immediately to my home following the visit with the gentleman who witnessed the exchange of what they felt was Johnny's body to the van. My detectives told me to keep that report to myself. Do not talk about it to anyone. Then if someone comes forward with information about this dark colored van and the kidnap car…we will know they are telling the truth. This information cannot be public knowledge at this time.

So, I did as he suggested and kept the file. Years later, when Paul Bonacci surfaced admitting he had helped kidnapped Johnny. In his description of everything that took place that morning. He said "And after we had Johnny in the car and heading down the street we pulled in where a dark BLUE VAN was waiting for us. We moved Johnny into the van, he was wrapped in a blanket and unconscious due to the chloroform we used on him. Then both vehicles headed North on 42nd street. The information was exactly as the man living in the house on that corner told us years before and was contained in the records I had been given.

Even though we had that information …It still did not reveal the name of the driver of the blue van. I literally prayed for an answer and the identity of this man who drove the van with my boy unconscious and wrapped in a blanket. It broke my heart to even think of what he must have gone through that day and for the remaining years after being kidnapped.

One day, I was given information and the name of the driver of the van. I believe Divine Intervention allowed this to happen. I decided to talk with someone from the police department about it. Because there was info to work with finally. I mentioned only the blue van. The officer I spoke to said, "we do not believe there ever was a van parked down a few blocks from where Johnny was taken"! Well, that ended the conversation. We have information, we have a driver, and they did not want to hear about it because according to them there was no van. However, it was seen and everything that took place was witnessed.

I refer to the LAST MAN STANDING occasionally. He is no stranger to illegal acts in his life. I am asked many times for his name. I do not share it but I feel Johnny's kidnapping was not his "first rodeo". I believe that just as miraculously as I found out about him then there will be something which will expose him. I don't have to do a thing. And since the police rejected any information or discussion. I have done my duty in trying to report it. The man in question is much older now… aren't we all.

I have noticed his name a few times posting information on Facebook. So possibly he is monitoring the site to see if anyone mentions his name but as for now, he remains: **THE LAST MAN STANDING!**

INTRODUCTION TO 2024

BILL

In the original book, a chapter explained a helping hand which came to me out of the blue. I call this man "BILL" and do not use his real name out of respect for his privacy. He stepped into my office and introduced himself one day. Then he said, "When you get tired of all the things the police are not doing on Johnny's case, call me I can help" Then he laid his business card down on the desk. I thanked him and tucked the card in my wallet.

The case was going downhill and a few weeks after Bill had come to my office the police called for a meeting with us and them. As we went to the police station, I had a feeling that it wasn't going to be a good meeting. I was right. The police chief started by saying "we are going to put this case on the back burner because it is draining our budget to continue working on it!" I spoke up first and said "This comes as a shock because you labeled Johnny as a runaway and didn't look for him. You told the FBI you didn't want their help. Basically, you have done little or nothing to find our son. And now you tell me all of this "inactivity" is draining the budget. How can it be both?" Everyone in this meeting just sat looking at one another. It was just an excuse to try and shut down the case. We left shortly after this information was given by police chief, Orval Cooney. He did not want anyone investigating Johnny's case.

That was the day I made the telephone call to "Bill" and asked for his help. He remained in touch with me after checking on individuals, running license plates and providing protection for me and my family. The atmosphere was becoming dangerous. The police shut down anything, no communication with us basically nothing. Not only did they not want to investigate but they did not want me delving into the case either. TOO LATE! I was already into it. Working with my private investigators, asking Bill to secure information when needed.

I was very grateful for the assistance I received for many years. If it had not been for the help, I received there is no way I would have learned what really took place in Johnny's kidnapping.

A few years later, Bill developed health problems and passed away. It was as though he had become a member of our family. He was missed greatly in terms of the investigation, how much he helped, and he became a friend.

INTRODUCTION TO 2024

JOHN DE CAMP

The first I ever heard of John DeCamp.... He was a very good attorney in Lincoln, Nebraska. When the Franklin Credit Union was being investigated it seemed so distant that it was not a part of Johnny's kidnapping. But that was before I learned that DeCamp had called our home saying a client of his had confessed to being part of Johnny's kidnapping. A young man named Paul Bonacci. I was at work and did not know about the phone call, Johnny's father took the call and did not tell me. It was over a year later when I heard about all of this on the radio during an interview with some man, I didn't know sharing all the details. Within minutes two FBI Agents came bursting into my office…demanding to know what I had heard about this young man. I had to tell them it was the first time I had heard about it also. Of course, they challenged that and did not believe me. So, they finally left. It was a long night as Johnny's father never came home that night. Finally at five a.m. he showed up and when I asked where he was and did, he hear the news. He shouted, "I have known about this for over a year and did not tell you".

I made arrangements with Roy Stepehens, John DeCamp's P.I. to go to the prison and talk to Paul Bonacci myself. It was arranged by John De Camp. However, I still had not met him. A couple years later ABC"s 20/20 wanted to do a big story on Johnny, sort of a follow up. The year was 1997.

After doing interviews in Des Moines, the producer wanted to drive to Lincoln, Nebraska and interview John De Camp, she requested that I go too. When we got there John De Camp welcomed us … took my hand and said it was so good to see me again. I must have looked shocked because when I told him I had never been there he too was shocked. His office manager cleared up and stated that "Johnny's father came with a woman and introduced her as his wife, Noreen but that it was not this woman (Me)" There was dead silence for a bit. No one knew what to say and I learned for the first time about the person who was impersonating me. It was a lot to take in at first. The situation was very strange and before the trip to Nebraska was over...I met twenty-five people who had all met the Fake Noreen being introduced by Johnny's father.

From that point on John De Camp became a good friend. He did everything he could to help me. He allowed me to go to his other building and go through all his records concerning the Franklin case, Paul Bonacci, and make copies if it was helpful to our case. He felt the cases in Des Moines were directly related to the Franklin Cover up.

John De Camp also very helpful when I was receiving a lot of threats, phone calls etc. He would call me nearly every day just to check and see if I was okay. Later he and Ted Gunderson would alternate days calling me. Both Ted and John knew I was living alone and since information had become public with a connection to the Franklin case. There were people who apparently did not want me involved in anything with Franklin and Paul Bonacci to share the truth. I guess it goes with the territory when one finds what I call "pay dirt"! People get nervous and react.

John offered his legal services to me if I should ever need assistance in that area. He also consented to being interviewed for the "Who Took Johnny "Documentary in 2015. Later I learned that John's health was failing, and he passed away a few years ago. I have been blessed with people who offered help at times when it was needed the most.

Thank you..., John De Camp!

INTRODUCTION TO 2024

TED GUNDERSON

Ted Gunderson was a long time Special Agent with the FBI... He was retired and spent time working, lecturing and helping families with missing or murdered children. I had heard the name shortly after Johnny was kidnapped but was told that his schedule was so full that it would be a long time to get help from him on Johnny's case. Some time went by and before I knew it Ted was in the area, and I got the opportunity to meet him. He was doing investigations, and I was able to meet with him and tell him about Johnny's case.

He was very attentive and offered to help wherever he could. He was also working at John De Camp at the time. And it was a couple of years before I met John. Ted offered advice, practical suggestions to try in my investigation of Johnny's case. Once again, I was blessed with someone appearing at the right time in the case.

After years had passed and Franklin Scandal had unfolded ... I noticed that every day, I would get a phone call from Ted Gunderson asking if I was okay and if I needed anything. Later on, he and John De Camp would alternate phone calls to me. Ted knew I was receiving threats and was living alone. Ted felt that the Franklin case was bigger than most people were aware of, and some very prominent people could be exposed, so to have it tied to a kidnapping in Des Moines Iowa was an obstacle they did not need or want. Others had been harmed at that time and suspicious deaths had taken place. Both Ted and John felt it was important to keep in touch with me and it was very much appreciated.

The FBI in Omaha, Nebraska were doing many things to try and keep the reach of the Franklin Scandal limited and protecting influential protecting influential. And the phone call which was made to the West Des Moines Police on the morning of Johnny's kidnapping... telling them to stand down and take no action on the Gosch case.... That phone call came from the Omaha FBI Office. Why would they do such a thing preventing any investigation by police. Then two FBI agents came to our home to tell us they would "not enter the case because I had not proven that Johnny's life was in danger"! What an absurd and stupid thing to say. Kidnapping is a federal crime, and it was a kidnapping.

INTRODUCTION TO 2024

SAM SODA…SODA POP

You will find the name Sam Soda throughout my original book. Sam was a very mysterious man and one I never trusted. Sam always wanted current information on the case from me and wanted to act as my Private Detective. I refused to give any information or permit him to act on behalf of the Johnny Gosch Foundation. Sam died on 1/16/20.

As mentioned in my original book, Sam was very persistent in coming after me for any information. Sam was also the one who "told" me there would be a second paper boy taken and gave me the exact day it would happen. How could this be? We (my husband George and I) went to DCI and talked to Brian London about Sam Soda, he found it very interesting and agreed with my husband Sam was just trying to keep tabs on how much we knew and was passing that information on. The "WHO" he was passing this on to was what I needed to find out. Unfortunately, Brian was asked to step down from his position.

Both Paul Bonacci and Rusty Nelson picked Sam Soda's photo out of twelve other photos as being a frequent visitor to Larry King's parties in Omaha. Paul identified Sam Soda as the man the kids called Soda Pop and acknowledged Sam was at the hotel in West Des Moines the night before Johnny's kidnapping and brought photos of Johnny to their hotel, so they made sure to pick the right paper boy. I have since found out through the DMV registration that Sam Soda did own a vehicle similar to one of the vehicles used in the Kidnapping of Johnny

There used to be (burnt down years ago) a lounge by the Des Moines Airport called Barry's Lounge. The main floor was the lounge, and the second floor was a cone shape and we have been told by investigators that the second floor is where Sam and others including Orval Cooney would gather to watch kiddy porn. God, forbid they abused children there, but I would not put anything pass these people. There were others on the list of people frequenting parties at Barry's Lounge that we are doing more fact checking on and could release later one of my Podcast on my website or on the Johnny Gosch Group on Facebook. Sam Soda lost his Private Investigator License due to the possession of kiddy porn.

One day, I received a call from a lady that was crying so hard I had to calm her down before I could understand her. She told me this is Theresa, I'm Sam Soda's sister Theresa and I'm so sorry for what he has done to your family. Theresa told me that Sam bragged about keeping Johnny's Paper Bag as a trophy. I feel sorry for Theresa having this knowledge eating at her insides every day plus living in fear of her brother Sam. Theresa is a very brave woman; people will read this and wonder why not sooner well she was afraid for her life and possibly others in her family's lives. I greatly appreciated her reaching out to me and hopefully now she can have some peace of mind.

Knowing what we know about Sam Soda we find the friendship between Sam Soda and Johnny's father to be a mystery. Several people saw the having dinner at well know Italian restaurant in Des Moines shortly before Sam died. We also have other sightings of the two of them but again we are fact-checking them.

INTRODUCTION TO 2024

JOHN GOSCH

In my original book, I mentioned the strange hang up calls very late at night before Johnny was kidnapped and the one brief conversation very early on the morning Johnny was kidnapped. It was very strange that he had a conversation with the wrong number.

That John had taken an imposter to Lincoln, Nebraska to meet with John DeCamp. He began making what he called business trips to Lincoln and Omaha and insisted on taking Johnny on an overnight trip to Offutt Air Force base. He was disengaged from the investigation, took his anger out on me and my children. John became a very different man than the one I first met. These disturbing changes led to a divorce in 1995.

When my husband George and I, Karen Burns and the rest of the 20/20 crew traveled to John DeCamp's office for the first time. John DeCamp to my surprise "said to me good to see you again. " I told him we had never met before. He called his office manager in, and she confirmed I was not the woman that John Gosch had been bringing to their office. We were all shocked and no one knew how to respond. It's been confirmed that not only was the imposter in John Decamps office more than once. But John also took her to the prison to see Paul Bonacci. We later learned that John Gosch also took the imposter to fund raisers in Omaha, Lincoln, Denver and other places. That money never made it back to the Johnny Gosch Foundation.

Rusty Nelson came to John DeCamps office the next day for an interview with Karen Burns and us. Rusty told us of his job as personal Photographer for Larry King and how his focus was to capture photos of people abusing children for the purpose of

extortion or future favors. During the interview we put 12 photos on a table and asked him if he recognized any of them to no one's surprise he pick out Sam Sodas photo out. Then to everyone's surprise he picked out John Gosch's photo and said he has seen him at Larry Kings Parties.

We asked if he could provide any photos proving this, he said he would get back to us, but we haven't heard from him again. I was shocked but not surprised. Could Sam have been the one calling our house the night of the kidnapping??? We know Sam was one of those involved it the physical kidnapping of Johnny. Did John Gosch know Sam Soda before the kidnapping???

That's something only John Gosch can answer.

We now know that Lt. Col. Michael Aquino was operating the MKUltra (Mind Control) Program on Children at Offutt Air Force base. Why take Johnny there is it just a coincidence?

There were several times during the investigation when it appeared as if John would go out of his way to sabotage the investigation, discredit me, become violent and just disengage from everything and everybody.

It reached the point where it was no longer safe for me and my children to be around him. People all deal with the hardship and loss of a child differently. I have talked to and tried to help many people when they reach out. Everyone's pain is different, but it is a deep everlasting pain. Perhaps John Gosch still hasn't found a way to have peace within himself and to be honest. My focus from day one has always been on my son and how we can help him and the other victims and their families. I keep in mind as I tell other parents of missing children…"Our child is the ultimate victim, but we are left with a heart ache"!

INTRODUCTION TO 2024

PAUL BONACCI

My original book went into detail of Paul's actual part in my sons kidnapping and I'm not going to go thru that again. What I want to do here may surprise a lot of people. I want Paul to understand how indebted and grateful to him I am for having the strength and courage to come forward and confirming what happened to Johnny and passing updates on to me.

Paul was also young victim at the time of Johnny's kidnapping. The torture and abuse Paul went through is hard to listen to let alone comprehend. When talking to him, I can see in his eyes the pain that has caused Paul but never have I heard the anger in Paul's voice come forward. Paul has weathered every storm and act of violence, torture and abuse thrown at him. In all our conversations Paul has always been very sincere, respectful and kind. I have the deepest respect for Paul surviving his past even though those memories are still haunting him he is doing the best he can to raise a family and live a normal life.

It's almost like the victims have formed their own brother/sister hood they feel the safest (for good reason) with each other and seldom do they trust anyone outside their own circle. I have talked to countless victims many have come through Boy's Town and thanks to Paul they can see the light at the end of the tunnel. Heroes come in all shapes and forms Paul has set an example for countless victims including Johnny to reach out and take control of their lives and not to let the demons take over. Paul, thank you for all you have done for Johnny and me.

Life Changing Experience

I have known Noreen since 1985. We started dating in 1997 and got married in October 2001. All I knew about Johnny's abduction was what I learned from the Media over the years. As I gained Noreen trust I was shocked about what really happened to Johnny. I was amazed at the amount of evidence Noreen had collected and couldn't understand the fact no one, other than Noreen, seemed to want Johnny's Abduction solved.

It's been an uphill battle to get the respect Noreen has and well deserves. Her reputation/quest is known worldwide as Noreen still gets emails every month from victims and supporters from around the world. When Noreen sends out a request for help, I'm amazed how fast her worldwide supporters come up with verified answers.

Johnny's Abduction was planned and coordinated... what those behind the abduction didn't count on is Noreen's inner strength and Noreen's relentless search for answers and her son.

I was with Noreen at John DeCamps office with 20/20 crew when he advised that she was not the same woman that John Gosch Sr. brought to his office numerous times saying she was Noreen. I have talked and sat in on interviews with Paul Bonacci and hearing some of the things he and others endured as a child makes you wonder how sick people are doing this to children.

I've talked with Rusty Nelson and was there when he picked out two photos out of 12 and advised that these people have been to Larry King's sex parties in Omaha, NE. I was at the Indian Reservation when Noreen was so close to Johnny, but it wasn't meant to be.

I have also accompanied Noreen on Countless National Speaking Engagements and TV appearances. We've had countless Victims show up in person or internet/phone that either knew Johnny or just wanted to talk about their suffering and had no one else to talk to. I like to refer to Noreen as the "Godmother to all the Victims" as Noreen is the one person they trust and that has always been there for them.

The past 26 years with Noreen have been a Life Changing Experience as I have been exposed to the dark side of our world. The horrifying stories of victims are more than a person can imagine. I would have never guessed that in 2000 when Noreen's book came out, we were talking about the same thing you now hear about every day "Human Trafficking". Johnny knows how much Noreen loves him and what Noreen has endured in her search for answers. We have all heard "that you can't judge a person until you walk a mile in their shoes" trust me I don't dare mess with Noreen's shoes, but I have been proud to walk behind Noreen and give whatever support I can to her. Noreen is one of a kind there will never be another like her I believe it was meant to be that we travel through our twilight years together.

George Hartney....

My Wonderful Husband George

For a few years after Johnny's kidnapping in 1982... I walked alone and had to be strong no matter what was happening around me. It wasn't easy but I knew Johnny's life depended upon it. Following my divorce from Johnny's father ... the pressures were even more staggering. It seemed I would get a little ahead and then push back farther. I continued the path trying to find Johnny. In time, he aged out of usefulness to traffickers. So, I felt it was time to focus on the people who committed this despicable crime.

When I began focusing on the guilty.... The threats really became dangerous....my home was broken into several times, my car was keyed and scraped, phone threats daily and even though all this was happening.... I felt I must have struck a nerve with someone who was involved. In the mid '90's. The America's Most Wanted program on Johnny's case opened even more activity on the case. Some good and some not so good. During those years, there was a great deal of criticism towards me. People challenging decisions I would make on the case. But being the one in the trenches and knowing what I was up against...I had to keep going. Someone said to me " you are burning the candle at both ends...just don't try to light it in the middle."

I had known George since 1985 and we began dating in 1997. It was such a such a wonderful feeling to know there was someone who was so kind, understanding and strong.

I had forgotten how to just have fun or laugh. George was there for me through thick and thin. The good and the bad of this situation. Many would not have wanted the extra stress of what was involved in my life. But George was different... he cared for and protected me.

Together, we went to many National TV interviews, conferences and other types of promotions for missing children. He was right beside me at the Indian Reservation when our investigation led us to that location. Many good ideas and suggestions have come from George through the years. George was with me in court and listened to Paul Bonacci's testimony...sharing what he knew about Johnny's kidnapping. It is hard to listen to all of this type of information. But I didn't have to go through it alone.... George was with me.

We have been there for each other during the deaths of both our mothers and other things that take place in life. He was so kind to my family. I remember visiting my mother at the nursing home. She had turned 100 years old. There was a big family picture on the wall. There were 12 children in my family, so with all of us and our spouses, grandchildren... the photographer suggested an outdoor setting to fit everyone in the picture. Mom looked at the picture and looked at George then said, "where were you when that picture was taken, Noreen is standing alone in the photo"? George looked at me and ... I said " Mom, George and I had not met yet when that picture was taken". Well, that made her feel better. It became a joke when we went again to see her. We all had a good laugh.

    I have a Facebook page for Johnny. It is where articles are posted, and people can share information. A couple years ago, George suggested that I start doing a Q& A for all the members. Thanks to George for the idea and to Frank LaBuda who organizes and handles all the questions and answers... We have a very efficient Johnny Gosch site. Because of it and the power of the internet this is going all over the world. People have come forward with information. It was one of the best ideas to start this project. Thank you to George for the idea... To date I have answered 2,370 questions. And we have approximately 8,500 members. It continues to grow and as a few people have said ... They feel like Johnny is everyone's son.

    George was there when victims of these horrible crimes come to our door and just want to talk to someone who understands... He has been so kind to those in need. They didn't ask for anything .... just a little time to talk. We both understand what these crimes do to young people. Sometimes they only want someone to listen. We can't change what has happened to them. But we can give them some time, encouragement and praise for surviving. When he refers to me as " the godmother of missing children".... It reinforces why I am still doing this type of work. None of these children have asked for this... they are the ultimate victims.

    There is a lot of stress and strain when one's child is kidnapped. And this goes on for the rest of one's life it seems. But George has brought so much happiness to our life together. I feel blessed, safe and thankful to have him in my life.

Thank you, George, for all that you do... you are "my wonderful husband"!

Noreen Gosch Hartney

WHY JOHNNY CAN'T COME HOME!

LARRY KING

In the earlier part of this book, you will see reference to Larry King, who was the Manager of the Franklin Credit Union in Omaha, Nebraska. He was involved in prostitution, money laundering and the abuse of young boys and girls. He had his group of boys, and they were called Kings Men. He was arrested and sent to prison for a number of years.

After Larry King was released from prison in April 2011, he moved to Reston, VA. One day an Internet detective from Australia called me and said photos of Johnny were being offered, a few at a time on a pedophile message board. The person posting bragged that he had 3,020 photos of Johnny Gosch and would continue to release a few at a time.

The detective asked what he could do to help. I asked him if he could get the guy posting these photos to write him an email. If he did, I could get the IP number traced. It took a few weeks before enough trust was established, and the man wrote a private email to the detective. We got the IP number and traced it to Larry King in Reston, VA.

I contacted the Missing Children's Center in DC to give them the information. They in turn contacted the FBI, a plan was made to raid Kings house, confiscate his computer and arrest King. Two hours before they were going to raid the King's house the FBI called off the raid, no one ever confiscated Kings computer and he was not arrested.

Following this fiasco, the National Center contacted me and said they were now willing to admit that Johnny's kidnapping was organized, and the FBI tried to cover it up as did The West Des Moines Police.

It appears whatever Larry King did or committed…he was always protected in some manner. It is very defeating when your child is taken and so many things were manipulated in the investigation. Every moment to a parent of a missing child means minutes out of their life.

INTRODUCTION TO 2024

JOHN DAVID NORMAN

Are you all familiar with John David Norman? I believe he is the key to understanding how all these children as networks operate and connect with each other.

For those not familiar with John David Norman, he's probably the most influential pedophile in history. Norman was convicted of child molestation in Colorado in 1988 and of distributing child pornography in California in 1995 and 1998. He's so important though because he connects all these different local operations from across the country on a national network level.

Throughout his life, Norman operated various direct mailing services dedicated to distributing child pornography and arranging sex trafficking. Among these operations were the Odyssey Foundation based out of Dallas; the Delta Project, Creative Corps and M-C Publications based out of Chicago; and Handy Andy based out of Pennsylvania. These were basically like magazines and/or newsletters where other pedophiles could connect with each other and see images of children engaged in sexually explicit acts and abuse.

Here's why this is so important to understand. In the Delta Project magazine, not only were there sexually explicit images of children, but there were classified ads in the magazine as well. In these classifieds, people could literally pay to arrange meet ups with children. There were also tutorials on how to groom and abduct victims through a wide verity of techniques that included drugs, alcohol, mental manipulation and the use of handcuffs and other restraints.

One of the people who was posting ads in the Delta Project classifieds was a millionaire pedophile named Francis Sheldon. I don't want to go into too much detail about Sheldon right now because this post isn't about him, but here's the general details. Sheldon owned a boy's camp that was located at North Fox Island in Lake Michigan. However, the boys camp facade was really a cover for a large-scale child sex trafficking operation and child material operation.

The only way on or off the island was through a private landing strip. On this island, wealthy people could pay large sums of money to fly to the island and abuse children, some of which was recorded for profit in the child material rings.

On August 13, 1973, Dallas police raided Norman's apartment at 3716 Cole Avenue based on a tip from a man in San Francisco that he was running a homosexual prostitution ring called the Odyssey Foundation. Police seized booklets bearing the name International and containing photographs and contact information of teenage boys and young men, as well as 30,000 index cards listing between 50,000 and 100,000 clients located in 35 U.S. states, some of which are rumored to be very powerful men. Conveniently, the FBI "lost" those index cards.

John David Norman was wanted on pedophile charges in several states and remained a fugitive for several years. Suspiciously, he was able to evade the authorities for decades before eventually being arrested and put away for good in 2009.

There is a strong suspicion that John David Norman probably was involved with Larry King, Alan Baer and others who were connected to the Franklin Cover Up or Johnny Gosch's case. John David Norman was heavily involved in distribution/spread of the material itself.

John David Norman started the Delta Project with a man named Phillip Paske. Phillip Paske was an American criminal, murderer, possible serial killer and child pornographer from Chicago, Illinois. He was closest associate and friend of sex trafficker John David Norman. Not only that, but he was briefly an employee of John Wayne Gacy's construction business. Which has led many to believe that John Wayne Gacy had accomplices and he may not be solely responsible for all the bodies that were found in his house.

John Wayne Gacy also had connections with the Democratic Party in the state of Illinois. There's that famous photo of him and Rosalynn Carter together as well. But wait, there's more. Paul Bonacci is the stepbrother of John Wayne Gacy's first victim, Timothy McCoy. Paul Bonacci's mom married his father, which I find to be a strange coincidence.

The handcuff trick technique that John Wayne Gacy would use to restrain his victims was a method that was published in John David Norman's magazines/newsletters. This same technique with the handcuff trick was also used by the Candyman serial killer Dean Corll. This is beautifully covered on "The Clown and the Candyman" podcast, if you'd like to learn more about it.

Images you can find those tutorials and many others circulating on the dark web in pedophile groups where images and videos of child abuse are uploaded. For more insight on how child rings operate on the dark web, I highly recommend checking out the "Hunting Warhead" documentary podcast series.

Keep in mind that Larry King was posting images of Johnny Gosch on the internet and many of his victims were used for child abuse material production as well.

Many of you will remember that it was reported by Paul Bonacci that a man called "The Colonel" came to where they were holding Johnny after he was kidnapped. This man paid in cash a large sum of money to buy Johnny. Paul was witness to this transaction.

The Colonel was always a mystery because it was a nickname. The kids who were kidnapped were never given real names for any of their abusers. It was made up of fake names or a nick name. We have worked for decades to learn the identity of the infamous Colonel.

The Colonel who purchased Johnny Gosch was none other than JOHN DAVID NORMAN. He is dead now but to learn that after all these years of searching is like finding a place for one more piece of a large jigsaw puzzle.

You will notice farther up in this chapter was the mention of a notorious pedophile named "Phillip Paske" which is his real name. However, he was using the name "Tony" the morning he helped kidnap my son. This information all came two days before I was to submit my book for publishing.

Many might wonder how the men got the titles of Colonel. Were they in the military giving service to our country. Absolutely not.... They gave themselves the titles. Perhaps to show control or to feel more important.

A few of the titles used by these criminals were:

The Colonel, The Captain, The Lieutenant, The General and one called the Chief. John Wayne Gacy was called the General!

All this information was shared in this book because it is important for everyone to know how widespread Human Trafficking is in our society. For many years people assumed that the Franklin Credit Union scandal which was a front for Human Trafficking was a small "Mom and Pop" organization. Wrong! It was connected, as explained earlier, into a huge network in our country. And believe me they are highly organized. I wish we were half as organized to be able to fully protect our children. This horrific crime could happen anywhere at anytime to any family.

INTRODUCTION TO 2024

THE LAST MAN STANDING

THE LAST MAN STANDING refers to the man who was driving the van the morning of my son's kidnapping. We learned of his presence and involvement in the kidnapping of Johnny within a few days after the crime was committed. We had an eyewitness to his presence and actions. Just because the police have disregarded your existence, we have not.

We know that in time the entire case will be wide open and there will not be any place to hide. There are many people who have put two and two together and know of your identity. Since those early days after Johnny was taken… it was a mystery as to who you were. We knew you were there and the part you played in the crime. Just as learning your identity was divine intervention. So will be the resolution of Johnny's kidnapping.

I am sure you feel as though you have escaped any responsibility for your actions. But whether you believe or not…. Justice will prevail. It always does in some fashion. Or you may in days to come feel it is time to do the "right thing"! No one is urging you to do so…that is entirely your choice. But your knowledge of what took place and your part in it is valuable. You could help spare many children the same violent horror. Give it some thought. You may even be given some type of leniency for your information and cooperation.

I may not ever see or meet you in person. But I know you are there every day of each year that has passed since my son was kidnapped. Nothing has changed you are still THE LAST MAN STANDING… others involved have already passed on to their final judgement. Is that what you want?

MY THANKS AND GRATITUDE TO

George Hartney *My Wonderful Husband... who has helped so much through the years. Thank you for suggesting the Q & A for the Official Johnny Gosch site on Facebook. It has been a tremendous success. For all your kindness, love and hard work on this case for 27 years. See the section on My Wonderful Husband.*

Frank LaBuda You stepped forward to manage the Official Johnny Gosch page. I had only seen Frank online sometimes when I was on Facebook. When the site needed someone to manage it all. Frank graciously agreed to do it. With his guidance, the number of members went from approx. 1200 and to 8,300 in two years. Those numbers are amazing. Frank organized and ran the Q & A which began on July 24, 2022. In that time, over 2,000 questions have been asked and answered by me. Frank does so much more for and with the Official Johnny Gosch site... He keeps order on the site. He has maintained a peaceful site.... no bickering or back biting is allowed. Some sites one must enter at their own risk. The Official Johnny Gosch Page on Facebook, where people can learn about the case, and what is happening in our world to innocent children. They may ask questions and receive answers. Some find comfort if they too have suffered horrific loss in their lives. Frank recognized

MY THANKS AND GRATITUDE TO

the need to continue a site like this and that the awareness would grow to make a difference. We have received very helpful information from members that have come forward. It is the awareness which spreads and grows. Thank you to my good friend, Frank LaBuda for all the many things he done for Johnny and me. It would not have happened without you!

Adrian Jackson Thank you, my friend, for starting the first Official Johnny Gosch page on Facebook. You began this site several years ago and brought it up to approximately 1,200 in its first stages. It attracted people who followed Johnny's Case and were interested in learning more. People posted articles and shared information among the membership. Thank you, I appreciate your work and the time that you managed the Official Johnny Gosch Page.

Monica.... Thank you for being a good friend. You were always there during some of the rough times in the past few years. Our communication was always something happy to look forward to each day. There was great opposition against me at the time we met. But you didn't let that stop you from being my friend. Thank you again for all the cheerful messages.

Kellie... You have been a good friend for 27 + years and counting. Thank you for being there so many times. Our communication continued daily ... barring a few sick days or vacation time. Always something to look forward to each morning. Whether it was a cherry message, solving an issue or our pondering information or events of interest. We did it all at one time or another. Thank you for all the cheerful messages.

David Bellingson ... Rumur Thank you David for taking a chance on Johnny's story and me. I appreciate the dedication by you and your crew to make "Who Took Johnny "! a success. Being able to condense 30 + years in the time frame of a movie. People still come up to me saying they watched it and how much it impacted their lives too. Thank you again, it was a pleasure to work with you.

Thomas Lake .... CNN Thomas thank you for the hours you put into the creation of the article you wrote about Johnny's case. You did very well write the information and coordinate many years of events into the article. It was easy to follow when reading it and provided answers for many people. Thank you again, it was a pleasure to work with you.

My Faithful Yoga Students.... Thank you for always showing up to class filling the room with happy vibes as we did our Yoga together. Everyone was a big part of my life and provided so much moral support for me over the past 40+ years. Thank you to all of you.

LOCKED UP AT ABC

After a succession of appearances over the years on Good Morning America, The Today Show, CBS Morning News, Charles Kuralt Sunday Morning, Phil Donahue, Inside Edition, 48 Hours, sharing my story about my son and alerting the public to the ever-present danger of child kidnapping. I received a phone call from Karen Burnes, a producer with ABC's 20/20, July of 1984, asking her to present an in-depth report on Johnny's story. This began a long-time relationship between ABC, Karen Burnes and me. Karen had been the producer over the years, as they had done a few updates when new information would surface.

Their previous shows depicted the search for Johnny and the effort I had made to cope with the loss of my son, which required me to become a public speaker, fundraiser, detective, and "thorn in the side of police, FBI and political bureaucrats". It seems the only way to get anything done on Johnny's case was to shout long and loud on any forum I could find from the stage of a church or school, newspaper, magazines to a radio or TV studio. To this day, I have worked two and more jobs to cover the expenses connected with this investigation. While Bill Clinton asked the American public to pay the 52 million in expenses for his "Monicagate"!

Before I knew it, fifteen years passed and Inside Edition contacted me wanting to do the "15-year anniversary story", I agreed. I announced my son was still alive and presented a computer-enhanced photo of my son at age 27, saying only to the media "that this came from a reliable source." Following the Inside Edition program. I received another call from Karen on 20/20, she saw the Inside Edition show. We talked for a while, catching up, then she asked me to come to New York to discuss doing another update on Johnny.

She wanted this update to depict the "my journey of fifteen years searching for my son". We decided for me to fly in and to meet at her office within a few days.

I met Karen, I decided to trust her with the secret that Johnny came to my home in the middle of the night on March 18, 1997. I had been afraid to share this with anyone up to that point.

I described how .... He knocked on the door, I was awakened, shaking, made my way to the door, looked out the security hole and I knew it was my son when I saw his eyes, but I asked anyway "who is there", he replied "Mom, it is me, Johnny". I opened the door and hugged him. He told me he could only stay a short time. He was asking for my help. No matter how much my son had changed over the years, I remembered that there was one identifying birthmark, which would have been impossible for anyone to duplicate. To make certain that this was my son, I asked to see this "birthmark in the shape of South America, which covered a large area on his chest". Johnny and I both a similar skin type and both tan so darkly that we can pass for Indians.

Johnny as I last saw him, is brushing six foot two, about 175 pounds, and had black hair. His hair is naturally a light brown, but he had darkened it ... his skin was also very dark, with the combination he did look Indian. I remarked about his new appearance, he then told me he had been living on Indian Reservations, and in hiding over the past few years.

He had a male companion with him that night, who remained silent during the entire visit. I asked his name, but it was not given to me. Both he and Johnny appeared very nervous ... when I asked which Indian

Reservation they had been living on, Johnny turned to his friend and the friend "shook his head, no!" It was as though Johnny needed approval from this other person before he could answer some of my questions.

Johnny told me many things about the kidnapping, including the names of people involved locally and that he was taken from Iowa by Col. Michael Aquino. Paul Bonacci had reported the same information… that the "Col" had taken Johnny to Colorado almost two weeks following the kidnapping.

Aquino, then an officer in the military reputedly in charge of Mind War for the U.S. government. I obtained a copy of the originally top-secret document "From Psyops to Mindwar…. The Psychology of Victory" written by Major Michael Aquino.

Karen Burnes became excited when I told her of Johnny's visit to my home. During our lunch meeting, she suggested that ABC 20/20 do a big update on Johnny. It would be an hour long special called " The Johnny Gosch Story." This would depict, at that time the 15-year journey, I had traveled in my search and intensive investigation to not only find my son but solve the case.

We rushed to her office, we spent the next three days researching information, and the names of people involved. ABC has a fantastic database in which they can enter names of people, it will give detailed information on people such as: addresses of property they own and owned, names of friends, names of business associates, money transactions etc. I was awed by the capability of this software program, to pull up this amount of information on people without having to leave an office. I thought to myself as I watched all this take place… this would be a wonderful piece of software to own if I ever decided to become a private detective. The Lord knows I have had enough experience in detective work after working on this case all these years.

We then decided upon filming dates to begin in November of 1997 when Karen and the film crew would travel to Des Moines to begin shooting this one-hour special. They brought in an enormous film crew. Due to the nature of this story, Karen reported to me that she, the associate producer, and the film crew all had to sign a "hold harmless clause" absolving ABC of any liability if any of them were to be killed in the process of telling this story. Never had this producer and crew been forced to sign such an agreement. The upper echelon of ABC obviously realized that this story was going to completely expose not only what happened to Johnny Gosch but many other children in this country.

She filmed a riveting four-hour interview with Paul Bonacci, who shared every detail of Johnny's kidnapping, as well as his own abuse. He explained how this powerful organization operates. It appeared to be comprised of the Defense Intelligence Agency, CIA, NAMBLA, and various Satanic organizations. Karen also learned that Bonacci had participated in another hour-long documentary "Conspiracy of Silence", produced by Yorkshire Television, Yorkshire England, which was not only prevented from airing on the Discovery Channel but also all copies were ordered to be destroyed.

I did not learn this documentary even existed until early in the year 2000. Information had been kept from me concerning this show, no doubt because it would have substantiated all the information Paul Bonacci had much earlier given in his confession, regarding his connection to Johnny's kidnapping.

In the process of her investigation, Karen Burnes uncovered 45 other victims of the same abuse, some of whom knew my son and were with him on many occasions. These individuals have all shared their story on film. Even though the victims were kidnapped in the same manner as Johnny, the common denominator among all of them was intimately knowing Michael Aquino and participating in ritual abuse and the MKUltra Mind War program. Karen had traveled all over the United States, meeting with victims, following leads and capturing it all on film. This project exceeded the budget and Karen was forced several times to stop and do other projects before ABC would allocate more money for the budget for Johnny's story.

I met Karen on one of the trips, which was to an Indian Reservation. Johnny was located on that Indian reservation by Bill (see the chapter on Bill and his connections to the Family). I got more help from the Mafia than I did from the FBI). His people had located Johnny and observed him for months before we traveled there. I drove all night and arrived in time to meet Karen's plane.

We called the priest, on the Reservation, asking him if we could meet with him and the Police Chief, Willie Strong. The priest agreed to set up a meeting. I had brought along a tape recording from me to Johnny, a letter and some family photos in a packet to give to my son. The priest greeted us warmly, he made coffee for us, and we began to try to explain this very complicated situation to him I showed him pictures of my son, clippings to help connect the story for him.

Soon there was a knock on the door, the priest opened the door and in walked Police Chief Willie Strong, a seven-foot tall Indian, who looked amazingly like the one in the movie "One Flew Over the Cuckoos' Nest"

At first, he was kind but reserved. I began to explain the story to him. He said, "How do I know you are Johnny's mother and are not someone coming here to hurt him?" I dug in my purse and got out all of my forms of identification to prove to him that I was Johnny's mom. He seemed satisfied with the information. He went on to say, "how can I help you?"

I told him I had information that my son was living on his reservation and I wanted to see him. He replied "you can leave your package with me and I can see that he gets it. Will you be in the area for a few days and where are you staying? I must get back to my office now." I told him we were staying in the next town and would be in the area for the next two days, giving him the number of the motel.

Willie left and returned within twenty minutes, in his hand was big manila envelope. He said, "please take this, it is a list of logging camps in our area where our people work... this will help you!" Then with tears streaming down his face, he stepped forward, towering over me, took both my hands in his massive hands and said, "No one should have to go through the pain that you have suffered!"

Karen and I said goodbye to the priest, as we walked out of the house, the wind was blowing leaves off the trees, I noticed the gray/ white building across the street and felt the same sensation I had when we drove through the gates of the reservation.... I knew we were being watched as we walked to the car and my son was nearby. Willie Strong was as helpful as possible while still being protective of Johnny. I wondered how many other young kids have taken refuge on reservations and were being protected on a sovereign state.

The first trip to the reservation had some success but I was not permitted to see my son. Willie Strong gave me clues in the packet of information. It was apparent we needed more investigation. Karen suggested bringing a private investigator in to investigate further. She placed a call to a Colorado Investigator, whom she had worked with in the past. He began doing background work, in phone calls to me, he stated,

" he was working for ABC and would not give me reports of his investigation." I consulted with Karen Burnes on a weekly basis.

I received a call from Karen, stating it was important for "us" to make a trip to the reservation once again, to attempt to see Johnny. It was Thanksgiving weekend 1998; I was to wait for a phone call then proceed with travel arrangements, to join the detective and Burnes at the reservetion. I waited and waited... no call from Burnes. However, I did receive a phone call from "Bill" (see chapter on Bill) stating, that the detective and Burnes had gone to the reservation without me, met with the Indian Council. Johnny heard of it and took off... he was on the run again. A few days later, Bonacci telephoned me saying the same thing... Johnny is on the run again... his cover was blown! Apparently, Johnny did not feel threatened when I went the first time to meet with the police chief but when Karen and the detective arrived it frightened him enough to take off.

It wasn't until two days later that I received a phone call from Karen and the detective saying they were at the "reservation". I told them "I already know, I got two reports telling me so". They were shocked that I already knew... I then explained it frightened Johnny and he was now on the run looking for another place of safety in which to live.

Despite this disappointing "misstep," I continued to work with 20/20 and Karen. It was very unfortunate, but the one-hour special was soon to be aired. This was the fourth and final episode of exactly what happened to Johnny Gosch...and thousands of other children, who have disappeared off America's streets in the last 30 years.

Readers Digest suggests that a hundred thousand children were taken in 1982 in the stranger abductions.... Others protest there were only hundreds. But does it matter whether it is thousands or hundreds... children are still being kidnapped.

The Johnny Gosch Story was scheduled for airing in April of 1998, but was postponed and postponed four different times. Little did I know during the process of filming that this show was doomed as was the "Conspiracy of Silence." The "powers that be" ....in this country felt it was unwise to allow people to see what happened to my son and to many other children.

I received word Karen Burnes was very ill, she had contacted me in an email and asked me if I thought, "someone had done something to make her sick?" Her illness was of unexplained origin; she was tested for many, many things, none of which proved to be the cause of her declineing health. She was confined to a hospital for a length of time and was out of communication with me. Some months later, I was able to reconnect with her and she has had to take a "medical leave of absence from ABC" as she is too ill to withstand the pressures of a work environment.

During the long investigation and filming Karen secured records and videos from the files of John DeCamp, Ted Gunderson and my private investigative reports all pertaining to the Franklin Cover Up and the connection to Johnny's case. This story was to my long journey of fifteen years, Karen was carefully putting together this story so the viewer would see how it evolved …. The struggle of a mother searching for her son. After Karen became ill, took the medical leave from ABC, I was informed by Ira Rosen, Senior Producer of 20/20 that all of the many boxes of records, tapes, videos belonging to DeCamp, Gunderson and myself, had been misplaced or lost and they did not know where they are located. I find this unbelievable that a television network such as ABC could lose that much material, which represented nearly $400,000 worth of expenses. Even for them it doesn't represent good business.

Ira Rosen, Senior Producer of 20/20 declared it could not be aired, and the show would be put on hold indefinitely. Which in their language means "sorry Charlie… no show".

I found Ira Rosen to be a very rude little man, who seemed to relish in the fact that he could be very short and snippy with people and not treating anyone with respect. After hearing the show was put on hold indefinitely, I asked if there could be someone at ABC who could finish the project in Karen's absence, as she was not coming back to work. Courtney Bullock, also of ABC, who did a show called "Vanished", had contacted me. She wanted to do Johnny's story. However, when she inquired with her Senior Producer after hearing the Johnny Gosch Story was put on hold, she was told "she was not allowed speak to me, to stay away from the Johnny Gosch story, as it was "classified and belongs to 20/20." I asked her "who gave the initial order to not communicate with me", during a phone call, she replied the order came from "Ira Rosen". She went on to say that she "could get into trouble for having the conversation with me." To me, the word "classified" generally means something to do with the military or national security, why would they be using it in reference to this show?

After a long hospital stay, I finally received a phone call from Karen Burnes, she told me she had asked Frank Snepp to help investigate, do leg work that she was unable to do because of her illness. She still believed that after a time, Johnny's story would eventually air. She explained Frank Snepp was a former CIA agent, was a friend of hers and could be trusted. She told me to expect a phone call from him soon and that Frank would work with me and "keep me in the loop".

A few days later, I received my first phone call from Frank Snepp

. He seemed nice enough, asking me a great many questions about the case and at times asking me to get information for him to evaluate. A few days later, Frank called and claimed the story had no validity, that Paul Bonacci was not credible. I reminded Frank that Paul had won a million-dollar judgment in a Civil Rights Case against Larry King, the man who abused him, by Federal Court Judge Urbom in February of 1999. In a very caustic manner, Frank said "none of that mattered and I would have to develop a new line of information to connect Johnny with the faction who took him".

Frank also claimed to have read every document concerning Johnny's case and knew more about it than I did. (Could Snepp have had access to the CIA Files on Johnny's case for some time?) I told him "if he had truly read all the documents, he wouldn't be making such stupid assumptions." Snepp then told me that "unless my son was turned over to "them" for Congressional protection, this story would never go on the air and that I was not allowed to speak to anyone at ABC." In essence, he wanted me to hand over my son to whoever "them" represented and I suspect it was CIA. At this point, not knowing who is connected to whom, I would not trust the safety of any member of my family to the CIA. Snepp warned me not to contact anyone at ABC, that he was in charge at this point.

I have not allowed anyone to tell me that "I cannot talk to whomever I please concerning my son's case," so I placed a phone call to Ira Rosen, the Senior Producer. When I reached Rosen, I told him of Frank Snepp's involvement and all that he had said to me. Rosen became outraged and began shouting on the phone, saying who brought Snepp into this and what is he doing? I told Rosen what I knew… he then told me he would get back to me in a few days.

Rosen returned my call two days later, saying "he been unable to reach Snepp." I then told Rosen that I was coming to New York within a week and wanted to schedule an appointment with him. He said, "he would much rather I just call him from the airport when I arrived." Even though it was against my better judgment, I could see that Rosen wasn't going to do it any other way…

A week later, I arrived in New York to film the Sally Jesse Raphael show, I telephoned Rosen from the airport. I reached his secretary; she informed me "Mr. Rosen is going to be out all day". Hmm, I thought this is odd, he knew I was arriving that day and would be calling. It appears he was dodging me. It made me more determined than ever to meet this man. To see what exactly I was dealing with… I wanted to look this man in the face and see how he reacted upon being faced with the mother of a child who had been subjected to such abuse.

My hotel was located just a few blocks from the ABC building on Columbus Ave, I decided to go to ABC anyway, even though Rosen was said to be out of the office. It was a nice day, so I decided to walk. As I neared the ABC building, I felt something hit me; I looked down and saw big white, slimly blobs of stuff all over my jacket, my dress and handbag. I wasn't sure if it was "bird poop or if someone had hurled from a tall building".

I looked around and spotted a dry-cleaning shop on the corner, I ran in and looked at this Oriental woman, I said, "is this bird poop or what". She grabbed a hold of my lapel and said, "It sure looks like bird poop to me." She motioned to the man working there to get something from the back room, he returned with a spray bottle and she immediately started to work to clean up the mess. Within a few minutes, I was back on my way towards ABC, very indebted to the nice Oriental lady, who had been so kind to me. Little did I know I was about to be "shit upon at ABC within minutes!"

I walked into ABC and went to the information desk, to ask for Ira Rosen, the guards told me to feel free to use the house phone to call his extension. Before dialing Rosen's extension, I buzzed Courtney Bullock, who does the Vanished program. She told me to come to her office. I told her I was going to buzz Rosen then I would be up.

I dialed Rosen's extension and to my surprise, he answered… (His secretary had told me he was going to be out all day and he couldn't see me). I said, "Ira, you are in today," He replied…" yes I am, who is this?" I said "This is Noreen Gosch and I am in the building too. I guess your secretary lied when she told me you weren't going to be in and could not see me today. I think under the circumstances you could spare 20 minutes to talk with me." He reluctantly agreed to meet me. I told him to meet me in Courtney Bullock's office. I arrived first in Courtney's office; she was very gracious and explained to me that she had been forbidden by Rosen to do anything with Johnny's story. She had been told to have no communication with me but knowing I had traveled all this way to come to their office she agreed to meet with me.

A few minutes later, the door opened and in walked a short little man all dressed in black, he was instantly rude and unpleasant to me. I sat there and wondered why he is being so nasty; I had never done anything to him. I had followed correct business procedure to set an appointment to discuss the project of Johnny's story. I had merely caught him in a lie when I dialed his extension on the house phone, and he answered personally. I suppose he didn't like it when he got "busted."

He proceeded to tell me that he had finally reached Frank Snepp and that Frank denied ever speaking to me. I looked at Rosen, got up off my chair and walked directly towards him until I was two inches from his face. I said to him, "hmm, you sounded much taller on the phone the many times I talked to you." First, why would you treat me in the manner you have when I have done nothing to you people? If you did not plan to do Johnny's story after spending $400,000 on it, why didn't you say so, instead of yanking me up and down like a yoyo!" Your behavior is inexcusable! By using those statements, I wanted to make him lose control and become the raging, shouting little tyrant that he had exhibited on the phone towards me. I wanted him to do it before witnesses. I had not gone to ABC alone; I had my Press Manager with me.

It worked, he popped like a cork from a bottle of champagne, losing his temper and I doubt whether he has found it to this day. I told Rosen ….

"You will continue to treat people in this nasty manner because it is your nature, but you will never have another opportunity to treat me this way." Rosen said "I was under an agreement with ABC 20/20 and could not take my story to any other form of media." I suggested a place "where they could put their agreement where it would never see the light of day. And that I would take my story to any other show I chose."

The agreement did not involve any money but an "exclusivity agreement" Rosen did not want any other network to have access to the entire Johnny Gosch story. This was only in effect until the story aired but they delayed it numerous times, still trying to enforce their agreement; I felt I had waited long enough.

Rosen, Senior producer for 20/20 released me from any obligation and suggested I could take my story elsewhere… the catch… they will release none of the information and film compiled by Karen Burnes. She had worked for over two years gathering the material.

I have gone on now to do two talk shows, Leeza Gibbons and Sally Jesse Raphael but the clout of a 20/20 or 60 Minute; one hour special might have resulted in Congressional Hearings. Or might aroused enough public anger, so that we the people might stop the abuse and experimentation with the world's children. If the children are the future, do we want them maimed and crippled by what the current generation is doing to them?

As this book goes to press, NBC's Today Show and Dateline have already scheduled me to tell Johnny's story. Johnny asked me to go public with his story, the night he came to see me, fourteen years after the kidnapping.

During the months which followed, John DeCamp, Ted Gunderson and I requested all of our files, records, videotapes etc, which were given to

Karen Burnes used for research in this story be returned. ABC has informed us all that these items have been misplaced and simply cannot be located.

How could ABC not do this story in the time frame planned, when they learned of the 45 other victims, who reluctantly shared their stories with Karen Burnes, they too have lived in fear for many years. Do not the upper echelon of producers and executives at ABC have children, know a child or were once a child themselves?

It makes an average citizen wonder at the level of responsibility, which simply does not exist for our fellow man, woman or child. The time, effort and money which was put into this project is enormous, it would have completely uncovered what has happened to Johnny and countless other victims of this sick, perverse, highly organized group of Pedophile Satanists.

Frank Snepp...CIA Spoiler

Frank Snepp is supposedly an ex-CIA man turned journalist. There are those who claim he is a CIA "spoiler," a plant whose job is to discredit those who would discredit the CIA or those connected to CIA.

Richard Brenneke, was real estate manager and arms dealer from Portland, Oregon.... He claimed, he was in Paris with the CIA team that arranged arms for Iran in exchange for keeping the hostages until Reagan was elected.

The book "The Mafia, CIA & George Bush" by Pete Brewton, got his book in print even though his original publisher, Simon & Schuster declined to publish. They had given him a $100,000 advance but told him to take his book somewhere else. SPI books, a division of Shapolsky Publisher, Inc., made the book available before going bankrupt. Perhaps they went bankrupt because they published a book with the name George Bush in the title. They also published "The Crimes of a President."

According to Brewton..." Snepp exposed in a story for the Village Voice that he supposedly lied about being in Paris during the alleged meetings." I think it significant that the author emphasized the word exposed. Snepp also convinced Brenecke not to talk to ABC's "20/20, which was preparing a program on the Houston Post's stories (I believe the ones Brewton was fired for writing). Brennecke's refusal to go on camera was a major factor in 20/20 decision not to air the story.

"So, it goes in the world of CIA contract agents (is he referring to Snepp) …journalists must cling particularly fast to the first rule of reporting. If your mother tells you she loves you, check it out!" Snepp's name seems to surface wherever there is trouble for the CIA. Especially where it is connected to George Bush and Iran Contra.

This is how a "spoiler" operates… they bring out information which contradicts information already disseminated. Whether it is true or not, makes no difference. If it is repeated often enough…. "Lies are accepted as truth".

VALIANT ATTEMPT

Karen Burnes and her associates made a valiant attempt to bring out the truth on Johnny's case. It would have solved the cases of many other kidnapped children in America. Unfortunately, when there are powerful people at the top making the cutting decisions… to protect their political friends. It is then riveting stories become "locked up."

UPDATE ON FILM PROJECT:

We have learned after many years that a very powerful man had financial Interest in Capital Cities, who owned ABC at the time. And information was given to us that the entire film project about Johnny and others to be shown on 20/20 had been destroyed.

GRIEF BY LOSS OF A CHILD BY NOREEN N. GOSCH

Someone you love is the victim of a kidnapping, possible homicide or some other tragedy has taken your child. This tragedy is sometimes more terrifying for the survivors than the actual victim. Your anger, frustration and pain will be extensive, and it will take a great deal of hard work to recover. This chapter was prepared for you by someone who has lived through the kidnapping.

SHOCK

Our minds are marvelous instruments, in that they take on only what we can handle. In the beginning, you will notice numbness. You will continually say to yourself, "this can't be real". Some liken it to being in a fog". In a kidnapping case, it is very important to become active in your child's search immediately. Time is precious for your child and every moment wasted is a moment of their life. Despite the pain and suffering you are enduring get involved in your child's search.

Hopefully the law enforcement will act quickly on your case… but in any event it is important for you to remember **"YOUR CHILD IS THE VICTIM,"** It will not help your child if you sink into depression at this time.

They need you more than ever before. Most parents are not alone in the possibility of a murder, and they may never find the child. Unfortunately, there are still some police departments that will not enter an investigation immediately. Work is being done in many states to correct this error.

Be prepared for the possibility that the police department may suspect you of your child's disappearance. Your pain is so intense for your child and the possibility of being considered a suspect destroys a great many parents. Try to remain as calm and strong as possible. ... Your child's life may well depend on it. This is not the time to be passive but rather move as quickly as possible... following the steps to assist in the search for your child.

The "fog" referred to earlier may last from three to six months. This numbness allows us to handle arrangements of many kinds and to deal with the initial loss of your loved one.

COPING WITH DISTANCE

Sooner or later... you come to realize, after the ground and air search has been completed, that your loved one may have been transported out of your county, state or even our country. This creates panic in the hearts of the parents. What chance do we have now? This is not the time to fall apart continued your efforts for publicity and searching for that child and working with your police department. We now have agencies to help parents – in past years the parents stood alone. For many parents coping with the possibility of distance in a kidnapping is the worst reality

FRIENDS

When we hurt, we turn to the people who have always been there, our friends. These are the people who came that awful day or night. They sat with us, answered our phone, made us eat and remained close if we needed anything.

During the search they were assisting with every aspect needed and if you did have to face a murder, your friends were there to assist with funeral arrangements, etc. but where are they now, a month, six months or a year after the tragedy? They have gone back to their lives, but you need to talk. If you bring up the kidnapping or murder, there are those who will change the subject, simply because "THEY CAN'T DEAL WITH THE DETAILS OF THE TRAGEDY". They can't bring themselves to talk about "IT". Unfortunately, it is human. Some feel so badly it is too difficult. But we are still in the throws of what has happened to our loved one.

REVENGE

Most of us are incapable of murder. It's something that we perhaps in a joking way said "Oh, I could kill you for that"! It's no longer a joke. For the first time in your life, you may be devising ways in your mind… revenge toward another human.

Understandably, some people are disturbed by this emotion. You may feel you are losing your mind. You are normal and human. Almost every person experiencing this emotion after a kidnapping or murder… does not act upon it. Our hearts go out to anyone experiencing this, we know your pain.

There will be those who will tell you that wanting revenge is unhealthy and that the only way to find peace is to forgive. If forgiveness is in your heart, fine, but do not allow these people to place unnecessary guilt on you. Chances are they have never been where you are. Could they forgive so easily? It is doubtful. You will come to that point yourself if that is heartfelt. I do not believe in revenge… it hurts the intended and the person seeking it. I however believe strongly in justice for our loved ones who have been harmed or killed.

FAMILY

Each of us is an individual. We like different foods, clothing, and select lifestyles unique to ourselves. It stands to reason that at the most painful time in our lives, we would also grieve in our own way. How we choose to grieve is determined by three things… our personal view of the crime and the loss, how society views our, and individual personalities.

When a kidnapping or murder happens to a family, we sometimes expect that it will pull us closer together. This is not always true. It is not unusual for us to see families separate, both physically and emotionally. After the loss of a loved one, some in the family may resent the rebuilding of your life in a different manner. Each of us recovers from grief in our own time frame. We can't expect any member of the family to completely understand the sense of loss of another.

Family members become possessive of one another and are also possessive of the relationship each had with the lost loved one. Each member of the family is attempting to comprehend the loss of this person in their life. The loved one represents something different to each individual. After a kidnapping or homicide, the personalities of the family members may change drastically. Some people find the need to block the horror of the crime with over-indulgence in drugs or alcohol.

Often, we see families argue about who hurts the most. For instance, a mother who cries easily may feel her husband, who doesn't cry, didn't really care about the victim because he shows no outward signs of grief. Or it may be the other way around – perhaps the mother shows more strength than the father.

In addition to experiencing the loss differently, families also become very protective – they have already lost one loved one and you may feel your own "potential mortality" and that of other family members. It has happened to us!

One must also consider the parent/stepparent situation. It may be difficult for a stepparent to feel the intensity of the parent's grief. The serious student who performed well in school prior to the kidnapping or murder may be failing in grades, dropping out and running away. The mother whose child has been abducted or murdered may become paranoid about allowing her remaining children out of her sight. The children caught in this situation, in time may feel stifled and may rebel or be socially inhibited. Communication currently is very important. Express the fears you have and discuss ways that one can protect oneself and still enjoy an active social life.

HOLIDAYS

Holidays are an accumulation of traditions. Traditions are habits made by families to be shared with family members. When a member of the family is no longer there to share the tradition that was once cherished it becomes a painful reminder instead of a thing of joy.

The first time we celebrate each holiday after a violent crime, it becomes a nightmare. Christmas gifts that once were ripped open immediately sit for days. Thanksgiving is hollow, "What do I have to be thankful for"? shouts a survivor. New Years Day "How can I begin a new year when I can't even get out of bed to start a new day"? Or birthdays, a celebration of another year of life is another reminder of your loss. You may find the need to develop new traditions. For some a trip out of town at Christmas time is beneficial. A birthday can be observed by donating to a charitable organization or doing something meaningful to you. There is no rule to follow on how to "GET THROUGH" a holiday. You will grieve. Allow yourself that, you deserve it.

SOCIETY

A general lack of understanding in our society about the impact of a kidnapping or homicide is often compounded by poor communication. One ten-year-old sibling responded to a reporter's question, "How do you feel about all of this?" by saying, "Well now I have a room to myself".

Society views this child's response as cold and cruel, when what the child was doing was denying the death of his older brother.

One mother of a homicide victim found, when speaking of her daughter's violent death that those whom she was addressing reacted with immediate withdrawal. What most people didn't realize was their rejections resulted in additional distress for the mother. One couple after the kidnapping of their child, developed programs and legislation and became national leaders in children's safety, only to be met with cruelty in their home community. The community was uncomfortable because now it was a reality.... If it has happened once, it may happen again. There is an element of our society which hides behind anonymity. They can possibly be more damaging than those who ignore us. They are the ones who call on the phone or write a letter condemning you for the loss of your loved one. Statements such as "If you were a better parent your child would still be here today", or in some cases accusing the survivor of committing the crime, even if there is no evidence to support the accusation.

Many people blame the victim for their own tragedy. We have been told, "Had they not been walking on that street at that time of the morning, this would not have happened!" The victim must be at fault for his own violent crime. If not, it could happen to anyone. Society simply cannot accept that this has happened to you, because if it happened to you, it could happen to them.

GUILT

In the beginning, after the kidnapping and during the long hours of waiting for an answer, many parents experience misplaced guilt. They deny themselves the normal, simple needs in life... because their child may be without these things. Perhaps they blame themselves because they were not there to protect and prevent this crime.

In the case of siblings, "If I hadn't run, my brother would still be here." Each survivor lives with the "What if's". What if I had been there.... This would not have happened." This is a very normal reaction. Unfounded, but normal. Please remember no one can predict the future or what might have been. We can't change the events that took place and to continue berating ourselves will only be destructive.

Misplaced guilt brings about anger, which may be vented on the very people you love and cherish.

ANGER

It is not uncommon to be angry at God. Do you ask, "Why does a just God allow this ugly thing to happen?" or "If there is a God, he would have prevented this from happening." Many people, prior to a violent crime had strong faiths and how they find going to their place of worship too painful. Some have been able to rebuild their faith, perhaps with a different cornerstone.

Before completely turning your back on God, I suggest reading the book, "When Bad Things Happen to Good People", by Rabbi Harold S. Kushner. It has helped others; I hope it will help you.

You may find that much of your anger is directed at the criminal justice system. Sometimes the system lacks sensitivity and understanding to the plight of the victims and their families. Consider the anger of the mother, whose daughter was murdered by a man who has been sentenced to die 8 years before her daughter was born. The criminal justice system failed to protect this young girl from a man who had previously committed murder.

Another family, their child kidnapped, no one would look, no one would work on the case… they did not consider the child's welfare or that it was a serious matter.

Victims see the aid and consolation given to the offender and his/her family. Churches often go into the prisons to comfort the offender and turn around and tell the victim he must forgive. Most churches do not provide long-term support and services for the victims of violent crime. They will, however, stand by an offender who continues committing one crime after another. A victim's anger stems from being treated indifferently by all facets of society.

Your anger is understandable and those of us who have been through this trauma care... you are not alone.

CRIMINAL JUSTICE SYSTEM

Are you angry with criminal justice or another authority system? You are not alone! Most victims initially are naïve to the working of the criminal justice system. As we progress through the various stages, we become angry and frustrated because the pre-conceived ideas of the justice system are false. We find that justice does not prevail. The guilty are released on technicalities and the only one serving the life sentence is the victim.

The criminal justice system, better known as "the victims' injustice system", can prolong your grief. Many kidnapping/murder cases are never solved, even when the identity of the offender is known. The family that seeks justice done through a timely resolution are more fortunate than those who never to trial or those that must wait for years to be resolved.

Plea bargaining often contributes to the miscarriage of justice. Families of the victims find plea bargaining dilutes the actual crime committed and leaves them dissatisfied with the criminal justice system.

Through the appeal process the unsuspecting survivors may find themselves going through the trial process two or more times. The additional trials may be more painful than the original trial because of the "shock or fog" which may have been protected the survivor's emotions during the earlier events is no longer there. Years after the crime your life is more stable. A retrial disrupts that stability and may very well destroy the progress you have made. Once again, you relive the horror of the crime on a day-to-day basis. Most kidnapping/homicide cases are automatically appealed, however, only a fraction of those find their way back to court.

Several years ago, survivors were merely a piece of evidence to be used in a trial. At last, there is hope for the victim in a system designed for the offender. Today, many prosecutors and district attorney's offices have started victim/witness units. The individuals running these programs are there to assist you, the victims. Contact your local prosecutor's office to see if there is such a program. In Seattle, they are fortunate to have not only a program in the prosecutor's office but also an excellent program is available through the Seattle Police Department. If you have no programs available… contact the Seattle Police Dept. or prosecutor's office about starting a program in your area.

CLICHES

Clichés are used by well-meaning people, who don't know what else to say to you. Clichés, in early grief and beyond, bring more aggravation and pain than comfort. Things people say and we wish they wouldn't:

It is God's will.
He will not have to suffer again.
She's better off, had she lived, she wouldn't have been the same. He's happier in heaven.
Aren't you lucky to have your remaining children? You will have another child.
Give up the search… He is probably dead anyway. Aren't you over that yet, it is time to get on with your life. Time heals all wounds.
Life goes on.
You were chosen… because you are strong, and you would bring progress out of this tragedy.
It is part of God's plan. Don't cry, It's okay.
What is the matter with you? Why don't you cry (Don't you have feelings?
I don't know how you can be so strong, if it were me, I couldn't survive.
It is divine to forgive.
You look too good; you can't be suffering.

These statements may both anger and hurt the survivors of violent crimes, it makes our road to rebuilding or recovering our loved one that much more difficult. To some parents, it cripples progress – for others it provokes angry reactions. It is the worst time of our lives, and we desperately try each day to survive. The time does not heal this wound – a violent crime leaves a mark that is not experienced in the passing of a loved ones by other circumstances.

THE DEATH CLAUSE

The subject is often neglected and not considered. When you are dealing with a kidnapping case, it is possible that your crime may never be solved. This leaves you and your family wondering "is he or she still alive" for the rest of your lives. In addition to the obvious pain this creates, it can also create some legal difficulties. Some states in their legislature deal with the kidnapping in terms of a missing person and the length of time before declaring that person dead, and others do not have any legislation, which addresses this situation. Some states address only the "missing in action or prisoner of war" – laws, which were written when our country had been at war. This is not helpful in your situation. You need the advice of an attorney, in terms of your will and arrangements to provide for your family. Insurance policies on the victim cannot be resolved until a death certificate is issued.

This is a dreaded and painful ordeal to face. It brings you to the reality all over again.... "WE WILL NEVER KNOW WHAT HAS HAPPENED TO OUR CHILD", This is an area where you need correct information and advice.

With the growing number of kidnappings and unsolved cases, many parents, for the first time in our country's history are having to face this legal technicality. The experts tell us it has never come up before. It is time we address this now, to afford the bet legal protection, which is possible for not only the victim but also the surviving family.

If this situation pertains to your case, contact the legal professionals in which you place your trust and listen to their advice.

EPILOG

The rest of your life is the epilog. Recently a survivor of a violent crime said "my life has been altered; I must rebuild it". A true statement. Everything in your life will be changed. You will see things differently now.

Incidents that were once catastrophe will be minor aggravations because you have already survived the worst. Your belief in your God may be shaken, you find trusting anyone impossible. You have found that the laws you thought were designed to protect you are really designed to protect the guilty. Listening to people define the rights of the offender, your mind will shout. **"BUT WHAT ABOUT THE RIGHT OF THE VICTIM TO LIFE, LIBERTY AND**

THE PURSUIT OF HAPPINESS?"

There is still happiness left in the world for you. You can laugh again, the first time it happens, you will be shocked for a moment at how good it feels. You can again feel warmth on a beautiful sunny morning. You will find for every negative, unkind person there are those who will stand by you and give you the support you need and deserve. You may find sensitivity for others you never realized you had and be moved to get involved with some type of activity which would bring progress and purpose out of tragedy. If you are a survivor, you have something to share with another who may be going through it. You will find joy in the memories you have been left with – the good memories, the quirks unique to your loved one. The special things they have said will leave a lasting imprint in your senses.

You may rediscover your mate – a marriage goes through a unique trauma during the tragedy of this nature. Sometimes we find couples reporting "THE ONLY THING HOLDING US TOGETHER IS OUR GRIEF AND IT IS NOT ENOUGH". It is true the divorce rate is very high among parents after a kidnapping or murder of their child. Each of you undergoes a transformation; you become different people due to this tragedy of a violent crime. No one else can understand how much you miss your child, too.

Some couples feel they need a marriage counselor and perhaps this will help. But the primary need is for someone to assist in dealing with the crisis before you can progress to the marriage. Arriving at the reality… that nothing will ever be the same again is a huge step. One cannot redo the past… we can only try to build and improve the future. If past hobbies or entertainment once enjoyed are too painful, try something different until you can derive some type of enjoyment together. It takes time and no one has a magic guarantee – but it is worth striving towards. The unique qualities which attracted the two of you perhaps have been altered and perhaps attempting to get acquainted with the new personality and accept that person at that level will be a way to begin rebuilding a very important relationship.

For some the need to be apart is greater and necessary. There are times when one partner becomes violent, and it is no longer safe to remain in the home and the marriage. Appropriate measures and decisions must be made to ensure the safety of yourself and if there are other children in the home.

This was written to offer help and hope to those who are suffering by someone who has been through the stages of grief.

RECOMMENDED READING

Multiple Journeys To One
Editors: Judy Dragon/ Terry Popp
Dancing Serpents Press
P.O. Box 8115
Santa Rosa, CA 95407
Email: danserpents@juno.com

Thanks For The Memories Brice Taylor
Brice Taylor Trust
P.O. Box 655
Landrum, SC 29356

The Franklin Cover-Up John DeCamp
AWT, Inc.
P.O. Box 85461
Lincoln, NE 68501
Email: decamplegal@inebraska.com

Check your local library for titles on Mind Control and the CIA. Inter-library loans will often bring titles from surrounding states, should your library not have it.

Printed in Great Britain
by Amazon